CW01142819

BASIC COMMUNITY CASES

Basic Community Cases

BERNARD RUDDEN

CLARENDON PRESS · OXFORD
1987

Oxford University Press, Walton Street, Oxford OX2 6DP
*Oxford New York Toronto Melbourne Auckland
Delhi Bombay Calcutta Madras Karachi
Petaling Jaya Singapore Hong Kong Tokyo
Nairobi Dar es Salaam Cape Town*

Associated companies in Beirut Berlin Ibadan Nicosia

OXFORD *is a trade mark of Oxford University Press*

*Published in the United States
by Oxford University Press, New York*

Introductory Material, Selection, and Notes © B. Rudden 1987

*All rights reserved. No part of this publication may be reproduced,
stored in a retrieval system, or transmitted, in any form or by any means,
electronic, mechanical, photocopying, recording, or otherwise, without
the prior permission of Oxford University Press.*

British Library Cataloguing in Publication Data
Rudden, Bernard
Basic Community cases.
1. European Economic Community   2. Law—
European Community countries
I. Title
341'.094   [LAW]
ISBN 0-19-876212-7
ISBN 0-19-876211-9 Pbk

Library of Congress Cataloging in Publication Data
Basic Community cases.
Includes index.
1. Law—European Economic Community countries—Cases.
I. Rudden, Bernard.
KJ947.B37   341.24'22   87-1717
ISBN 0-19-876212-7
ISBN 0-19-876211-9 (pbk.)

*Set by Butler & Tanner Ltd, Frome and London
Printed in Great Britain
at the University Printing House, Oxford
by David Stanford
Printer to the University*

PREFACE

THE art of learning is to get as much benefit from as little study as possible. In the case of the European Community, the development of its law has been largely the work of the European Court of Justice (ECJ), but the official law reports are not easy reading. Common-lawyers, in particular, may face several difficulties, being accustomed to lawsuits whose facts are interesting, and whose judgments are the work of individual human beings, each with a distinctive voice. By contrast, the events which provoke much Community litigation, when intelligible at all, seem quite remote from everyday life; and the judgments are the work of an impersonal institution ('The Court') writing the cold language of a committee.

In reality, in the major cases, the Court of Justice has been bold, vigorous, and far-sighted. Its contribution to the creation of a common law which governs all Community citizens and their rulers was made both possible and necessary by a number of factors. First, the Treaty of Rome is largely a set of principles, to be brought to life by the Community institutions. Secondly, the planned initial balance between the legislative organs quickly changed in favour of the Council, at whose table national interests or political caution frequently prevailed; and, with the Commission thus muzzled, a gap was left to be filled by the Court. Thirdly, and inherent in the foregoing, the pace of the Community's legislative development was much slower than expected; consequently, the ECJ, time and again, turns back to the Treaty itself, and finds there its authority to do what the Council has not, and to make the Community work. Yet, for the beginner, the judicial achievement in the foundation of a genuine economic and legal community is often difficult to discern beneath the dull surface of the law reports.

This book attempts to help the student, first to grasp the basic principles which have grown up over the last thirty years, and secondly to see just how important the Court has been. It does so by three tactics: selection, explanation, and concentration. Far from attempting to be a comprehensive digest of European case-law, the work deliberately goes to the other extreme. In the belief that it is better to read intensively than extensively, this is an attempt to pick out only leading cases, that is to say those decisions which are crucial at several levels.

The fundamental level concerns the nature of EEC law for, since it is the common law of the Community, it must be autonomous, uniform, and supreme. Next comes the notion of its direct effect on the officials, courts, and subjects of the national legal systems; and then its application in various sectors. Most of these features are to be found in each of the texts presented, so that they may need to be read more than once before their full range becomes clear.

To make the process easier, each extract is prefaced by suggestions as to how the case should be studied in order to make it yield the most. The prefatory explanations normally follow the same pattern, covering a checklist which readers may find useful. First, it is made clear who is bringing the action (national court, Commission, other institution, individual, or firm) and for what: an interpretation, a declaration, judicial review, damages. The facts are then summarized in a way which deliberately suppresses detail and sometimes descends to a certain dramatization. Thirdly, the legal issues (there will usually be several) are then outlined. After extracts from the case itself, some Comments provide guidance towards understanding the implications of the lawsuit as a whole.

The tactic of concentration has been used to try to save the reader from having to grapple with many distinct, and complex, sets of facts. Fortunately, one single recent scientific discovery has given rise to numerous lawsuits, some of which go to the roots of Community law. The newcomer is isoglucose, a natural sweetener produced from grain, whose introduction into the Community threatened chaos to the cereal and, in particular, to the sugar sectors of the common agricultural policy. The Community's attempts to control production have faced the ECJ with several fundamental problems. Consequently, Part III selects from the isoglucose litigation, so that the reader need master only one set of facts in order to understand problems in several crucial areas.

The work is not meant to be self-sufficient, and gives cross-references to the legislative texts printed in *Basic Community Laws*, edited by Bernard Rudden and Derrick Wyatt (2nd edition, OUP 1986), and to the treatise by T. C. Hartley, *The Foundations of European Community Law*, (OUP 1981). The materials given are extracts from the Opinions and Judgments; omissions are not indicated. Most of the texts are taken from the official European Court Reports, though, with some of the more recent decisions, the official mimeographed advance sheets have been used. Case 34/86 (extract no. 18) is taken from the law report in *The Times* of 4 July 1986; and Case 145/83 (extract no. 26) from [1986] 1 CMLR 506. Grateful thanks are due to Times Newspapers Ltd. and to the European Law Centre. Both the correct title of, and the reference to, the cases selected or cited are set out in the Table, while the text itself gives only the docket number and the name by which the case is usually known.

A selection of so small a fraction of the Court's case-law is bound to provoke questions both as to the enterprise itself, and to the choice made. All Community lawyers will have their favourites, which they may well not find here. In response, it should be said that exclusions stem partly from constraints of space and price, but mainly from personal judgment. They are not necessarily the result of ignorance, for the compiler has had the resources of the Bodleian Law Library and the advice of its learned staff; and, above all, has been able to draw upon the wise counsel of Claudine Lévy of the University of Leeds, John Davies of Brasenose College, and Derrick Wyatt of St Edmund Hall, Oxford. Any faults of selection, emphasis, or analysis which remain may be imputed only to the undersigned.

B.R.

Brasenose College, Oxford
Midsummer 1986

CONTENTS

Table of Community Laws	xi
Table of Cases and Opinions	xv
Abbreviations	xxi
Introduction: Reading Community Cases	1
I The Law Common to the European Economic Community	7
1 Case 26/62 *Van Gend en Loos*	9
2 Cases 28–30/62 *Da Costa en Schaake*	31
3 Case 6/64 *Costa v. ENEL*	41
4 Case 106/77 *Simmenthal*	54
5 Case 11/70 *Internationale Handelsgesellschaft*	61
II The Development of Community Law	69
A The Internal Market	71
(1) Goods	72
6 Case 120/78 *Cassis de Dijon*	73
7 Case 249/81 *Commission v. Ireland*	78
8 Cases 56 and 58/64 *Consten and Grundig v. Commission*	81
(2) People	87
9 Case 41/74 *Van Duyn*	87
10 Case 2/74 *Reyners*	99
11 Case 33/74 *Van Binsbergen*	108
12 Case 293/83 *Gravier v. Liège*	115
13 Case 43/75 *Defrenne 2*	122
14 Case 152/84 *Marshall*	137
B Constitutional Checks and Balances	147
15 Case 22/70 *ERTA*	149
16 Case 13/83 *Parliament v. Council*	161
17 Case 294/83 *Les Verts v. Parliament*	171
18 Case 34/86 *Council v. Parliament*	177
III Community Blunders	183
The Isoglucose Story: Prologue	186
Act I: Production Refunds	188
19 Case 101/76 *KSH v. Council and Commission*	190
20 Case 125/77 *KSH v. Netherlands Intervention Agency*	192
Act II: Production Levies	196

x   *Contents*

    21 Joined Cases 103 and 145/77 *Royal Scholten-Honig* v.
        Agricultural Intervention Board   197
  Act III: Actions for Compensation   201
    22 Joined Cases 116 and 124/77 *Amylum and Tunnel* v.
        Council and Commission   202
  Act IV: The Parliament Slighted   207
    23 Case 138/79 *Roquette Frères* v. *Council*   210
  Act V: Retroactive Regulations   216
    24 Case 108/81 *Amylum* v. *Council*   218

IV Judicial Technique   223
    25 Case 155/79 *AM & S Europe Limited* v. *Commission*   225
    26 Case 145/83 *Adams* v. *Commission* (no. 1)   236

Index   253

TABLE OF COMMUNITY LAWS

Citation references are given only for those not printed in Rudden and Wyatt, *Basic Community Laws*.

ECSC TREATY

Article	Page
38	160, 171

EEC TREATY

Article	Page
3	161, 164, 230
4	3, 29, 163, 164, 213, 226
5	46, 80, 142, 153, 160
6	123
7	46, 51, 67, 87, 117–20
8	46, 103, 112
9	23, 25
12	9, 11, 12, 14, 18, 19, 20, 23, 26, 29, 31, 38, 42, 54, 88, 122
13	12
14	25
15	46
17	46
25	46
26	46
30	54, 73, 74, 76, 77, 78, 80
31	12
36	73, 77, 97
37	41, 48–9, 51, 52, 73, 77
39	65, 67, 186, 197
40	65, 186, 193, 197, 198
43	66, 186, 207, 210, 214
48	87, 90, 91, 93, 96–7, 116, 122, 143
49	116
52	48, 99, 100, 101–3, 116
53	41, 48, 51, 99
54	99, 101, 102
55	99, 100, 104–6
56	90, 91, 98
57	101, 102, 105
59	108, 109, 110–13, 116, 118, 161, 168
60	108, 109, 110–13, 116, 118

Article	Page
61	116, 161, 164, 168
62	116
63	108, 112, 113
65	114
66	98, 112, 113
71	12
73	46
74	153, 164
75	150, 152, 155, 157–60, 161, 164, 166, 168–9
84	164
85	26, 81, 82, 83–6, 225, 229, 230
86	26, 51, 86, 225, 229, 230, 238
87	26, 230
89	26
92	48, 78
93	41, 46, 48, 51
95	12, 40
100	98, 132
100A	72, 98
102	41, 47, 51
113	129, 152
114	152
116	158, 159
117	127
118	116
119	67, 122, 124, 127–33
125	116
128	115, 119
137	163, 209
138	172, 174
139	209, 214
142	171
149	215
155	131, 133
164	1, 61, 129, 155, 172, 226
169	11, 12, 17, 21, 22, 23, 25, 42, 44, 51, 78, 122, 131, 134
170	11, 12, 17, 21, 22, 23, 25, 42, 44, 51
171	30, 44
173	44, 61, 81, 149, 151, 154–5, 161, 162, 163, 171, 172–3, 176, 177, 183–4, 188, 190, 196, 199, 210, 216, 225
174	156, 178, 180, 199, 209, 220
175	161, 162, 163, 164–6, 184

Article Page
176   166, 176, 199, 200, 220
177   4, 9, 11, 13, 14, 17, 21, 22, 25, 27, 31, 34, 36, 37, 38, 40, 41, 44, 45,
         47, 50, 54, 56, 58, 59, 61, 73, 87, 94, 99, 108, 122, 137, 184, 189, 196,
         208
178   184, 201, 236
183   3
184   44, 184, 206
185   234
186   234
189   10, 46, 51, 54, 56, 57, 88, 93, 94, 100, 138, 143, 149, 154, 162, 184,
         190
190   149, 150, 188, 216, 221
203   177, 178–9
204   181
210   150, 152
214   243, 244–5
215   184, 201, 202–3, 204, 236, 250
216   181
219   30
222   67, 82, 86
223   46
224   46
225   46
226   46
228   149, 150, 157–60
235   98, 133, 136, 145, 157
236   132
238   152

STATUTE OF THE COURT OF JUSTICE (EEC)

2   5
17   232, 235
20   9, 16, 17, 37, 213
37   208, 213, 225
43   184, 236, 242, 248–9

SINGLE EUROPEAN ACT 1986   2, 67, 72, 98, 215

EEC REGULATIONS

17/62   81, 225–6, 227, 228, 229, 230–1, 243
1612/68 116, 119

2742/75 OJ 1975 L281/57   188
1862/76 OJ 1976 L206/3   188, 190, 192–5
2158/76 OJ 1976 L241/21 (Commission)   188, 190, 192–5
1110/77 OJ 1977 L134/1   196
1111/77 OJ 1977 L134/4   196, 197–9, 202, 204, 210
1293/79 OJ 1979 L162/10   207, 210–15
1592/80 OJ 1980 L160/12   216
387/81 OJ 1981 L44/1   216, 220
388/81 OJ 1981 L44/4   216
1983/83   86

EEC DIRECTIVES

64/221   87, 90, 93, 94, 96–7
70/50   77, 78
75/117   131, 133, 134
75/362 OJ 1975 L167/1   107
76/207   136, 137, 139–45
77/249   114, 233, 235
79/7   136, 140

COUNCIL DECISION

1976 Direct Elections   172, 175, 207, 211

TABLE OF CASES and OPINIONS

(Bold numbers indicate extracts)

Case

25/62	Plaumann & Co. v. Commission [1963] ECR 95	206
26/62	NV Algemene Transport en Expeditie Onderneming Van Gend en Loos v. Nederlands Administratie der Belastingen [1973] ECR 1	**9,** 31, 32, 33, 38, 39, 42, 45, 55, 60, 72
28–30/62	Da Costa en Schaake NV, Jacob Meijer NV and Hoechst-Holland NV v. Nederlandse Belastingadministratie [1963] ECR 31	31, 199
6/64	Flaminio Costa v. ENEL [1964] ECR 585	**41,** 56
56 and 58/64	Etablissements Consten SARL and Grundig-Verkaufs-GmbH v. Commission [1966] ECR 299	**81,** 184
16/65	Firma C. Schwarze v. Einfuhr und vorratsstelle für Getreide und Futtermittel [1965] ECR 877	199, 200
5, 7, and 13–24/66	Firma E. Kampffmeyer et al. v. Commission [1967] ECR 245	206
28/67	Firma Molkereizentrale Westfalen-Lippe GmbH v. Hauptzollamt Padenborn [1968] ECR 143	40
4/69	Alfons Lütticke GmbH v. Commission [1971] ECR 325	206
29/69	Stauder v. City of Ulm [1969] ECR 419	67
9/70	Franze Grad v. Finanzamt Traunstein [1970] ECR 825	98
11/70	Internationale Handelsgesellschaft mbh v. Einfuhr- und Vorrattstelle für Getreide und Futtermittel [1970] ECR 1125	**61**
22/70	Commission v. Council [1971] ECR 263	**149**
31/70	Deutsche Getreide und Futtermittel Handelsgesellschaft mbH v. Hauptzollamt Hamburg Altona [1970] ECR 1055	200
33/70	Sp.A. SACE v. Italian Finance Ministry [1970] ECR 1213	98
5/71	Aktien-Zuckerfabrik Schöppenstedt v. Council [1971] ECR 975	206
20/71	Luisi Sabbatini, née Bertoni v. European Parliament [1972] ECR 345	135, 184
7/72	Boehringer Mannheim GmbH v. Commission [1972] ECR 1281	67
155/73	Giuseppe Sacchi [1974] ECR 409	52, 121
185/73	Hauptzollamt Bielefeld v. Offene Handelsgesellschaft in Firma H.C. König [1974] ECR 607	200

2/74	Jean Reyners v. Belgian State [1974] ECR 631	52, **99**, 108, 114
8/74	Procureur du Roi v. Benoit and Gustave Dassonville [1974] ECR 837	77
9/74	Donato Casagrande v. Landeshauptstadt München [1974] ECR 773	121
17/74	Transocean Marine Paint Association v. Commission [1974] ECR 1063	67
21/74	Jeanne Airola v. Commission [1975] ECR 221	135
33/74	Johannes Henricus Maria Van Binsbergen v. Bestuur van de Bedrijfsvereniging voor de Metaalnijverheid [1974] ECR 1299	**108**, 116, 162
36/74	B. N. O. Walrave, L. J. N. Koch v. Association Union Cycliste Internationale, Koninklijke Nederlandsche Wielren Unie and Federacion Española Ciclismo [1974] ECR 1405	121
41/74	Yvonne Van Duyn v. Home Office [1974] ECR 1337	**87**, 122, 138, 145
48/74	Mr Charmasson v. Minister for Economic Affairs and Finance [1974] ECR 1383	28, 77
67/74	Carmelo Angelo Bonsignore v. Oberstadtdirektor der Stadt Köln [1975] ECR 297	98
74/74	CNTA SA v. Commission [1975] ECR 533	67, 206
36/75	Roland Rutili v. Minister for the Interior [1975] ECR 1219	98
43/75	Gabrielle Defrenne v. SABENA [1976] ECR 455	28, **122**, 145
48/75	Jean Noël Royer [1976] ECR 497	98
59/75	Pubblico Ministero v. Flavia Manghera et al. [1976] ECR 91	52
91/75	Hauptzollamt Göttingen and Bundesfinanzminister v. Wolfgang, Miritz GmbH & Co. [1976] ECR 217	52
3, 4, and 6/76	Cornelis Kramer et al. [1976] ECR 1279	160
13/76	Gaetano Donà v. Mario Mantero [1976] 1333	121
33/76	Rewe-Zentralfinanz eG and Rewe-Zentral AG v. Landwirtschaftskammer für das Saarland [1976] ECR 1989	5
35/76	Simmenthal S.p.A. v. Italian Minister of Finance [1976] ECR 1871	54, 56
64 and 113/76, 167 and 239/78, and 27-8 and 45/79	P. Dumortier Frères SA et al. v. Council [1979] ECR 3091	206
71/76	Jean Thieffry v. Conseil de l'Ordre des Avocats à la Cour de Paris [1977] ECR 765	107
83 and 94/76, and 4, 15, and 40/77	Bayerische HNL Vermehrungsbetriebe GmbH & Co. KG et al v. Council and Commission [1978] ECR 1209	206

Table of Cases and Opinions xvii

85/76	*Hoffman-Laroche & Co. AG* v. *Commission* [1979] ECR 461	238
101/76	*Koninklijke Scholten-Honig NV* v. *Council and Commission* [1977] ECR 797	**190**
112/76	*Renato Manzoni* v. *Fonds National de Retraite des Ouvriers Mineurs* [1977] ECR 1647	200
11/77	*Richard Hugh Patrick* v. *Ministre des Affaires Culturelles* [1977] ECR 1199	107
30/77	*Regina* v. *Pierre Bouchereau* [1977] ECR 1999	98
103 and 145/77	*Royal Scholten-Honig (Holdings) Ltd and Tunnel Refineries Ltd.* v. *Intervention Board for Agricultural Produce* [1978] ECR 2037	**197**, 210, 216
106/77	*Amministrazione delle Finanzo dello Stato* v. *Simmenthal S.pA.* [1978] ECR 629	**54**
116 and 124/77	*G. R. Amylum NV and Tunnel Refineries Ltd.* v. *Council and Commission* [1979] ECR 3497	**202**
125/77	*Koninklijke Scholten-Honig NV* v. *Hoofdproduktschap voor Akkerbouwprodukten* [1978] ECR 1991	**192**
143/77	*Koninklijke Scholten-Honig NV* v. *Council and Commission* [1979] ECR 3583	201
92/78	*Simmenthal S.p.A.* v. *Commission* [1979] ECR 777	184
110 and 111/78	*Ministère Public and Chambre Syndicale des Agents Artistiques et Impresarii de Belgique ASBL* v. *Willy Van Wesemael et al.* [1979] ECR 35	121
120/78	*Rewe Zentral AG* v. *Bundesmonopolverwaltung für Branntwein* [1979] ECR 649	**73**
148/78	*Pubblico Ministero* v. *Tullio Ratti* [1979] ECR 1629	98
238/78	*Ireks-Arkady GmbH* v. *Council and Commission* [1979] ECR 2955	206
241, 242, and 245–50/78	*DGV, Deutsche Getreidverwertung et al.* v. *Council and Commission* [1979] ECR 3017	206
261 and 262/78	*Interquell Stärke-Chemie GmbH & Co KG and Diamalt KG* v. *Council and Commission* [1979] ECR 3045	206
32/79	*Commission* v. *UK* [1980] ECR 2403	11
52/79	*Procureur du Roi* v. *Marc J.V.C. Debauve et al.* [1980] ECR 833	121
62/79	*SA Société Générale pour la diffusion de la Télévision Coditel et al.* v. *SA Ciné Vog Films et al.* [1980] ECR 881	121
104/79	*Pasquale Foglio* v. *Maria Novello* (no. 1) [1980] ECR 745	39
138/79	*SA Roquette Frères* v. *Council* [1980] ECR 3333	**210**, 216, 221
139/79	*Maizena GmbH* v. *Council* [1980] ECR 3393	216, 221
155/79	*AM & S Europe Ltd* v. *Commission* [1982] ECR 1575	**225**

Table of Cases and Opinions

66/80	S.p.A. International Chemical Corporation v. Amministrazione delle Finanza dello Stato [1981] ECR 1191	200
113/80	Commission v. Ireland [1981] ECR 1625	80
244/80	Pasquale Foglio v. Maria Novello (no. 2) [1981] ECR 3045	39
19/81	Arthur Burton v. British Railways Board [1982] ECR 555	136, 141
108/81	G. R. Amylum v. Council [1982] ECR 3107	**218**
110/81	SA Roquette Frères v. Council [1982] ECR 3159	217
114/81	Tunnel Refineries Limited v. Council [1982] ECR 3189	217
115 and 116/81	Rezguia Adoui v. Belgian State and City of Liège; Dominique Cornuaille v. Belgian State [1982] ECR 1665	98
230/81	Grand Duchy of Luxemburg v. European Parliament [1983] ECR 255	160, 181
242/81	SA Roquette Frères v. Council and Commission [1982] ECR 3213	216
249/81	Commission v. Ireland [1982] ECR 4005	**78**
283/81	Srl CILFIT and Lanificio di Gavardo S.p.A. v. Ministry of Health [1982] ECR 3415	40
152/82	Sandro Forcheri and his wife Marisa Forcheri, née Marino v. Belgian State and ASBL Institut Supérieur de Sciences Humaines Appliquées [1983] ECR 2323	121
264/82	Timex Corporation v. Council and Commission [1985] 3 CMLR 550	199
271/82	Vincent Rodolphe Auer v. Ministère Public [1984] ECR 2727	98
286/82 and 26/83	Graziana Luisi and Giuseppe Carbone v. Ministero del Tesoro [1984] ECR 377	116
13/83	Parliament v. Council [1986] 1 CMLR 138	**161**
63/83	Regina v. Kent Kirk [1984] ECR 2689	160
108/83	Grand Duchy of Luxemburg v. European Parliament [1984] ECR 1945	160, 181
145/83	Stanley Adams v. Commission [1986] 1 CMLR 506	**236**
177/83	Theodor Kohl KG v. Ringelhan & Rennett SA et al. [1984] ECR 3651	77
216/83	Parti Ecologiste, Les Verts v. Parliament [1984] ECR 3325	171
293/83	Françoise Gravier v. City of Liège [1985] ECR 593	**115**
294/83	Parti Ecologiste, Les Verts v. Parliament	**171**, 178, 183, 208
152/84	M. H. Marshall v. Southampton and South West Hampshire Area Health Authority (Teaching) [1986] 2 ALLER 602	98, **137**
170/84	Bilka-Kaufhaus GmbH v. Karin Weber von Hartz [1986] 2 CMLR 701	136

181/84	*R* v. *Intervention Board for Agricultural Produce, ex parte E. D. & F. Man (Sugar) Ltd.* [1986] 2 ALLER 115	68, 200
209–13/84	*Ministère Public* v. *Lucas Asjes* [1986] 3 CMLR 173	169
121/85	*Conegate Ltd* v. *Customs & Excise Comrs.* [1986] 2 ALLER 688	77
15, 17, 18, 19, and 23/86	*Netherlands and other States* v. *Parliament*	177
34/86	*Council* v. *Parliament* [1986] 3 CMLR 94	177
51/86	*France* v. *Parliament*	181
Opinion 1/75	*Local Cost Standard* [1975] ECR 1355	160
Opinion 1/76	*Laying-up Fund* [1977] ECR 741	160

ABBREVIATIONS

AG	Advocate-General
AETR	Accord Européen sur les Transports Routiers (see ERTA)
ALLER	All England Law Reports
BCL	*Basic Community Laws*
CCBE	Consultative Committee of the Bars and Law Societies of the European Community
CMLR	Common Market Law Reports
DGIV	Directorate-General for Competition
EAEC	European Atomic Energy Community
ECJ	European Court of Justice
ECSC	European Coal and Steel Community
ECR	European Court Reports
ECU	European Currency Unit
EEC	European Economic Community
ERTA	European Road Transport Agreement
FCL	*Foundations of Community Law*
NCE	Non-compulsory expenditure
OJ	Official Journal of the European Communities
WLR	Weekly Law Reports

Introduction: Reading Community Cases

As a prelude to the extracts which follow, it may be useful to set out a few hints aimed specifically at preparing the student whose only experience so far has been in an English-speaking country.

THE READER

1. One should begin by trying to become aware of the unconscious assumptions of students in such a system—the things they take for granted and are likely to assume (quite erroneously) must be found everywhere. The first is endemic to English (though rare among American or Commonwealth, and unknown among Scottish) students: that there is only one legal system. The sensible study of Community law involves the realization that it involves the interrelation of different 'legal orders': classical international law, Community law, and the domestic law of twelve Member States. Of the latter, one—Germany—is a federal system, while others have distinct legal subsets: on the continent there are Andorra, Monaco, and San Marino, while the United Kingdom covers the law of England and Wales, Scotland, and Northern Ireland, but not those of the Channel Islands or the Isle of Man. It is neither possible, nor desirable, to master each of these systems; but a sense of their coexistence is essential.

2. The second assumption peculiar to common-lawyers is that the basic legal system is the work, not of the legislator, but of the courts. In the Community, however, it is the Treaties—above all, the Treaty of Rome creating the EEC—which lay the legal foundations. The Treaty of Rome acts as an international Treaty between High Contracting Parties and as the Constitution of a new and distinct legal entity, conferring and allocating law-making power among its institutions, and providing 'checks and balances' between them; it lays down the internal legal structure of a vast market where products, people, services, and money move freely; and it governs the relations of this economic community with the rest of the world. Over all these areas sits the European Court of Justice (ECJ), whose mission is to ensure that 'the law is observed' (EEC 164). As is made clear in the texts which follow, this 'law' is not to be found only in the Treaty and Community sources.

THE COURT

A full description of the composition, functions, and procedure of the ECJ may be found in any of the standard works on Community law or on the

Court itself. The following are merely a few remarks designed to emphasize certain features which are useful to an understanding of the case-law.

3. Although there is only the one Court of Justice, its jurisdiction and powers derive from three separate Treaties, each with its own Protocol on the Court Statute. In practice, the major differences are between actions brought under ECSC and those under the other two Treaties.

4. The Court consists of thirteen judges and six Advocates-General. They are chosen from persons whose independence is beyond doubt, and must either be qualified for high judicial office in their own countries or be learned jurists. Strictly speaking, they need not be Community nationals but, since they are appointed by 'common accord' of the Member States, in practice they always are; 'common accord' means that each State must positively approve. So far, the only common-lawyer on the Bench has been the Irish judge. The judge appointed on the accession of the UK is a Scot, although two Advocates-General have been English. The student from an anglophone country, accustomed to having as senior judges only experienced advocates, should realize that many members of the Court have never practised as such. On the other hand, at some time before their appointment, about a third have been members of their national Parliaments, and several have been Ministers.

5. Under the EEC Treaty, the ECJ has numerous judicial functions. It acts as an international court handling breaches by Member States; as a public-law court with sole powers of judicial review over legal measures and acts of the institutions; as the ultimate interpreter of Community laws; as the court with complete jurisdiction over the liability of the Community and penalties imposed by the Commission; and as adviser to the institutions on the compatibility with the Treaty of proposed agreements between the Community and other States or international organizations.

6. In all these weighty tasks, the ECJ was, until 1986, the tribunal of first and last resort. There is no higher court to which appeal can be made, although the ECJ itself can be asked to explain a judgment or even to 'revise' it if new and decisive facts come to light. The Single European Act of February 1986, however, amends the Treaties to provide for the creation of a separate court of first instance to hear cases brought by persons or firms, with an appeal on points of law to the ECJ. At the time of writing, it seems likely that one of the new court's main tasks will be to hear actions brought by the staff of the Community institutions.

7. The ECJ itself sits either in plenary session, or in Chambers. Broadly speaking, the most important matters come before the Full Bench, while Chambers of five or three judges deal with matters of middling or minor

importance. If, however, the action is brought by a Member State or an institution of the Community, the Court must decide it in plenary session.

8. Despite its numerous and weighty tasks, the ECJ has no inherent general jurisdiction. It is not, in that sense, a 'common-law' court, which can hear any case unless the legislator takes away its power in certain areas. The Treaty, by contrast, first lists the tasks of the Community and then entrusts their fulfilment to four institutions, stipulating that each 'shall act within the limits of the powers conferred upon it by this Treaty' (EEC 4(1)). In the case of the first three—Parliament, Council, and Commission—this provision in no way curtails their agenda; they may consider anything they like, and are restricted only in the things they can do at the end of the day. By contrast, in the case of the Court, the provision limits its jurisdiction not merely in the kinds of judgment it may give but in the types of case it may hear. For instance, actions by one citizen or firm against another, or against a Member State, even though based squarely on Community law, can never be entertained by the ECJ; and, even where the Community itself is a party, national courts have jurisdiction save where the Treaty specifies the ECJ (EEC 183). Thus general jurisdiction belongs to the national judges: it is they who administer and enforce the common Community law, whereas the ECJ is a court of great stature and considerable power, but limited jurisdiction.

UNFAMILIAR FEATURES

9. At a more humdrum level, several features of Community cases pose difficulty for the common, or Scots, lawyer. The first is simply the reporting. Since Edmund Plowden in the sixteenth century, common-lawyers have been accustomed to reports which are themselves the work of a powerful organizing intelligence. Although not all English reporters are of the same calibre, the general standard ensures that legal issues are normally presented with clarity, and that conflicting arguments are coherently marshalled. The European Court Reports do not belong to this tradition. The reporter may have to cope with different languages (and alphabets) and with pleadings framed by lawyers from disparate legal backgrounds, while the end product has to be produced in similar format in nine languages.

10. A second hindrance for the English student is that the Court's working language, in which its judgments are drafted, is French; and (unless that is the language of the case) the final version will have to be put into the language of the case. Thus the student will almost always be reading a translation, (or a translation of a translation) which will inevitably not stand comparison with the vigour of original native speech. This last word points to another contrast: the characteristic tone of the common-law judgment is that of the speaking voice of an individual who was once an advocate. European Court

decisions are invariably written, and are the work of a committee, not all of whose members practised at the bar.

11. Not only is French the language of the draft judgment, the French judicial style is also the model. The keynote of this style is austerity: a glance at the French text of the first case selected here will reveal that a great deal is written as one sentence with facts, procedural steps, arguments, and reasons, all drafted as subordinate clauses leading with an air of cold inevitability to the ruling. Some hint of this flavour appears in the English version of the final ruling in the text below. In later years the style becomes slightly more relaxed, but the Court never attempts to achieve verbal bite or pungency.

PROCEDURE

12. The Court adopts its own Rules of Procedure, which require the unanimous approval of the Council. Details may be found in the Rules themselves, but it should be noted that the steps leading up to judgment differ considerably from the common-law method. After an action has begun and the parties have exchanged their arguments of fact and law, it is the Court, guided by an advocate-general and by one of its members acting as *juge rapporteur*, which decides if further evidence is needed. If it is, witnesses are examined by a Chamber of the Court and their testimony added to the file. This written procedure overshadows the oral stage; for the latter, the reporting judge prepares a statement of the facts and summary of the legal arguments; counsel may then, of course, briefly address the court, and answer questions put by the Bench, but the facts and the main legal contentions will already be on file. At a later date, the Advocate-General delivers his submissions, on which the parties are not allowed to comment.

13. Proceedings under EEC 177 requesting a preliminary ruling on interpretation or validity are not, strictly speaking, contentious. The national court's reference is notified to the parties, the Member States, the Commission, and the Council; the addressees may submit written or oral observations or both. There is, however, no 'exchange of pleadings' as in a contested action, so that the oral hearing provides the only opportunity to reply to arguments put forward by other participants.

14. Judgment is always reserved and the reporting judge's draft is discussed by the judges alone and in secrecy. The Rules of Procedure specify what the judgment must contain; essentially it consists of three parts. The first states the facts and summarizes the arguments of the parties (but not the submissions of the Advocate-General); the second gives the Court's reasons for its decision and, since the mid-1960s, is usually set out in numbered paragraphs; and the third, and briefest, part is the actual ruling. This last is the only section read out by the Court, although the whole text is, of course, given to the parties.

15. The Court follows the common civil-law practice of delivering its decision as a collegiate body. There is never a concurring, much less a dissenting, opinion and, as to the court's own deliberations, the judges are—literally—sworn to secrecy (Court Statute, art. 2; see Rudden and Wyatt, *BCL*, 113). To a common-lawyer, the result of this technique of anonymity and unanimity is to present a chain of reasoning which is compelling only in syntax, while, in terms of judicial reasoning, what is framed as deduction sometimes reads like mere assertion. The position taken may well be satisfactory—as when the ECJ assumed jurisdiction to hear and decide the first case below—but readers must often supply for themselves the 'policy' reasons.

16. The first part of the judgment will recount the arguments of the parties to the dispute, but the reasoning which follows will rarely refute those of the loser, as a common-law judge (trained as an advocate) would instinctively do: that is, by spelling out their consequences in other, hypothetical situations and thus demonstrating their weakness. One striking feature is that the Court will summarize the arguments of the parties, but not that of its Advocate-General. Frequently, in fact, the ECJ follows his submissions. But in the great cases where it does not—extracts nos. 1, 13, and 15 below—it never explains why.

17. Yet it is in the submissions of the Advocate-General that common-lawyers will see most resemblance to their own judgments. It is he who discusses the facts, the prior decisions, the choices open to the Court, and any relevant considerations of policy.

18. A particular puzzle for the common-lawyer may be the role of precedent. Formally speaking, this is no problem. As nothing in the Treaty provides that the ECJ is bound by its own judgments, then it is not so bound; the extent to which it must be followed by domestic courts is discussed in the notes to extract no. 2, below. At a practical level, however, it is unlikely that the ECJ would reverse itself on a fundamental matter. Indeed, after a while, certain paragraphs recur so often that they become familiar: for instance, those dealing with the nature of Community law, with fundamental rights, or with the characteristics of a regulation. Thus there has grown up a settled body of case-law which, for all practical purposes, has as much normative authority as the Treaty.

19. Nonetheless, the view is still sometimes expressed that the ECJ must not—nay, cannot—make law. In Case 33/76 *Rewe*, for instance, Warner A-G said (at p. 2005): 'A ruling of this Court declares the law; it does not make it.' To what extent—if at all—this is true, is a question which must be answered by each reader.

I
The Law Common to the European Economic Community

1 Case 26/62 *Van Gend en Loos*

INTRODUCTION

Van Gend en Loos is undoubtedly the richest and most creative of all Community cases, and one in which virtually every later development can—at least with hindsight—be seen to have its germ. For this reason extensive extracts are printed below. The major omission is the opinion of the Advocate-General which, on the crucial points, was not accepted by the ECJ.

Unfortunately, although this case is arguably the most important ever decided by the ECJ, the student who begins conscientiously at the beginning, determined to read to the end, may soon be discouraged by an encounter with tedious lists of 'phenoplasts, aminoplasts, alkyds', and the like. One solution would have been to excise large portions of the facts and arguments. However, at some point, students must learn to face for themselves the raw material of Community case-law. Consequently, very little of it has been cut, but the introductory explanation goes to some lengths to prepare the reader.

1. *The action.* The Amsterdam 'Customs Court' (*Tariefcommissie*) asked the ECJ to explain EEC 12. EEC 177 gives the ECJ jurisdiction to interpret the Treaty and provides that any national court, if it considers that, in order to decide a case, it needs help from the ECJ, may request a ruling. Under the ECJ's Statute, art. 20, briefs were filed in the case by three Member States, the Commission, the Netherlands customs authorities, and the firm involved.

2. *The salient, simplified facts*

2.1 The EEC Treaty came into force in 1958.

2.2 It provides for the gradual dismantling of existing customs duties, but meanwhile sets out to stop new ones in their tracks. EEC 12 says: 'Member States shall refrain from introducing between themselves any new customs duties on imports or exports or any charges having equivalent effect, and from increasing those which they already apply in their trade with each other.'

2.3 Before 1958, the firm Van Gend en Loos had been importing glue from Germany and paying customs duties of 3 per cent of its value.

2.4 In 1957 a Dutch law had ratified the EEC Treaty, but in 1959 another law ratified a Benelux customs protocol, under whose Tariff Schedule the product attracted duty at 8 per cent.

2.5 The firm's protest at the 5 per cent extra, made to the Customs Inspector, was unavailing, so it brought an action in the Amsterdam Customs Court. The parties seem to have argued mainly questions of fact as to the correct classification of the import under the Tariff Schedule. The Court, however, realizing that the product had come from one Member State into another, decided that, before reaching a decision, it needed help as to the effect of the Treaty on this import. Consequently, it sent to the ECJ two questions about EEC 12. They will be discussed in more detail later, but at this stage it is enough to say that the essence of the questions concerns whether the Treaty article has a direct effect on the legal position of individuals and firms.

2.6 It should also be explained that nothing in the Treaty itself deals expressly with this problem. EEC 189 says that regulations are directly applicable, but no article of the Treaty says that any article of the Treaty has similar effect.

3. *The legal issues.* The contentions set out in the various briefs filed with the Court are, naturally, summarized very concisely in the law report, and so what follows is an attempt to reconstruct, organize, and set out at greater length the relevant legal arguments.

3.1 *The proper forum.* The Customs Court is seeking the views of the ECJ. As we shall see, the questions submitted are not meticulously drafted. But, before even considering them, it is evident that the crucial issue is going to be this: Van Gend en Loos is obviously affected by its own national law; so the question whether the firm's legal position is also affected by EEC 12 raises the issue of the relationship (and possible conflict) between a Treaty provision and national legislation. Now, it is agreed by both international, and national, law that the effect of a Treaty on municipal legislation is a matter, not of international law, but of national *constitutional* law.

The Netherlands Constitution then in force had a (somewhat obscure) provision (art. 66) dealing with the topic. Its lack of clarity, however, is not relevant here: what matters is not what it means, but *who decides* what it means. For it would be accepted by everyone as certain that the ECJ cannot (whether under international, national, or Community law) decide what the Netherlands Constitution means. Consequently, the powerful (and potentially very dangerous) argument put forward by Belgium is that a reference under EEC 177 is impossible because the ECJ *has no jurisdiction* to rule on the effect of an international Treaty on a Dutch subject; that question is exclusively a matter for a Netherlands court applying its own constitutional law.

3.2 *The proper plaintiff.* The defence of the customs authorities (apart from arguments on the facts) was the Dutch customs Order. The firm might well admit that this legislation was valid as a purely national measure, but pointed to EEC 12, arguing that this Treaty provision somehow overrode the later, inconsistent, national law. To this, the Netherlands Government answered, 'So what?' The EEC Treaty, it said, 'does not differ from a standard international treaty'; even supposing that the Netherlands is in breach of the Treaty, that is a matter of purely international misbehaviour giving rise only to an action before the ECJ (and not before a national court) brought by

Germany under EEC 170 or by the Commission under EEC 169 (and certainly not by a Dutch firm). This argument deserves respect, in terms both of what the Member States understood when they signed the Treaty, and of how their alleged infringements are to be judged. From their point of view, a request for interpretation under EEC 177 leads to a purely juridical, and rather academic, exercise. If, however, they are sued directly under EEC 169 or 170 they have the opportunity, in their defence, to plead the facts of what may be a highly complicated, or even critical, situation, of great importance to their citizens, and to mount arguments as to the choices open to them. (For instance, in the EEC 169 action in Case 32/79 *Commission* v. *UK*, certain fisheries measures were held to constitute a breach of the Treaty, but only after the UK as defendant, and four other Member States (particularly Denmark), had filed extensive and detailed briefs as to fish stocks.)

3.3 *The dilemma.* The first two issues, therefore, try to put the firm in a dilemma. If the plaintiff has a cause of action which calls into question the Netherlands legislation, then the proper forum is a national court, applying its own constitutional law. If, however, the ECJ is to have jurisdiction then the firm is not the proper plaintiff; the action should be brought by Germany or the Commission (under EEC 169, 170).

3.4 *The purpose of EEC 177.* A start may be made in dealing with the arguments so far set out by noting that EEC 177 says the ECJ may give a ruling if asked to do so by a national court. Now such a court will be hearing suits by citizens against public authorities, and will be dealing with numerous routine actions—say in contract—by one person against another. Why, in this event, should it need an interpretation of an international Treaty? Before the Treaty came into force, the domestic court would simply have applied its own national public, private, or conflicts law to the dispute. The answer seems to lie in EEC 177, which expressly covers the situation where the national court thinks an ECJ ruling is 'necessary to enable it to give judgment'. Now a ruling on the meaning of a Treaty can be necessary to the resolution of a dispute between two individuals only if the Treaty itself affects their legal position. This conclusion does not, of course, of itself entail that EEC 12 has this effect.

3.5 *The direct effect of EEC 12.* Even if (as submitted by the Advocate-General and the Commission) the ECJ has jurisdiction to respond to the request for a ruling on the effect of EEC 12, the Governments, while accepting that the article imposed an obligation on Member States, argued nonetheless that the correlative right to enforce, or sanction breach of, that obligation was vested only in the other parties to the Treaty and in the community 'policeman', the Commission. There were three reasons for this contention.

The first was the general assertion (with which the Advocate-General agreed) that where the Treaty dealt with the Member States—the High Contracting Parties—then it set up an agreement which took effect merely between them (i.e. internationally), but not between them and their citizens. The second was argued strongly by the Netherlands Government: EEC 169 and 170 provide remedies in the ECJ for breach of the Treaty; if, in addition, a Member State could find itself sued in its own courts by its own citizens 'the legal protection of that state would be considerably diminished'. The third objection (again the view of the Advocate-General) was directed to the wording of article 12 itself, which was said to be too complex to give citizens direct rights.

3.6 *Analysis of EEC 12.* At this stage it is useful to reread EEC 12 (above, 2.2) and to note its characteristics as a norm. They are as follows:

(i) It imposes an obligation only on Member States.

(ii) It does not spell out precisely to whom this obligation is owed; but, from EEC 169 and 170, it must, at the very least, be owed to the other Member States and to the Community (with the Commission empowered to enforce performance on the latter's behalf).

(iii) It enjoins, not action, but inaction; that is to say, the obligation does not require any positive act—on the contrary, the duty imposed is merely 'to refrain'. The State which does nothing complies scrupulously with EEC 12.

(iv) The duty is strict or, as the ECJ often says, it is an obligation 'to attain a precise result'. What this means is that the article does not merely require Member States to do their best not to increase customs duties; it tells them not to do it at all. Most negative obligations (or 'restrictive covenants') are like this. It is true that, by careful drafting, a duty may be only to *try* not to act, and EEC 71 provides an example: Member States 'shall endeavour to avoid introducing ... new exchange restrictions on the movement of capital ...'. EEC 12, however, imposes an absolute prohibition, and its technique is repeated in other 'standstill' provisions of the Treaty (e.g. EEC 31, 37(2), 53, 62, 95).

(v) The sentence which makes up EEC 12 forbids two things. One of them is quite clear—new customs duties. The other covers 'charges having equivalent effect', an area which is more difficult to define, and where there may be room for doubt. But it does not follow (as the Advocate-General seemed to think) that this makes the whole sentence too vague to be understood and directly applied. We may grant that there are some charges on which the effect of EEC 12 is uncertain, for those already in existence were to be dismantled, not by a simple timetable as for customs duties, but by Commission directives under EEC 13(2) (and, by 1965, 357 such doubtful charges had been found). Nonetheless, at least the prohibition of customs duties under EEC 12 is instantly comprehensible. There may be twilight, but we can still tell high noon.

3.7 *The drafting of the Dutch court's questions.* EEC 177 provides the means under which national courts ask the ECJ to interpret the Treaty (and other Community acts). Naturally, it does not give the ECJ power to interpret national law, nor does it expressly allow the Court to rule on the compatibility of one with the other, nor to apply its interpretation to the facts of the particular case. Yet it is precisely these problems which are likely to lead national courts to make a reference to the ECJ. This was the situation in *Van Gend en Loos*, with the consequence that the Amsterdam court's two questions seem, on one reading, to be inadmissible. They were (slightly abridged):

1. whether EEC 12 has direct application within the territory of a Member State, in other words, whether nationals of such a State can, on the basis of this article, lay claim to individual rights which the court must protect; and
2. if so, whether the application of an import duty of 8 per cent to the import into the Netherlands from the Federal Republic of Germany represented an unlawful increase within the meaning of EEC 12 or whether it was in this case a reasonable alteration of the duty applicable before 1 March 1960—an alteration which, although amounting to an increase from the arithmetical point of view, is nevertheless not to be regarded as prohibited under the terms of Article 12.

As the Advocate-General admitted, the wording of the first question—whether Article 12 has direct application—seems to pose a problem of national, as well as Community, law. But it is possible to rephrase it as asking the question, what—in the whole context of the Community, with its six Member States and numerous importers and exporters—does EEC 12 mean? It thus becomes, at least formally, a problem of how to interpret the Treaty.

The second question seems to ask the ECJ to read the Dutch tariff classifications and to decide whether the increase is real or merely numerical, a process which, as even the firm accepted, would clearly involve applying EEC 12 to the facts of the particular dispute. It is however possible (admittedly with some difficulty) to distil a more general question as to what EEC 12 means by 'new' or 'increased' duties as opposed to those that 'already apply'. Thus the two questions can be reformulated so as to relate more clearly to the only thing—treaty interpretation—which is within the ECJ's jurisdiction on this reference. The Court does reformulate them in order to show what, in the case of the second question, it describes as the 'real meaning'.

3.8 *The Dutch court's need for a ruling.* It will be recalled that EEC 177 allows a national court to refer only when 'it considers that a decision on the question is necessary to enable it to give judgment'. Consequently the Belgian Government argued that the ECJ had no jurisdiction to answer the first question because an answer was not necessary to enable the Dutch court to decide the lawsuit; all that the domestic court need do was to decide whether it could ignore the 1959 *national* law increasing the duty on the grounds of its conflict with the 1957 *national* law ratifying the EEC Treaty. As the Advocate-General demonstrated, however, and as the Court held, the vital problem was not 'Is a ruling necessary?' but *who decides* whether a ruling is necessary. There are only two possibilities—the ECJ or the referring court—and EEC 177 itself says that a reference may be made by a national court when '*it* decides'.

TEXT

In Case 26/62

Reference to the Court under subparagraph (*a*) of the first paragraph and under the third paragraph of Article 177 of the Treaty establishing the European Economic Community by the Tariefcommissie, a Netherlands administrative tribunal having final jurisdiction in revenue cases, for a preliminary ruling in the action pending before that court between

NV Algemene Transport- En Expeditie Onderneming Van Gend en Loos, having its registered office at Utrecht, represented by H. G. Stibbe and L. F. D. ter Kuile, both Advocates of Amsterdam, with an address for service in Luxemburg at the Consulate-General of the Kingdom of the Netherlands

AND

Nederlandse Administratie Der Belastingen (Netherlands Inland Revenue Administration), represented by the Inspector of Customs and Excise at Zaandam, with an address for service in Luxemburg at the Netherlands Embassy.

on the following questions:

1. whether Article 12 of the EEC Treaty has direct application within the territory of a Member State, in other words, whether nationals of such a State can, on the basis of the Article in question, lay claim to individual rights which the courts must protect;
2. in the event of an affirmative reply, whether the application of an import duty of 8 per cent to the import into the Netherlands by the applicant in the main action of ureaformaldehyde originating in the Federal Republic of Germany represented an unlawful increase within the meaning of Article 12 of the EEC Treaty or whether it was in this case a reasonable alteration of the duty applicable before 1 March 1960, an alteration which, although amounting to an increase from the arithmetical point of view, is nevertheless not to be regarded as prohibited under the terms of Article 12;

THE COURT

composed of: A. M. Donner (President), L. Delvaux and R. Rossi (Presidents of Chambers), O. Riese, Ch. L. Hammes (Rapporteur), A. Trabucchi and R. Lecourt (Judges),

Advocate-General: K. Roemer

Registrar: A. Van Houtte

gives the following

JUDGMENT

Issues of fact and of law

I FACTS AND PROCEDURE

The facts and the procedure may be summarized as follows:

1. On 9 September 1960 the Company NV Algemene Transport- en Expeditie Onderneming Van Gend en Loos (hereinafter called 'Van Gend en Loos'), according to a customs declaration of 8 September on form D. 5061, imported into the Netherlands from the Federal Republic of Germany a quantity of ureaformaldehyde described in the import document as 'Harnstoffharz (U. F. resin) 70, aqueous emulsion of ureaformaldehyde'.

2. On the date of importation, the product in question was classified in heading 39.01-a-1 of the tariff of import duties listed in the 'Tariefbesluit' which entered into force on 1 March 1960. The nomenclature of the 'Tariefbesluit' is taken from the protocol concluded between the Kingdom of Belgium, the Grand Duchy of Luxemburg, and the Kingdom of the Netherlands at Brussels on 25 July 1958, ratified in the Netherlands by the Law of 16 December 1959.

3. The wording of heading 39.01-a-1 was as follows:

Product of condensation, poly-condensation, and poly-addition, whether modified or not, polymerized, or linear (phenoplasts, aminoplasts, alkyds, allylic polyesters and other non-saturated polyesters, silicones, etc....):

(*a*) Liquid or paste products, including emulsions, dispersions, and solutions:

	Duties applicable	
	gen. %	spec. %
1 Aminoplasts in aqueous emulsions, dispersions, or solutions	10%	8%

4. On this basis, the Dutch revenue authorities applied an *ad valorem* import duty of 8 per cent to the importation in question.

5. On 20 September 1960 Van Gend en Loos lodged an objection with the Inspector of Customs and Excise at Zaandam against the application of this duty in the present case. The company put forward in particular the following arguments:

On 1 January 1958, the date on which the EEC Treaty entered into force, aminoplasts in emulsion were classified under heading 279-a-2 of the tariff in the 'Tariefbesluit' of 1947, and charged with an *ad valorem* import duty of 3 per cent. In the 'Tariefbesluit' which entered into force on 1 March 1960, heading 279-a-2 was replaced by heading 39.01-a.

Instead of applying, in respect of intra-Community trade, an import duty of 3 per cent uniformly to all products under the old heading 279-a-2, a subdivision was created: 39.01-a-1, which contained only aminoplasts in aqueous emulsions, dispersions, or solutions, and in respect of which import duty was fixed at 8 per cent. For the other products in heading 39.01-a, which also had been included in the old heading 279-a-2, the import duty of 3 per cent applied on 1 January 1958 was maintained.

By thus increasing the import duty on the product in question after the entry into force of the EEC Treaty, the Dutch Government infringed Article 12 of that Treaty, which provides that Member States shall refrain from introducing between themselves any new customs duties on imports or exports or any charges having equivalent effect, and from increasing those which they already apply in their trade with each other.

6. The objection of Van Gend en Loos was dismissed on 6 March 1961 by the Inspector of Customs and Excise at Zaandam on the ground of inadmissibility, because it was not directed against the actual application of the tariff but against the rate.

7. Van Gend en Loos appealed against this decision to the Tariefcommissie, Amsterdam, on 4 April 1961.

8. The case was heard by the Tariefcommissie on 21 May 1962. In support of its application for the annulment of the contested decision Van Gend en Loos put forward the arguments already submitted in its objection of 20 September 1960. The Nederlandse Administratie der Belastingen replied in particular that when the EEC Treaty entered into force the product in question was not charged under the heading 279-a-2 with a duty of only 3 per cent but, because of its composition and intended application, was classified under heading 332 bis ('synthetic and other adhesives, not stated or included elsewhere') and charged with a duty of 10 per cent so that there had not in fact been any increase.

9. The Tariefcommissie, without giving a formal decision on the question whether the product in question fell within heading 332 bis or heading 279-a-2 of the 1947 'Tariefbesluit', took the view that the arguments of the parties raised questions concerning the interpretation of the EEC Treaty. It therefore suspended the proceedings and, in conformity with the third paragraph of Article 177 of the Treaty, referred to the Court of Justice on 16 August 1962, for a preliminary ruling on the two questions set out above.

10. The decision of the Tariefcommissie was notified on 23 August 1962 by the Registrar of the Court to the parties to the action, to the Member States, and to the Commission of the EEC.

11. Pursuant to Article 20 of the Protocol on the Statute of the Court of Justice of the EEC written observations were submitted to the Court by the parties to the main action, by the Government of the Kingdom of Belgium, the Government of the

Federal Republic of Germany, the Commission of the EEC, and the Government of the Kingdom of the Netherlands.

12. At the public hearing of the Court on 29 November 1962, the oral submissions of the plaintiff in the main action and of the Commission of the EEC were heard. At the same hearing questions were put to them by the Court. Written replies to these were supplied within the prescribed time.

13. The Advocate-General gave his reasoned oral opinion at the hearing on 12 December 1962, in which he proposed that the Court should in its judgment only answer the first question referred to it and hold that Article 12 of the EEC Treaty imposes a duty only on Member States.

II ARGUMENTS AND OBSERVATIONS

The arguments contained in the observations submitted in accordance with the second paragraph of Article 20 of the Protocol on the Statute of the Court of Justice of the European Economic Community by the parties to the main action, the Member States, and the Commission may be summarized as follows:

A THE FIRST QUESTION

Admissibility

The Netherlands Government, the Belgian Government, and the Nederlandse Administratie der Belastingen (which in its statement of case declared that it was in complete agreement with the observations submitted by the Netherlands Government) confirm that the main complaint of Van Gend en Loos against the Governments of the Benelux countries is that by the Brussels protocol of 25 July 1958 they infringed Article 12 of the EEC Treaty by increasing after its entry into force a customs duty applied in their trade with other Member States of the communities.

The Netherlands Government disputes whether an alleged infringement of the Treaty by a Member State can be submitted to the judgment of the Court by a procedure other than that laid down by Article 169 and 170, that is to say on the initiative of another Member State or of the Commission. It maintains in particular that the matter cannot be brought before the Court by means of the procedure of reference for a preliminary ruling under Article 177.

The Court, according to the Netherlands Government, cannot, in the context of the present proceedings, decide a problem of this nature, since it does not relate to the interpretation but to the application of the Treaty in a specific case.

The Belgian Government maintains that the first question is a reference to the Court of a problem of constitutional law, which falls exclusively within the jurisdiction of the Netherlands court.

That court is confronted with two international treaties both of which are part of the national law. It must decide under national law—assuming that they are in fact contradictory—which treaty prevails over the other or more exactly whether a prior national law of ratification prevails over a subsequent one.

This is a typical question of national constitutional law which has nothing to do with the interpretation of an Article of the EEC Treaty and is within the exclusive jurisdiction of the Netherlands court, because it can only be answered according to the constitutional principles and jurisprudence of the national law of the Netherlands.

The Belgian Government also points out that a decision on the first question referred to the Court is not only unnecessary to enable the Tariefcommissie to give its judgment but cannot even have any influence on the solution to the actual problem which it is asked to resolve.

In fact, whatever answer the Court may give, the Tariefcommissie has to solve the same problem: Has it the right to ignore the law of 16 December 1959 ratifying the Brussels Protocol, because it conflicts with an earlier law of 5 December 1957 ratifying the Treaty establishing the EEC?

The question raised is not therefore an appropriate question for a preliminary ruling, since its answer cannot enable the court which has to adjudicate upon the merits of the main action to make a final decision in the proceedings pending before it.

The Commission of the EEC, on the other hand, observes that the effect of the provisions of the Treaty on the national law of Member States cannot be determined by the actual national law of each of them but by the Treaty itself. The problem is therefore without doubt one of interpretation of the Treaty.

Further the Commission calls attention to the fact that a finding of inadmissibility would have the paradoxical and shocking result that the rights of individuals would be protected in all cases of infringement of Community law except in the case of an infringement by a Member State.

On the substance

Van Gend en Loos answers in the affirmative the question whether the article has internal effect.

It maintains in particular that:

—Article 12 is applicable without any preliminary incorporation in the national legislation of Member States, since it only imposes a negative obligation;
—it has direct effect without any further measures of implementation under Community legislation, as all the customs duties applied by Member States in their trade with each other were bound on 1 January 1957 (article 14 of the Treaty);
—although the Article does not directly refer to the nationals of Member States but to the national authorities, infringement of it adversely affects the fundamental principles of the Community, and individuals as well as the Community must be protected against such infringements;
—it is particularly well adapted for direct application by the national court which must set aside the application of customs duties introduced or increased in breach of its provisions.

The Commission emphasizes the importance of the Court's answer to the first question. It will have an effect not only on the interpretation of the provision at issue in a specific case and on the effect which will be attributed to it in the legal systems of Member States but also on certain other provisions of the Treaty which are as clear and complete as Article 12.

According to the Commission an analysis of the legal structure of the Treaty and of the legal system which it establishes shows on the one hand that the Member States did not only intend to undertake mutual commitments but to establish a system of Community law, and on the other hand that they did not wish to withdraw the application of this law from the ordinary jurisdiction of the national courts of law.

However, Community law must be effectively and uniformly applied throughout the whole of the Community.

The result is first that the effect of Community law on the internal law of Member States cannot be determined by this internal law but only by Community law, further that the national courts are bound to apply directly the rules of Community law, and finally that the national court is bound to ensure that the rules of Community law prevail over conflicting national laws even if they are passed later.

The Commission observes in this context that the fact that a community rule is, as regards its form, directed to the States does not of itself take away from individuals who have an interest in it the right to require it to be applied in the national courts.

As regards more particularly the question referred to the Court, the Commission is of the opinion that Article 12 contains a rule of law capable of being effectively applied by the national court.

It is a provision which is perfectly clear in the sense that it creates for Member States a specific unambiguous obligation relating to the extension of their internal law in a matter which directly affects their nationals and it is not affected or qualified by any other provision of the Treaty. It is also a complete and self-sufficient provision in that it does not require on a Community level any new measure to give concrete form to the obligation which it defines.

The Netherlands Government draws a distinction between the question of the internal effect and that of the direct effect (or direct applicability), the first, according to it, being a precondition of the second.

It considers that the question whether a particular provision of the Treaty has an internal effect can only be answered in the affirmative if all the essential elements, namely the intention of the contracting parties and the material terms of the provision under consideration, allows such a conclusion.

With regard to the intention of the parties to the Treaty the Netherlands Government maintains that an examination of the actual wording is sufficient to establish that Article 12 only places an obligation on Member States, who are free to decide how they intend to fulfil this obligation. A comparison with other provisions of the Treaty confirms this finding.

As Article 12 does not have internal effect it cannot, *a fortiori*, have direct effect.

Even if the fact that Article 12 places an obligation on Member States were to be considered as an internal effect, it cannot have direct effect in the sense that it permits the nationals of Member States to assert subjective rights which the courts must protect.

Alternatively the Netherlands Government argues that, so far as the necessary conditions for its direct application are concerned, the EEC Treaty does not differ from a standard international treaty. The conclusive factors in this respect are the intention of the parties and the provisions of the Treaty.

However the question whether under Netherlands constitutional law Article 12 is directly applicable is one concerning the interpretation of Netherlands law and does not come within the jurisdiction of the Court of Justice.

Finally the Netherlands Government indicates what the effect would be, in its view, of an affirmative answer to the first question put by the Tariefcommissie:

—it would upset the system which the authors of the Treaty intended to establish;
—it would create, with regard to the many provisions in Community regulations which expressly impose obligations on Member States, an uncertainty in the law of a kind which could call in question the readiness of these States to co-operate in the future;
—it would put in issue the responsibility of States by means of a procedure which was not designed for this purpose.

The Belgian Government maintains that Article 12 is not one of the provisions:

—which are the exception in the Treaty
—having direct internal effect.

Article 12 does not constitute a rule of law of general application providing that any introduction of a new customs duty or any increase in an existing duty is automatically without effect or is absolutely void. It merely obliges Member States to refrain from taking such measures.

It does not create therefore a directly applicable right which nationals could invoke and enforce. It requires from Governments action at a later date to attain the objective fixed by the Treaty. A national court cannot be asked to enforce compliance with this obligation.

The German Government is also of the opinion that Article 12 of the EEC Treaty does not constitute a legal provision which is directly applicable in all Member States. It imposes on them an international obligation (in the field of customs policy) which must be implemented by national authorities endowed with legislative powers.

Customs duties applicable to a citizen of a Member State of the Community, at least during the transitional period, thus do not derive from the EEC Treaty or the legal measures taken by the institutions, but from legal measures enacted by Member States. Article 12 only lays down the provisions with which they must comply in their customs legislation.

Moreover the obligation laid down only applies to the other contracting Member States.

In German law a legal provision which laid down a customs duty contrary to the provisions of Article 12 would be perfectly valid.

Within the framework of the EEC Treaty the legal protection of nationals of Member States is secured, by provisions derogating from their national constitutional system, only in respect of those measures taken by the institutions of the Community which are of direct and individual concern to such nationals.

B THE SECOND QUESTION

Admissibility

The Netherlands and Belgian Governments are of the opinion that the second as well as the first question is inadmissible.

According to them the answer to the question whether in fact the Brussels Protocol of 1958 represents a failure by those states who are signatories to fulfil the obligations laid down in Article 12 of the EEC Treaty cannot be given in the context of a preliminary ruling, because the issue is the application of the Treaty and not its interpretation. Moreover such an answer presupposes a careful study and a specific evaluation of the facts and circumstances peculiar to a given situation, and this is also inadmissible under Article 177.

The Netherlands Government emphasizes, furthermore, that if a failure by a state to fulfil its Community obligations could be brought before the Court by a procedure other than those under Articles 169 and 170 the legal protection of that state would be considerably diminished.

The German Government, without making a formal objection of inadmissibility, maintains that Article 12 only imposes an international obligation on States and that the question whether national rules enacted for its implementation do not comply with this obligation cannot depend upon a decision of the Court under Article 177 since it does not involve the interpretation of the Treaty.

Van Gend en Loos also considers that the direct form of the second question would necessitate an examination of the facts for which the Court has no jurisdiction when it makes a ruling under Article 177. The real question for interpretation according to it [the firm] could be worded as follows:

Is it possible for a derogation from the rules applied before 1 March 1960 (or more accurately, before 1 January 1958) not to be in the nature of an increase prohibited by Article 12 of the Treaty, even though this derogation arithmetically represents an increase?

Grounds of judgment

I PROCEDURE

No objection has been raised concerning the procedural validity of the reference to the Court under Article 177 of the EEC Treaty by the Tariefcommissie, a court or tribunal within the meaning of that Article. Further, no grounds exist for the Court to raise the matter of its own motion.

II THE FIRST QUESTION

A JURISDICTION OF THE COURT

The Government of the Netherlands and the Belgian Government challenge the jurisdiction of the Court on the ground that the reference relates not to the interpretation but to the application of the Treaty in the context of the constitutional law of the Netherlands, and that in particular the Court has no jurisdiction to decide, should the occasion arise, whether the provisions of the EEC Treaty prevail over Netherlands legislation or over other agreements entered into by the Netherlands and incorporated into Dutch national law. The solution of such a problem, it is claimed, falls within the exclusive jurisdiction of the national courts, subject to an application in accordance with the provisions laid down by Articles 169 and 170 of the Treaty.

However in this case the Court is not asked to adjudicate upon the application of the Treaty according to the principles of the national law of the Netherlands, which remains the concern of the national courts, but is asked, in conformity with subparagraph (*a*) of the first paragraph of Article 177 of the Treaty, only to interpret the scope of Article 12 of the said Treaty within the context of Community law and with reference to its effect on individuals. This argument has therefore no legal foundation.

The Belgian Government further argues that the Court has no jurisdiction on the ground that no answer which the Court could give to the first question of the Tariefcommissie would have any bearing on the result of the proceedings brought in that court.

However, in order to confer jurisdiction on the Court in the present case it is necessary only that the question raised should clearly be concerned with the interpretation of the Treaty. The considerations which may have led a national court or tribunal to its choice of questions as well as the relevance which it attributes to such questions in the context of a case before it are excluded from review by the Court of Justice.

It appears from the wording of the questions referred that they relate to the interpretation of the Treaty. The Court therefore has the jurisdiction to answer them.

This argument, too, is therefore unfounded.

B ON THE SUBSTANCE OF THE CASE

The first question of the Tariefcommissie is whether Article 12 of the Treaty has direct application in national law in the sense that nationals of Member States may on the basis of this Article lay claim to rights which the national courts must protect.

To ascertain whether the provisions of an international treaty extend so far in their effects it is necessary to consider the spirit, the general scheme, and the wording of those provisions.

The objective of the EEC Treaty, which is to establish a Common Market, the functioning of which is of direct concern to interested parties in the Community, implies that this Treaty is more than an agreement which merely creates mutual obligations between the contracting states. This view is confirmed by the preamble to the Treaty which refers not only to governments but to peoples. It is also confirmed more specifically by the establishment of institutions endowed with sovereign rights, the exercise of which affects Member States and also their citizens. Furthermore, it must be noted that the nationals of the states brought together in the Community are called upon to co-operate in the functioning of this Community through the intermediary of the European Parliament and the Economic and Social Committee.

In addition, the task assigned to the Court of Justice under Article 177, the object of which is to secure uniform interpretation of the Treaty by national courts and tribunals, confirms that the states have acknowledged that Community law has an authority which can be invoked by their nationals before those courts and tribunals.

The conclusion to be drawn from this is that the Community constitutes a new legal order of international law for the benefit of which the States have limited their sovereign rights, albeit within limited fields, and the subjects of which comprise not only Member States but also their nationals. Independently of the legislation of Member States, Community law therefore not only imposes obligations on individuals but is also intended to confer upon them rights which become part of their legal heritage. These rights arise not only where they are expressly granted by the Treaty, but also by reason of obligations which the Treaty imposes in a clearly defined way upon individuals as well as upon the Member States and upon the institutions of the Community.

With regard to the general scheme of the Treaty as it relates to customs duties and charges having equivalent effect it must be emphasized that Article 9, which bases the Community upon a customs union, includes as an essential provision the prohibition of these customs duties and charges. This provision is found at the beginning of the part of the Treaty which defines the 'Foundations of the Community'. It is applied and explained by Article 12.

The wording of Article 12 contains a clear and unconditional prohibition which is not a positive but a negative obligation. This obligation, moreover, is not qualified by any reservation on the part of States which would make its implementation conditional upon a positive legislative measure enacted under national law. The very nature of this prohibition makes it ideally adapted to produce direct effects in the legal relationship between Member States and their subjects.

The implementation of Article 12 does not require any legislative intervention on the part of the States. The fact that under this Article it is the Member States who are made the subject of the negative obligation does not imply that their nationals cannot benefit from this obligation.

In addition the argument based on Articles 169 and 170 of the Treaty put forward by the three Governments which have submitted observations to the Court in their statements of case is misconceived. The fact that these Articles of the Treaty enable the Commission and the Member States to bring before the Court a State which has not fulfilled its obligations does not mean that individuals cannot plead these obligations, should the occasion arise, before a national court, any more than the fact that the Treaty places at the disposal of the Commission ways of ensuring that obligations imposed upon those subject to the Treaty are observed, precludes the possibility, in actions between individuals before a national court, of pleading infringements of these obligations.

A restriction of the guarantees against an infringement of Article 12 by Member States to the procedures under Articles 169 and 170 would remove all direct legal protection of the individual rights of their nationals. There is the risk that recourse to the procedure under these Articles would be ineffective if it were to occur after the implementation of a national decision taken contrary to the provisions of the Treaty.

The vigilance of individuals concerned to protect their rights amounts to an effective supervision in addition to the supervision entrusted by Articles 169 and 170 to the diligence of the Commission and of the Member States.

It follows from the foregoing considerations that, according to the spirit, the general scheme, and the wording of the Treaty, Article 12 must be interpreted as producing direct effects and creating individual rights which national courts must protect.

III THE SECOND QUESTION

A THE JURISDICTION OF THE COURT

According to the observations of the Belgian and Netherlands Governments, the wording of this question appears to require, before it can be answered, an examination by the Court of the tariff classification of ureaformaldehyde imported into the Netherlands, a classification on which Van Gend en Loos and the Inspector of Customs and Excise at Zaandam hold different opinions with regard to the 'Tariefbesluit' of 1947. The question clearly does not call for an interpretation of the Treaty but concerns the application of Netherlands customs legislation to the classification of aminoplasts, which is outside the jurisdiction conferred upon the Court of Justice of the European Communities by subparagraph (*a*) of the first paragraph of Article 177.

The Court has therefore no jurisdiction to consider the reference made by the Tariefcommissie.

However, the real meaning of the question put by the Tariefcommissie is whether, in law, an effective increase in customs duties charged on a given product as a result not of an increase in the rate but of a new classification of the product arising from a change of its tariff description contravenes the prohibition in Article 12 of the Treaty.

Viewed in this way the question put is concerned with an interpretation of this provision of the Treaty and more particularly of the meaning which should be given to the concept of duties applied before the Treaty entered into force.

Therefore the Court has jurisdiction to give a ruling on this question.

B ON THE SUBSTANCE

It follows from the wording and the general scheme of Article 12 of the Treaty that, in order to ascertain whether customs duties of charges having equivalent effect have been increased contrary to the prohibition contained in the said Article, regard must be had to the customs duties and charges actually applied at the date of the entry into force of the Treaty.

Further, with regard to the prohibition in Article 12 of the Treaty, such an illegal increase may arise from a rearrangement of the tariff resulting in the classification of the product under a more highly taxed heading and from an actual increase in the rate of customs duty.

It is of little importance how the increase in customs duties occurred when, after the Treaty entered into force, the same product in the same Member State was subjected to a higher rate of duty.

The application of Article 12, in accordance with the interpretation given above, comes within the jurisdiction of the national court which must enquire whether the dutiable product, in this case ureaformaldehyde originating in the Federal Republic of Germany, is charged under the customs measures brought into force in the Netherlands with an import duty higher than that with which it was charged on 1 January 1958.

The Court has no jurisdiction to check the validity of the conflicting views on this subject which have been submitted to it during the proceedings but must leave them to be determined by the national courts.

IV COSTS

The costs incurred by the Commission of the EEC and the Member States which have submitted their observations to the Court are not recoverable, and as these proceedings are, in so far as the parties to the main action are concerned, a step in the action pending before the Tariefcommissie, the decision as to costs is a matter for that court.

On those grounds,

upon reading the pleadings;
upon hearing the report of the Judge-Rapporteur;
upon hearing the parties;
upon hearing the opinion of the Advocate-General;
having regard to Articles 9, 12, 14, 169, 170, and 177 of the Treaty establishing the European Economic Community;
having regard to the Protocol on the Statute of the Court of Justice of the European Economic Community;

having regard to the Rules of Procedure of the Court of Justice of the European Communities;

THE COURT

in answer to the questions referred to it for a preliminary ruling by the Tariefcommissie by decision of 16 August 1962, hereby rules:

1. Article 12 of the Treaty establishing the European Economic Community produces direct effects and creates individual rights which national courts must protect.
2. In order to ascertain whether customs duties or charges having equivalent effect have been increased contrary to the prohibition contained in Article 12 of the Treaty, regard must be had to the duties and charges actually applied by the Member State in question at the date of the entry into force of the Treaty.

   Such an increase can arise both from a rearrangement of the tariff resulting in the classification of the product under a more highly taxed heading and from an increase in the rate of customs duty applied.
3. The decision as to costs in these proceedings is a matter for the Tariefcommissie.

COMMENTS

THE ECJ'S MODE OF REASONING

1. It will be obvious to the common-law reader that the methods of reasoning used by the ECJ are more limited in range than those of his own judges. The Court's legal logic combines a certain wintry elegance with great brevity. Thus, the Member States contended (for reasons both legal and practical) that the firm cannot plead a breach of the Treaty in its own courts because the Commission can do so in the ECJ under EEC 169, where they will have the chance to defend themselves on the merits. This is dealt with by a counter-argument which is, in terms, addressed only to legal deduction and not to the policy, or propriety, of the Member States' claim. The ECJ merely points out that the Commission can enforce against individuals certain Treaty obligations (EEC 87 2 (*a*) and 89 must be meant, though they are not cited) and yet, before a national court, one individual may plead another's breach of the Treaty (again, EEC 85 and 86 must be meant). Similarly, the Court answers the argument that the Member States never intended to give their citizens rights under EEC 12 by pointing out that, by giving jurisdiction to the ECJ under 177, the States have 'acknowledged that Community law has an authority which can be invoked by their nationals before [their] courts'.
2. Other passages, however, may seem to a common-lawyer less satisfactory. Let us consider one brief example:

the Court is not called upon to adjudicate upon the application of the Treaty according to the principles of the national law of the Netherlands ... but is asked, in conformity with Article 177(a) of the Treaty, to interpret the scope of Article 12 as of the Treaty within the context of Community law and with reference to its effect on individuals.

To the reader accustomed to English-language law reports, this reads more like assertion than argument, and the style seems curiously opaque (though this may be caused partly by the difficulty of translating the original).

3. Furthermore, to one accustomed to the forensic skill of the common-law judge, the ECJ's most telling point seems couched in rather stilted language. The Court does spell out the very important basic fact that the Treaty, in setting up a common market, is concerned directly with the activities of ordinary people—workers, the self-employed, firms which trade across borders—and it would make no sense at all to divide the impact of Community law in the market-place along the boundaries of national legal systems: German citizens must be able to trade on the same terms as their counterparts in Italy, and so on. But all these 'policy' considerations have to be read into the reference to the Treaty's 'effect on individuals' and in the Court's later statement that the subjects of the Community legal order 'are not only the Member States but individuals as well'.

4. In this, (as in its main ruling that EEC 12 has direct effects) the ECJ does not follow the Advocate-General who could not believe that firms would rely on a Treaty rather than their national customs provisions. Perhaps the Court was signalling to traders in the common market-place that, from now on, they could rely on at least the standstill clauses of the Treaty.

5. The ECJ deduces from this 'effect on individuals' that 'the Community constitutes a new legal order of international law, for the benefit of which the States have limited their sovereign rights, albeit within limited fields, and the subjects of which comprise not only Member States but also their nationals.' It is not entirely clear from this sentence whether the ECJ identifies the Community as an entirely *sui generis* legal system, something which is not international, federal, or national, or whether it means that here we have a new subclass of international law. The latter reading raises serious doubts, for a system which gives rights directly to individual citizens runs counter to the long-standing general principles of classical international law. In any event, although in later cases the ECJ has often repeated the substance of this sentence, it has never again described the Community as an order 'of international law'.

6. One powerful type of reasoning comes so naturally to common-lawyers that they are hardly aware of it. It is the method which tests a possible solution by supposing that it were not adopted and then asking what the results would be. This style of argument comes automatically to the advocate

who attacks his opponent's case by drawing attention to its baleful consequences. It is a powerful tool which the ECJ hardly ever uses explicitly, though one sees it employed in the Commission's arguments. Yet this method of reasoning makes the result of the case almost inevitable.

7. First—and most important—of all, the ECJ assumes jurisdiction to hear the case, although powerful arguments were raised against this on the grounds that the problem was one of Netherlands constitutional law. Suppose the Court had, on this ground, declined jurisdiction. It is still perfectly possible that Van Gend en Loos would have won the day in their own courts; but that would have been because of their courts' interpretation of the Netherlands Constitution. Very satisfactory for a Dutch firm; but what would be the fate of a Belgian or Italian firm, whose country (like the UK) did not recognize the internal primacy of international Treaties? The result would be that EEC 12—which is supposed to cover all trade in the Community—would directly protect some traders and not others, depending on the constitution of their country. So EEC 12 would not be a rule of common Community law, that is to say it would not be a rule common to the whole Community.

8. Secondly, suppose the ECJ had taken the case but had followed the Advocate-General and held that EEC 12 was too complex directly to confer rights. A host of problems would have arisen, both practical and legal. As to the first, various Member States might have introduced new duties or otherwise broken their Treaty obligations. They could, of course, be sued in the ECJ by the Commission or the other States, but there is no obligation to sue. Other Member States might themselves be in breach, and dog would not eat dog. The Commission is supposed to 'ensure that the Treaty is applied' (EEC 155), but might prefer to try persuasion, delay, or simple inaction. For instance, in Case 48/74 *Charmasson*, a French banana importer had no success at all with his complaints to the Commission about his government's breach of the Treaty, which was not found (indirectly) until he persuaded the Conseil d'Etat to make a reference under EEC 177; and in Case 43/75 *Defrenne* 2 (below, extract no. 13), the Court courteously rebuked the Commission for its inaction on equal pay.

9. Even if an action were brought in the ECJ, the only result would be a finding of the State's misbehaviour. It is very important to recall that, while the ECJ can quash Community acts under EEC 174, it has no such power against Member States. It would be up to the defaulter, under EEC 171, to put things right, but this would not necessarily help the traders who had paid the duties in the meantime. An action in their own courts, on the other hand, (as the ECJ says) gives them direct legal protection and the means of policing their country's compliance with the common Community law.

SOME IMPLICATIONS OF THE JUDGMENT

10. Although the Dutch court's drafting has been criticized, its first question performs the vital function of calling attention to the implications of the interpretation decided in *Van Gend en Loos*. The first problem is whether EEC 12 directly affects individuals by giving them rights, and one can begin to answer it by a formal analysis on the lines set out in 3.6 above, and by a consideration of the function of the provision within a common market affecting traders in six countries. The ECJ makes use of both these techniques; but, if EEC 12 be interpreted as giving direct rights to citizens, a whole range of problems opens up.

11. Rights against whom? The answer must be, first, against their own country and then, presumably, against other Member States. Who is to protect these rights? Nothing in Community law allows citizens to go straight to the ECJ to complain about Member States' breach of the Treaty. So the answer must be—as the Netherlands court realized and the ECJ states—that it is the national judge who is to enforce the community rights of individuals against the very State of which they are citizens and he a judge. But if this be the case—as it must be—then EEC 12 does more than confer rights on people; it imposes duties on the officials of a State, especially its judges, to respect and enforce the numerous individual rights, liberties, and duties which flow from the Treaty.

12. In short, it is the national court which becomes the main upholder of the Community, since the ECJ's jurisdiction is restricted to a small number of precisely defined situations, and EEC 4(1) says that 'each institution must act within the limits of the powers conferred upon it by this Treaty'. All other cases must be handled by national courts which thus become the residual jurisdiction for the *common Community law*.

13. However, this task of upholding Community law may conflict with the obligation (usually sworn to in the judicial oath) to enforce the law of the country of which the official is judge. He is bound to be faced with the problem of what to do about a valid statute of his own country which infringes a litigant's Community rights. And, if a Dutch judge must uphold the litigant's Community rights against the Netherlands, then must he uphold them against France if she breaks Article 12 by putting a new duty on imports from the Netherlands? If so, how?

14. This last question broaches a further set of problems. Community law may directly give people rights but, as a great American judge once observed, a right without a remedy is like the hole in a doughnut. What remedy is the national judge to deploy against the defaulting State: judicial review, injunction, damages? And logically prior to this is the question of what system of law is to determine the appropriate remedy? There is no Community law

spelling out the remedies available to an individual against a Member State, since the ECJ has no jurisdiction in such cases; though it is not without significance that where, in an action by the Commission or another Member State, it has jurisdiction, the only thing it can do is to 'find that a Member State has failed to fulfil an obligation' (EEC 171)—i.e., the ECJ can merely make a declaration.

15. So, if Community law does not help the national judge to devise the appropriate remedy, he must use his own system. This has the strange result that the right is determined by Community, but the remedy by national, law. It has the further consequence that the right conferred by one and the same article of the Treaty may give rise to as many different remedies as there are legal systems within the Community.

16. The most urgent problem raised by this great case concerned the effect, not of EEC 12, but of the simple handing down of the preliminary ruling. The Amsterdam court is bound by the ECJ's decision that EEC 12 has direct effect and must, if its finding of fact makes this necessary, enforce the right which the Article confers directly on the firm. This binding effect on the referring court is not spelled out by, but seems inherent in, EEC 177: it says that the ECJ has jurisdiction to interpret the Treaty and other Community Acts, and EEC 219 stops Member States from using any other method of settlement of a dispute on (*inter alia*) interpretation of the Treaty. In any case, the EEC 177 procedure would be pointless if the national court which asked the question could ignore the answer.

17. But what is the effect of the ruling on the Amsterdam court in other cases involving EEC 12, and on *all* other national courts? Does it become what a common-lawyer would call a precedent, so that, in any disputes on EEC 12, all courts must, as a matter of law, hold that the Article is directly effective? Fortunately, some sort of answer to this problem was given very soon after, and in the context of, Case 26/62 *Van Gend en Loos*, so it may conveniently be dealt with in the next extract.

2 Cases 28–30/62 *Da Costa en Schaake*

1. *The action.* These three cases were all references under EEC 177 (*a*) by the Amsterdam Customs Court asking the ECJ to interpret EEC 12. The ECJ considered the issues raised to be identical in all three, and ordered them to be joined.

2. *The salient, simplified facts*

2.1 The Netherlands Customs Order which caused the dispute in Case 26/62 *Van Gend en Loos* applied to a range of products. Other importers of goods from Germany protested to the Customs Authorities and, when this failed, appealed to the Customs Court.

2.2 The Court made references similar to that in Case 26/62 *Van Gend en Loos*, so that four cases had been begun.

2.3 The Commission and Germany filed briefs. The arguments of the former were those it had put forward in Case 26/62 *Van Gend en Loos*, while the Government repeated the view that, from the viewpoint of Community law, EEC 12 imposed a solely international obligation, so whether it also gave individuals rights was a matter for national constitutional law.

2.4 Judgment in Case 26/62 *Van Gend en Loos* was given a fortnight before oral argument in the three remaining cases.

2.5 Consequently, at the hearing, the Commission advanced a view that would gladden the heart of English lawyers. They would call it *precedent*.

3. *The main issues*

3.1 The main issue in this case is *not* the interpretation of EEC 12.

3.2 It was conceded that the problem of interpretation was the same in the four cases—in fact the referring court's two questions were virtually identical in all of them.

3.3 Thus we have the same issue, referred by the same court. The only difference (at the national level, and surely unimportant) is in the products and their importers.

3.4 The new, and major, problem can be presented most simply by asking the following question. If the Amsterdam court, faced with four virtually identical lawsuits, had referred only Case 26/62 *Van Gend en Loos* and reserved judgment in the others, would it, after receiving the ECJ's answer in the main case, have been *bound* to apply to the other disputes the rule laid down therein?

3.5 In other words we were faced with two possible rules of Community law. The primary rule has just been laid down: EEC 12 has direct effect. Is there, therefore, a second-order rule that the primary rule must be applied to all similar fact-situations?

3.6 Nothing in the Treaty deals explicitly with either rule.

3.7 If there is such a doctrine of 'precedent', it must be a Community rule common to the whole EEC territory, so the answer given to a Netherlands court will have to be applied by those in the other Member States.

3.8 Furthermore, if this rule exists, is a national court even *allowed* to refer the same question once again? Can an answer be, in the words of EEC 177 'necessary to enable it to give judgment'?

3.9 At the oral hearing, the Commission argued that the case should be 'dismissed for lack of substance'. In other words, they seem to have tried to persuade the ECJ to adopt the view that, as its decision in Case 26/62 *Van Gend en Loos* was generally binding, it should not even answer the other requests for interpretation.

3.10 A common-lawyer can see some point in this. After all, the ECJ has just announced that Community law 'confers on individuals rights which become part of their legal heritage', has told national courts that they must protect these rights, and has said that this includes EEC 12. Individuals are presumably entitled to expect that their national courts (and other officials) will follow and obey. A (somewhat theoretical) reply, however, is that nothing in the Treaty says that the ECJ is bound by its *own* decisions, so it is free to reverse its previous interpretative rulings.

3.11 One possible answer to this last objection might be to say that, within Community law, the relationship of the ECJ and national courts in the operation of EEC 177 is like that of the English House of Lords and the lower courts: they are bound by its decisions, but it is not.

3.12 Advocate-General Lagrange discusses the above issues with Gallic clarity, albeit with some subtlety, and fairly generous extracts from his submissions are printed below.

TEXT

OPINION OF MR ADVOCATE-GENERAL M. LAGRANGE

I

As you know, the three cases, of which I have to give my analysis today, came before us in exactly the same circumstances as Case 26/62, which led to your judgment of 5 February 1963. Now, as then, the Tariefcommissie is referring to the Court for a preliminary ruling under Article 177 of the EEC Treaty two questions relating to the interpretation of Article 12 of the Treaty. The questions posed are in the same terms; the written observations presented both by the parties to the main actions and by the Governments and the Commission are the same; finally, no new circumstance has occurred since the judgment, and no new argument has been presented. The only difference from the procedural point of view is that reference was made to the Court by the Tariefcommissie on different dates: 16 August 1962 in Case 26/62 and 19 September 1962 in the three other cases—those which are at present before you. Thus it would seem that you have merely to reply as you did on 5 February last, and to the same effect, for there exists no apparent reason to hold differently.

However, such an approach would imply that the effect of *res judicata* resulting from your judgment of 5 February 1963 does not extend to the present actions; for otherwise you would be required, if not to dismiss the requests of the Tariefcommissie as inadmissible (since they are prior to your judgment), at least to declare them as unfounded by dismissing the cases for lack of grounds. A matter of principle is involved here which is not without importance to the future application of Article 177 and the relationships between the Court of Justice and the national courts which flow from it.

I think that this problem should be resolved by a normal application of the principles which govern *res judicata*, on the one hand, and the system of references for preliminary rulings, on the other. I do not think that I should go at length into these principles, which are common to the six Member States, at least in essence; I shall confine myself to recalling them briefly.

1. As regards *res judicata*, the principle is that its binding effect is only relative and exists only in so far as there is identity of parties, cause, and object. Apart from the special case of the annulment of administrative measures (and also, according to some, the 'declaration of illegality' of such measures), which applies *erga omnes*, there are no exceptions to the rule unless the law provides otherwise. In the Treaty of Rome I find no special provision derogating from the principle that *res judicata* binds only the case in question, when the Court is called upon to interpret the provisions of the Treaty, whether by way of preliminary ruling or otherwise.

2. As regards the principles which govern the system of references for preliminary rulings, they depend essentially on absolute respect by each of the two judicial systems for the jurisdiction of the other. Thus the court before which the main action is pending is required to defer to the judgment given by the court to which the case has been referred, as regards the point of law on which the latter court has given a decision: within this limit, the judgment given on reference has binding effect. But the court before which the main action is pending remains free to draw from the preliminary judgment the relevant legal conclusions for a definitive settlement of the case, even to the extent of not drawing any conclusions at all if, for example, it afterwards discovers that the consultation was not necessary and that it can give a decision on other grounds.

As for the court referred to for the preliminary ruling, it has but one power—which is also a duty—and that is to confirm its own jurisdiction: once it has recognized this, it is required to give a decision without having to confirm whether the reference was justified, whether it was really necessary for the adjudication of the main action, etc. These were the principles which the Court applied in its judgment in Case 26/62 where we read this:

> In order to confer jurisdiction on the Court in the present case, it is necessary only that the question raised should clearly be concerned with the interpretation of the Treaty. The considerations which may have led a national court or tribunal to its choice of questions as well as the relevance which it attributes to such questions in the context of a case before it, are excluded from review by the Court.

II

If we apply simultaneously the two principles just described, we reach the conclusion that the Court's judgment of 5 February 1963, given in Case 26/62, does not have binding effect in the three other disputes. I say 'the three other disputes' advisedly, meaning that for each of them it is necessary to regard all the proceedings as a whole, which includes the reference ordered by the Dutch court and the consequences which this reference entails before the Court of Justice. The whole of these proceedings, including the stage which is taking place now here in Luxembourg, has in the last resort but one purpose: to allow a judgment to be delivered, as far as the respective jurisdictions extend, in the cases properly brought before a national court—that is, in this instance, the three cases between importers and the Nederlandse Belastingadministratie. Although the legal issue (*causa petendi*) may be the same in the four cases, the subject-matter (*petitum*) is different, and furthermore there is no identity of parties; therefore, the binding effect of your judgment of 5 February does not extend to the three other cases which are the subject of separate requests by the Tariefcommissie, on which you have not yet given judgment.

Doubtless it could be argued, in support of the contrary view, that the aspect of 'public policy' in the system provided for in Article 177 (obligation to refer in the case of the third paragraph of Article 177, direct reference to the Court of Justice by the national court) is emphasized, the aim clearly being to ensure a unified interpretation of the Treaty as far as possible. But I think that care should be taken not to confuse the *ratio legis* (which is in fact to be sought in such interpretation) and the process by which it may be affected. This process is embodied in the system of reference for a preliminary ruling, which is based, as I have mentioned, on respect by the courts of each of the two legal systems for the limits of their respective jurisdictions. It is thus a collaboration between the Court of Justice and the national courts which ought to result, by way of case-law, in that unity of interpretation which is so desirable: through decisions and not through regulations. In other words, the Court of Justice should, in this as in all other matters, remain free when giving its future judgments. However important the judgment which it is led to give on some point may be, whatever may be the abstract character which the interpretation of some provision of the Treaty may present—or appear to present—, the golden rule of *res judicata* should be preserved; it is from the moral authority of its decisions, and not from the legal authority of *res judicata*, that a jurisdiction like ours should derive its force. Clearly no one will expect that, having given a leading judgment, such as the judgment in Case 26/62, the Court will depart from it in another action without strong reasons, but it should retain the legal right to do so. The rule that *res judicata* binds only the particular case is a wise rule; rather than enabling the court to shelter formally behind a previous judgment, as one shelters behind a law or regulation, it obliges it unceasingly to retain awareness of its responsibility, that is, to confront the realities of the situation with the legal rule in each action, which can lead it in appropriate cases to recognize its errors in the light of new facts, of new arguments, or even of a spontaneous rethinking, or more frequently to alter its point of view subtly without changing it fundamentally, thus being party in the light of experience and the evolution of legal theories and economic, social, or other phenomena, to what is called the evolution of case law. The rule that *res judicata* binds only the particular case is the weapon which permits courts to do this. Of course, they should in their wisdom only use this weapon prudently, on pain of destroying legal certainty, but it is necessary for them and they should not abandon it.

Could one then envisage making a distinction between the binding effect of a judgment by the Court of Justice with regard to itself—an effect which would only be relative—and the binding effect which would only be relative—and the binding effect with regard to national courts—which would on the contrary be absolute? In other words, so long as the Court did not overrule itself—which it would always have the right to do—national courts would be required to conform to the judgment in every case which comes before them, as is the case with judgments given by the Karlsruhe Court. I do not think so. This would be, in effect, to recognize a jurisdiction of a truly constitutional nature in the Court. Although our Court, in certain respects, plays the role of a constitutional court within the Communities, the Treaties have not given it all the prerogatives of a court of that nature.

It should be added that the argument which I am seeking to refute would also risk involving serious disadvantages. It would result in giving a contentious character to the scope of the Court's judgments in the matter. Does this or that later action pose exactly the same question of interpretation as that already settled, or does it involve new elements which justify a new request for interpretation? The Court, rather than having to settle (in the same terms or, if necessary, by supplementing its previous judgment) a question relating to the interpretation of the Treaty, which is its normal role, would first have to ask whether the question posed had or had not already been previously settled by it, which in many cases would lead to interpreting the judgment instead of the Treaty. I find here the disadvantage of giving up the freedom which the rule that *res judicata* binds only the particular case gives to the court: it is better to repeat a leading judgment several times, apart from slight alterations in the text in accordance with new elements or arguments, than to refuse to reply and have to give reasons for the refusal. Once again, better for a court to interpret the law (the purpose for which it is set up) than to interpret its own decisions.

III

But then—and this is the last question I wish to consider—does not the Court run the risk of being encumbered with unnecessary actions, because they concern matters which have already been settled? This problem has two aspects—one of fact, the other of law.

In fact, I believe that national courts will in general refrain from referring to the Court questions which are really unnecessary. The natural tendency of a court is to exercise its jurisdiction to the full rather than to abdicate it in favour of another; the parties, for their part, in so far as they can influence this procedure which is regarded as a matter of public policy, will not in general have any interest in prolonging it unnecessarily, with the extra costs and delays involved. In particular the assumption that the very court which has already made a reference to this Court and received a reply will make a further reference is, in the absence of relevant reasons, unlikely to be fulfilled.

But—and this is the legal aspect of the problem—does not the third paragraph of Article 177 compel the national courts or tribunals to which it refers (those 'against whose decisions there is no judicial remedy under national law') to refer to the Court as soon as a 'question' on the interpretation of the Treaty 'is raised in a case pending before' one of them, since, according to the same provision, the court or tribunal in question in such a case 'shall bring the matter before the Court of Justice'? Does this obligation to refer to the Court exist even when the question of interpretation which has arisen has already led to a judgment of the Court, or even been the subject of a whole line of decisions?

This is a question which you do not have to decide, for it comes within the jurisdiction of the national courts. You could decide it only if a request were referred to you for an interpretation of Article 177 itself, which is not the case here.

I merely say that this problem—which is not the only one raised by the interpretation of Article 177—seems capable of settlement by the national courts without great difficulty if they follow one of the rules which govern the matter of preliminary rulings. This rule is very simple: before the procedure of referring a question for a preliminary ruling on interpretation can be set in motion, there must clearly be a question, and that question must be relative to the interpretation of the provision involved; otherwise, if the provision is perfectly clear, there is no longer any need for interpretation but only for application, which belongs to the jurisdiction of the national court whose very task it is to apply the law. This is what is sometimes described, not perhaps very accurately and in a way which is often misunderstood, as the theory of the 'acte clair' (a measure whose meaning is self-evident): really, it is simply a question of a demarcation line between the two jurisdictions. Of course, as always in such a case, there can be doubtful cases or borderline cases. When in doubt, obviously, the court should make the reference.

If a national court is faced with a question of interpretation of the Treaty, but this question has been applied by the competent court as a matter of what may be considered as established case-law, it must be accepted that there is no longer really any 'question' requiring a reference, the case being comparable with the preceding one: a provision which is obscure in itself, but the meaning of which has consistently been interpreted in the same way by the competent court, is equivalent to a provision which has no need of interpretation. This is a rule of good sense and wisdom, which happily combines respect for jurisdictional limits with the need to avoid multiplying reference proceedings unnecessarily.

In short, I consider that if the national courts of Member States follow the principle which I have just outlined—and I have every hope that they will, since these principles are generally recognized in both national and international law—a satisfactory system of collaboration between these courts and the Court of Justice can be created on the basis of Article 177.

In this system it is to be expected that the Court should sometimes have to give a decision on questions of interpretation of the Treaty or Community regulations which it may already have settled before, but for the reasons which I have given I do not think that this risk will be very great. However that may be, it is infinitely less serious to have several judgments of the Court reproducing previous judgments than to be faced with refusals to accept references from national courts, refusals based on a perhaps questionable interpretation of the scope of a previous judgment which would be the source of conflicts for which the Treaty provides no solution.

GROUNDS OF JUDGMENT

The regularity of the procedure followed by the Tariefcommissie in requesting the Court for a preliminary ruling under Article 177 of the EEC Treaty has not been disputed and there is no ground for the Court to raise the matter of its own motion.

The Commission, appearing by virtue of the provisions of Article 20 of the Statute of the Court of Justice of the EEC, urges that the request should be dismissed for lack of substance, since the questions on which an interpretation is requested from the Court in the present cases have already been decided by the judgment of 5 February 1963 in Case 26/62, which covered identical questions raised in a similar case.

This contention is not justified. A distinction should be made between the obligation imposed by the third paragraph of Article 177 upon national courts or tribunals of last instance and the power granted by the second paragraph of Article 177 to every national court or tribunal to refer to the Court of the Communities a question on the interpretation of the Treaty. Although the third paragraph of Article 177 unreservedly requires courts or tribunals of a Member State against whose decisions there is no judicial remedy under national law—like the Tariefcommissie—to refer to the Court every question of interpretation raised before them, the authority of an interpretation under Article 177 already given by the Court may deprive the obligation of its purpose and thus empty it of its substance. Such is the case especially when the question raised is materially identical with a question which has already been the subject of a preliminary ruling in a similar case.

When it gives an interpretation of the Treaty in a specific action pending before a national court, the Court limits itself to deducing the meaning of the Community rules from the wording and spirit of the Treaty, it being left to the national court to apply in the particular case the rules which are thus interpreted. Such an attitude conforms with the function assigned to the Court by Article 177 of ensuring unity of interpretation of Community law within the six Member States. If Article 177 had not such a scope, the procedural requirements of Article 20 of the Statute of the Court of Justice, which provides for the participation in the hearing of the Member States and the Community institutions, and of the third paragraph of Article 165 of the Treaty, which requires the Court to sit in plenary session, would not be justified. This aspect of the activity of the Court within the framework of Article 177 is confirmed by the absence of parties, in the proper sense of the word, which is characteristic of this procedure.

It is no less true that Article 177 always allows a national court, if it considers it desirable, to refer questions of interpretation to the Court again. This follows from Article 20 of the Statute of the Court of Justice, under which the procedure laid down for the settlement of preliminary questions is automatically set in motion as soon as such a question is referred by a national court.

The Court must, therefore, give a judgment on the present application.

The interpretation of Article 12 of the EEC Treaty, which is here requested, was given in the Court's judgment of 5 February 1963 in Case 26/62. This rules that:

1. Article 12 of the Treaty establishing the European Economic Community produces direct effects and creates individual rights which national courts must protect.
2. In order to ascertain whether customs duties or charges having equivalent effect have been increased contrary to the prohibition contained in Article 12 of the Treaty, regard must be had to the duties and charges actually applied by the Member State in question at the date of the entry into force of the Treaty. Such an increase can arise both from a rearrangement of the tariff resulting in the classification of the product under a more highly taxed heading and from an increase in the rate of customs duty applied.

The questions of interpretation posed in this case are identical with those settled as above and no new factor has been presented to the Court.

In these circumstances the Tariefcommissie must be referred to the previous judgment.

On those grounds the Court in answer to the question referred to it, for a preliminary ruling, by the Tariefcommissie on 19 September 1962, hereby rules:

1. There is no ground for giving a new interpretation of Article 12 of the EEC Treaty.
2. It is for the Tariefcommissie to decide as to the costs of the present proceedings.

COMMENTS

THE ADVOCATE-GENERAL'S SUBMISSIONS

1. Not surprisingly, M. Lagrange's approach is not that of a common-lawyer. Coming from a system with no formal rule of precedent, he accepts that normally a given decision is binding as a matter of law—*res judicata*—only if the parties, the cause of action, and the remedy sought are identical. In that narrow form the rule exists, of course, in the common law.

2. He explains clearly the two principles of jurisdiction, Community and national, to be deduced from EEC 177. On the one hand the ECJ, faced with an apparently genuine reference, cannot question the reasons which led the lower court to request a ruling; on the other hand, the latter, having received

its answer, cannot itself then differ, for that would be to assume a jurisdiction it does not possess, namely to interpret the provision involved.

3. From these he concludes that there is no rule of Community law that the decision in Case 26/62 *Van Gend en Loos* constitutes a precedent unequivocally binding on other national courts. The first principle mandates the ECJ to comply with a new request for interpretation; the second limits only the court which made the first reference.

4. Recognizing that the ECJ is not bound by its own judgments, he asks whether they could still not be precedents for all other courts. This is the position of the German Constitutional Court but Lagrange A-G (who does not mention the situation in Britain, then a non-Member State, with its House of Lords, nor that of the US Supreme Court) sees this as a jurisdiction of a constitutional nature, whose existence would be stretching the EEC too far.

5. He then adds two consequentialist arguments which are acute, but very civilian. If some rule of precedent existed, then much of a later reference would be taken up with arguments, not about the Treaty or other Community Act, but about the earlier judgment dealing with them. The ECJ, he says, instead of interpreting the Treaty, would spend its time interpreting its previous judgments. Furthermore if, on the grounds that a previous ruling was a precedent, it refused a reference, it would have to give reasons for the refusal. These reasons would relate to the scope and meaning of its earlier decision so that its judgment would have to deal with its own case-law *whether it accepted or refused the reference*. The idea that a court should devote much of its energy to explaining, and distinguishing, its own case-law is, of course, taken for granted by common-lawyers. To others, it seems a waste of time.

6. EEC 177 appears to say, and Lagrange A-G to accept, that the decision to make a reference is entirely for the national court. There must be some limit to this: if—to imagine a simple case—a domestic Divorce Court were to request an interpretation of EEC 12, the ECJ must surely be able to refuse the reference. At a much more complex level, the problem has arisen in Case 104/79 *Foglio* v. *Novello* 1, and Case 244/80 *Foglio* v. *Novello* 2.

THE ECJ'S JUDGMENT

7. The Court states that it cannot, as the Commission proposed, simply dismiss the case, because EEC 177 clearly gives the decision about making a reference to the national court. Nonetheless, the dispositive part of its actual judgment contains only two sentences, of which the second is about costs.

8. The Court's supporting reasoning deduces the wide range of potential application of an interpretation under EEC 177 from the power given to Member States and all Community institutions to participate in argument, and from the fact that the Court must sit in plenary session. (This last

requirement no longer holds good; since 1974 such references may be heard by a Chamber.)

9. The Court also states that the fact that an interpretative ruling has already been given may absolve national courts from their duty to refer. Even the supreme national court need not do so if, in the light of the earlier ruling, the meaning of the disputed provision is clear: Case 283/81 *CILFIT*. No national court, however, can be denied the chance to refer a question on a provision which has already been interpreted. This is so for three reasons.

The first is the text of EEC 177 itself. The second is the fact that a national court may find it difficult to understand an interpretation already given. But courts cannot simply say to the ECJ 'What does such-and-such a decision mean?', and nothing in the Treaty gives the Court power to conduct seminars on its own judgments. So, if some later court wants clarification of an interpretative ruling, it has to cite the Treaty provision or Community act in question.

The third reason is more important. It is perfectly possible that a later national court may understand all too well the interpretation handed down by the ECJ, but may consider the ruling wrong, and be anxious to give the ECJ the opportunity to think again and to reverse itself. This happened in references made by German courts after the ECJ had declared EEC 95 to be directly effective: see, for instance, Case 28/67 *Molkereizentrale*.

10. What emerges are seven second-order rules of Community law. Firstly, there is no strict doctrine of precedent. Secondly, national courts cannot ignore an earlier preliminary ruling given under EEC 177. Thirdly, if, in their estimation, it applies to the facts before them, they cannot refuse to follow it. This does not mean, however, that they have to apply it because, fourthly, the ECJ cannot refuse to hear a new reference. Fifthly, therefore, national courts have only two choices: follow the previous decision, or refer the same question. Sixthly, even the highest court may simply follow an interpretative ruling and decline to make a reference, even though the last sentence of EEC 177 appears to oblige it to refer.

11. The seventh rule is that the six rules stated in the preceding paragraph must themselves be of direct effect upon the judges of Member States. Even the fourth, by imposing a duty on the ECJ, confers a power on national courts.

12. The rules of UK law are the same as those in 10 above. The European Communities Act 1972, s 3(1) says that any question as to the meaning or effect of the Treaties or Community instruments, or as to the validity of the latter, is one of law, which must either be referred, or decided 'in accordance with the principles laid down by and any relevant decision of the European Court'.

3 Case 6/64 *Costa* v. *ENEL*

INTRODUCTION

1. *The action*. This was a reference under EEC 177 made by the Milanese *giudice conciliatore*, the lowest rung in the Italian judicial hierarchy, and something similar to a small claims court. He did not frame a question, but simply sent the case file to the ECJ, citing EEC 177 and referring to the allegation of one of the parties that a 1962 Italian law infringed the following articles of the Treaty:

—102 (before adopting national provisions which may distort the Common Market, a Member State must consult the Commission);
—93 (paragraph (3) whereof enjoins Member States who plan to grant aids to inform the Commission in good time);
—53 (the standstill clause forbidding Member States to impose new restriction on the establishment of nationals of other Member States);
—37 (which provides for the progressive elimination of existing discriminatory provisions protecting State commercial monopolies and, in 37 (2), lays down a standstill clause forbidding new measures contrary to this principle).

Briefs were filed by the Italian Government, the Commission, and Mr Costa, but a private electricity company was not permitted to do the same, since, although it was interested in the outcome, it was not involved in the national lawsuit.

2. *The salient, simplified facts*

2.1 In 1962, by statutes and subsequent decrees, Italian private electricity undertakings were nationalized and their assets transferred to the National Electricity Board, ENEL.

2.2 Mr Costa was a shareholder in one of the private firms, a user of electricity, and a lawyer. He was against nationalization.

2.3 Consequently, he refused to pay the electricity bill (of about £1) sent him by ENEL.

2.4 When sued, he pleaded that the nationalization legislation was (*a*) unconstitutional under Italian law; and (*b*) a breach of Community law, as it was incompatible with the Treaty Articles listed above.

3. *The legal issues*. These fell into three categories. The first concerns the reference itself, the second the relation between Community and Italian law, and the third the Treaty Articles.

3.1 *The drafting of the reference*. The Italian Court's covering letter sent with the file appears only to ask the ECJ to decide whether the Italian nationalization laws infringe the Treaty. Naturally, the Court could not address itself to that problem. Instead, it distilled from the request the question whether the Articles cited above are of direct effect and create individual rights which national courts must protect.

3.2 *The need for a reference.* Italy argued that the Milan judge did not need an explanation of the Treaty of Rome in order to decide a dispute about a trifling sum. As in Case 26/62 *Van Gend en Loos*, however, the problem is not whether a reference is necessary, but who decides whether it is needed.

3.3 *The admissibility of the reference.* This was the most dangerous objection put forward by Italy. The judge, it was argued, had to apply to the dispute the rules of only one system: his own. If by any chance, the nationalization laws were incompatible with the Treaty, that was a matter of international law to be resolved under EEC 169 and 170. As, therefore, the national judge had to apply only domestic law, his questions about an international Treaty were 'absolutely inadmissible'.

3.4 *Lagrange A-G has two answers to this argument.* The first is familiar, namely that it is for the national court alone to decide whether a reference is necessary. The second is more fundamental: a particular situation may be subject to two legal rules, one of national, and one of Community, law. This may become clearer if we think, for a moment, of *Van Gend en Loos*'s payment of the extra duty: that was subject both to Dutch customs law and, because it was charged on an import *from another Member State*, to EEC 12.

3.5 *Community and national law.* Because the two rules just mentioned may contradict each other in their application to the same situation, one must prevail. Once again, the prior question arises of who decides which prevails; and, before that, come the questions of which legal system determines who decides; and of who decides which legal system determines who decides; and so on for ever: there thus arises the spectre of an infinite regression. As one might expect, the ECJ insists that these problems are to be solved by Community law and does so, not by logic-chopping, but, in a most powerful summary of the Community's *real powers*, by insisting that the EEC Treaty has created its own legal system, and by omitting the little phrase 'of international law' which it had incautiously uttered in Case 26/62 *Van Gend en Loos*.

3.6 *Subsequent national legislation.* It might be argued—as has been the case in the UK—that, whatever the effect of the Treaties on prior national law, the courts must give effect to a clear conflicting, but subsequent, statute. Lagrange A-G observes, that, confronted with such a statute, the national court would be faced with a constitutional problem. This issue is covered more fully in the next case; here it will suffice to call attention to the careful language of the ECJ which observes that the State's Treaty obligations would not be unconditional if they could be undermined by subsequent legislation. At the very beginning of the dispositive part of the judgment, the ECJ is even more forthright, saying that a subsequent unilateral measure cannot take precedence over Community law.

3.7 *The effect of the Treaty Articles.* The ECJ gives its reasons for distinguishing those which do, and those which do not, have direct effect. As might be expected, the two standstill provisions—like EEC 12, obligations on Member States not to act—are held to be capable of producing direct effects on the relations between Member States and individuals, imposing on their courts a duty of protection and giving the latter rights.

TEXT

OPINION OF MR ADVOCATE-GENERAL LAGRANGE

The preliminary question upon which you have to give a ruling under Article 177 of the EEC Treaty does not, for once, come from a Netherlands court, but from an Italian one, and it is no longer a question of social security or of Regulation no. 3, but rather of a certain number of provisions of the Treaty itself, in respect of which your interpretation is requested in circumstances that are such as to bring in issue the constitutional relations between the European Economic Community and its Member States. This highlights the importance of the judgment you are called upon to pronounce in this case. The facts are known to you: Mr Costa, a lawyer practising in Milan, claims that he is not under an obligation to pay an invoice amounting to 1,925 lire demanded of him in respect of the supply of electricity by the 'Ente Nazionale per l'Energia Elettrica (ENEL)'. He objected to this payment before the Giudice Conciliatore (which has sole jurisdiction by virtue of the amount involved) claiming that the Law of 6 December 1962 nationalizing the electricity industry in Italy was contrary to a certain number of provisions of the Treaty of Rome, and was unconstitutional. In this connexion he requested—and obtained—a reference of the case, on the one hand to the Italian Constitutional Court, and on the other hand to this Court for a preliminary ruling pursuant to Article 177 of the Treaty.

Two preliminary questions in connection with the validity of the reference to this Court must be resolved.

A. The first is the question whether the Milan court has referred to you questions which really relate to the interpretation of the Treaty. The order contained in the judgment in question does no more than mention 'the allegation that the Law of 6 December 1962 and the presidential decrees issued in pursuance of that Law infringe Articles 102, 93, 53, and 37 of the Treaty' and, as a consequence, suspends proceedings and orders the 'transmission of a certified copy of the file to the Court of Justice of the European Economic Community in Luxemburg'. However, in its reasoning, the judgment shows in a brief but nevertheless precise manner, how the law nationalizing the electricity industry in Italy might constitute an infringement of each of the relevant Articles of the EEC Treaty and hence be incompatible with the Treaty. I think that this Court can and must make the necessary effort to select from the four points of difficulty set out in the judgment that which is relevant to the interpretation of the Treaty. You have been willing to make such efforts in other cases with a view to enabling a national court to give a decision within the limits of its jurisdiction, whilst remaining within the sphere of your own; and this, after all, is quite reasonable in view of the fact that the abstract interpretation of the wording of the Treaty or of Community regulations always takes place in connection with concrete cases which are the subject of litigation. What must be avoided—and this is a danger which becomes apparent as cases under Article 177 multiply—is that this Court, under the guise of interpretation, might more or less substitute itself for the national court which, let us not forget, retains jurisdiction to apply the Treaty and the regulations of the Community which have been incorporated into national law by ratification.

B. This brings me to an examination of the second preliminary question which is concerned precisely with the constitutional difficulties to which I have just referred. In its observations, the Italian Government contends that the question referred to you by the Milan court is absolutely inadmissible because, it declares, the question is not, as is required by Article 177, the premise of the legal syllogism which the court must normally formulate to decide the dispute before it. In this dispute the court merely has to apply a domestic law of the Italian State; there is therefore as little cause to interpret the Treaty of Rome as to apply it. The Italian Government expressed the position as follows:

> In this case, the court has no provision of the Treaty of Rome to apply and cannot therefore have any of the doubts on the interpretation of the Treaty that Article 177 of the Treaty itself clearly requires; it merely has to apply the national law (that concerned precisely with ENEL) which governs the question before it.

On the other hand, the Italian Government continues, an examination of a possible infringement by a Member State of its community obligations through a domestic law can only take place in accordance with the procedure laid down in Articles 169 and 170 of the Treaty in which individuals have not, even indirectly, any standing: '... the rules of law remain valid even after the judgement of the Court, until such time as the State, in pursuance of the general obligation undertaken under Article 5, itself takes the necessary measures to comply with such judgment.'

I must first dispose of the objection, that infringement of the Treaty by a subsequent domestic law which conflicts with the Treaty can only be pleaded under the procedure for a finding of default by a Member State as laid down in Articles 169 to 171, a procedure which is not open to individuals and which does not affect the validity of the impugned law until it has been finally repealed following a judgment of the Court declaring its incompatibility with the Treaty. In fact, that is not the problem; it is that of the coexistence of two opposing legal rules (as a hypothesis) which both apply to the domestic system, one deriving from the Treaty or the Community institutions, the other from the national legislature and institutions: which must predominate until such time as the conflict is resolved? Therefore we cannot avoid the problem which results from the coexistence within each Member State of two systems of law, domestic and Community, each operating in its own sphere of competence, nor can we avoid the question what sanction should follow the encroachment by one into the sphere of competence reserved to the other.

For encroachments on the part of the institutions of the Community, there is no difficulty. They are dealt with by the Court under one of the procedures envisaged in the Treaty both at the instance of Member States and of individuals, in particular the application for annulment (Article 173) and the plea of illegality (Article 184).

For encroachments on the part of national authorities, there must also be a sanction and this too must be available not only at the instance of the States, but also in favour of individuals when the latter derive individual rights from the Treaty or Community regulations. As the Court has said, the protection of these rights falls upon the national courts.

GROUNDS OF JUDGMENT

By Order dated 16 January 1964, duly sent to the Court, the Giudice Conciliatore of Milan, 'having regard to Article 177 of the Treaty of 25 March 1957 establishing the EEC, incorporated into Italian law by Law no. 1203 of 14 October 1957, and having regard to the allegation that Law no. 1643 of 6 December 1962 and the presidential decrees issued in execution of that Law ... infringe Articles 102, 93, 53, and 37 of the aforementioned Treaty', stayed the proceedings and ordered that the file be transmitted to the Court of Justice.

On the application of Article 177

ON THE SUBMISSION REGARDING THE WORDING OF THE QUESTION

The complaint is made that the intention behind the question posed was to obtain, by means of Article 177, a ruling on the compatibility of a national law with the Treaty.

By the terms of this Article, however, national courts against whose decisions, as in the present case, there is no judicial remedy, must refer the matter to the Court of Justice so that a preliminary ruling may be given upon the 'interpretation of the Treaty' whenever a question of interpretation is raised before them. This provision gives the Court no jurisdiction either to apply the Treaty to a specific case or to decide upon the validity of a provision of domestic law in relation to the Treaty, as it would be possible for it to do under Article 169.

Nevertheless, the Court has power to extract from a question imperfectly formulated by the national court those questions which alone pertain to the interpretation of the Treaty. Consequently a decision should be given by the Court not upon the validity of an Italian law in relation to the Treaty, but only upon the interpretation of the above-mentioned Articles in the context of the points of law stated by the Giudice Conciliatore.

ON THE SUBMISSION THAT AN INTERPRETATION IS NOT NECESSARY

The complaint is made that the Milan court has requested an interpretation of the Treaty which was not necessary for the solution of the dispute before it.

Since, however, Article 177 is based upon a clear separation of functions between national courts and the Court of Justice, it cannot empower the latter either to investigate the facts of the case or to criticize the grounds and purpose of the request for interpretation.

ON THE SUBMISSION THAT THE COURT WAS OBLIGED TO APPLY THE NATIONAL LAW

The Italian Government submits that the request of the Giudice Conciliatore is 'absolutely inadmissible', inasmuch as a national court which is obliged to apply a national law cannot avail itself of Article 177.

By contrast with ordinary international treaties, the EEC Treaty has created its own legal system which, on the entry into force of the Treaty, became an integral part of the legal systems of the Member States and which their courts are bound to apply.

By creating a Community of unlimited duration, having its own institutions, its own personality, its own legal capacity and capacity of representation on the international plane, and, more particularly, real powers stemming from a limitation of sovereignty or a transfer of powers from the States to the Community, the Member States have limited their sovereign rights, albeit within limited fields, and have thus created a body of law which binds both their nationals and themselves.

The integration into the laws of each Member State of provisions which derive from the Community, and more generally the terms and the spirit of the Treaty, make it impossible for the States, as a corollary, to accord precedence to a unilateral and subsequent measure over a legal system accepted by them on a basis of reciprocity. Such a measure cannot therefore be inconsistent with that legal system. The executive force of Community law cannot vary from one State to another in deference to subsequent domestic laws, without jeopardizing the attainment of the objectives of the Treaty set out in Article 5 (2) and giving rise to the discrimination prohibited by Article 7.

The obligations undertaken under the Treaty establishing the Community would not be unconditional, but merely contingent, if they could be called in question by subsequent legislative acts of the signatories. Wherever the Treaty grants the States the right to act unilaterally, it does this by clear and precise provisions (for example Articles 15, 93 (3), 223, 224, and 225). Applications, by Member States for authority to derogate from the Treaty are subject to a special authorization procedure (for example Articles 8 (4), 17 (4), 25, 26, 73, the third subparagraph of Article 93 (2), and 226) which would lose their purpose if the Member States could renounce their obligations by means of an ordinary law.

The precedence of Community law is confirmed by Article 189, whereby a regulation 'shall be binding' and 'directly applicable in all Member States'. This provision, which is subject to no reservation, would be quite meaningless if a State could unilaterally nullify its effects by means of a legislative measure which could prevail over Community law.

It follows from all these observations that the law stemming from the Treaty, an independent source of law, could not, because of its special and original nature, be overriden by domestic legal provisions, however framed, without being deprived of its character as Community law and without the legal basis of the Community itself being called into question.

The transfer by the States from their domestic legal system to the Community legal system of the rights and obligations arising under the Treaty carries with it a permanent limitation of their sovereign rights, against which a subsequent unilateral act incompatible with the concept of the Community cannot prevail. Consequently Article 177 is to be applied regardless of any domestic law, whenever questions relating to the interpretation of the Treaty arise.

The questions put by the Giudice Conciliatore regarding Articles 102, 93, 53, and 37 are directed first to enquiring whether these provisions produce direct effects and create individual rights which national courts must protect, and, if so, what their meaning is.

On the interpretation of Article 102

Article 102 provides that, where 'there is reason to fear' that a provision laid down by law may cause 'distortion', the Member State desiring to proceed therewith shall 'consult the Commission'; the Commission has power to recommend to the Member States the adoption of suitable measures to avoid the distortion feared.

This Article, placed in the chapter devoted to the 'Approximation of Laws', is designed to prevent the differences between the legislation of the different nations with regard to the objectives of the Treaty from becoming more pronounced. By virtue of this provision, Member States have limited their freedom of initiative by agreeing to submit to an appropriate procedure of consultation. By binding themselves unambiguously to prior consultation with the Commission in all those cases where their projected legislation might create a risk, however slight, of a possible distortion, the States have undertaken an obligation to the Community which binds them as States, but which does not create individual rights which national courts must protect. For its part, the Commission is bound to ensure respect for the provisions of this Article, but this obligation does not give individuals the right to allege, within the framework of Community law and by means of Article 177, either failure by the State concerned to fulfil any of its obligations or breach of duty on the part of the Commission.

On the interpretation of Article 93

Under Article 93 (1) and (2), the Commission, in co-operation with Member States, is to 'keep under constant review all systems of aid existing in those States' with a view to the adoption of appropriate measures required by the functioning of the Common Market.

By virtue of Article 93 (3), the Commission is to be informed, in sufficient time, of any plans to grant or alter aid, the Member State concerned not being entitled to put its proposed measures into effect until the Community procedure, and, if necessary, any proceedings before the Court of Justice, have been completed.

These provisions, contained in the section of the Treaty headed 'Aids granted by States', are designed, on the one hand, to eliminate progressively existing aids and, on the other hand, to prevent the individual States in the conduct of their internal affairs from introducing new aids 'in any form whatsoever' which are likely directly or indirectly to favour certain undertakings or products in an appreciable way, and which threaten, even potentially, to distort competition. By virtue of Article 92, the Member States have acknowledged that such aids are incompatible with the Common Market and have thus implicitly undertaken not to create any more, save as otherwise provided in the Treaty; in Article 93, on the other hand, they have merely agreed to submit themselves to appropriate procedures for the abolition of existing aids and the introduction of new ones.

By so expressly undertaking to inform the Commission 'in sufficient time' of any plans for aid, and by accepting the procedures laid down in Article 93, the States have entered into an obligation with the Community, which binds them as States but creates no individual rights except in the case of the final provision of Article 93 (3), which is not in question in the present case.

For its part, the Commission is bound to ensure respect for the provisions of this Article, and is required, in co-operation with Member States, to keep under constant review, existing systems of aids. This obligation does not, however, give individuals the right to plead, within the framework of Community law and by means of Article 177, either failure by the State concerned to fulfil any of its obligations or breach of duty on the part of the Commission.

On the interpretation of Article 53

By Article 53 the Member States undertake not to introduce any new restrictions on the right of establishment in their territories of nationals of other Member States, save as otherwise provided in the Treaty. The obligation thus entered into by the States simply amounts legally to a duty not to act, which is neither subject to any conditions, nor, as regards its execution or effect, to the adoption of any measure either by the States or by the Commission. It is therefore legally complete in itself and is consequently capable of producing direct effects on the relations between Member States and individuals. Such an express prohibition which came into force with the Treaty throughout the Community, and thus became an integral part of the legal system of the Member States, forms part of the law of those States and directly concerns their nationals, in whose favour it has created individual rights which national courts must protect.

The interpretation of Article 53 which is sought requires that it be considered in the context of the chapter relating to the right of establishment in which it occurs. After enacting in Article 52 that 'restrictions on the freedom of establishment of nationals of a Member State in the territory of another Member State shall be abolished by progressive stages', this chapter goes on in Article 53 to provide that 'Member States shall not introduce any new restrictions on the right of establishment in their territories of nationals of other Member States'. The question is, therefore, on what conditions the nationals of other Member States have a right of establishment. This is dealt with by the second paragraph of Article 52, where it is stated that freedom of establishment shall include the right to take up and pursue activities as self-employed persons and to set up and manage undertakings 'under the conditions laid down for its own nationals by the law of the country where such establishment is effected'. Article 53 is therefore satisfied so long as no new measure subjects the establishment of nationals of other Member States to more severe rules than those prescribed for nationals of the country of establishment, whatever the legal system governing the undertaking.

On the interpretation of Article 37

Article 37 (1) provides that Member States shall progessively adjust any 'State monopolies of a commercial character' so as to ensure that no discrimination regarding the conditions under which goods are procured and marketed exists between nationals of Member States. By Article 37 (2), the Member States are under an obligation to refrain from introducing any new measure which is contrary to the principles laid down in Article 37 (1).

Thus, Member States have undertaken a dual obligation: in the first place, an active one to adjust State monopolies, in the second place, a passive one to avoid any new measures. The interpretation requested is of the second obligation together with any aspects of the first necessary for this interpretation.

Article 37 (2) contain an absolute prohibition: not an obligation to do something but an obligation to refrain from doing something. This obligation is not accompanied by any reservation which might make its implementation subject to any positive act of national law. This prohibition is essentially one which is capable of producing direct effects on the legal relations between Member States and their nationals.

Such a clearly expressed prohibition which came into force with the Treaty throughout the Community, and so became an integral part of the legal system of the Member States, forms part of the law of those States and directly concerns their nationals, in whose favour it creates individual rights which national courts must protect. By reason of the complexity of the wording and the fact that Articles 37(1) and 37(2) overlap, the interpretation requested makes it necessary to examine them as a part of the chapter in which they occur.

This chapter deals with the 'elimination of quantitative restrictions between Member States'. The object of the reference in Article 37(2) to 'the principles laid down in paragraph (1)' is thus to prevent the establishment of any new 'discrimination regarding the conditions under which goods are procured and marketed... between nationals of Member States'. Having specified the objective in this way, Article 37(1) sets out the ways in which this objective might be thwarted in order to prohibit them.

Thus, by the reference in Article 37(2), any new monopolies or bodies specified in Article 37(1) are prohibited in so far as they tend to introduce new cases of discrimination regarding the conditions under which goods are procured and marketed. It is therefore a matter for the court dealing with the main action first to examine whether this objective is being hampered, that is whether any new discrimination between nationals of Member States regarding the conditions under which goods are procured and marketed results from the disputed measure itself or will be the consequence thereof.

There remain to be considered the means envisaged by Article 37(1). It does not prohibit the creation of any State monopolies, but merely those 'of a commercial character', and then only in so far as they tend to introduce the cases of discrimination referred to. To fall under this prohibition the State monopolies and bodies in question must, first, have as their object transactions regarding a commercial product capable of being the subject of competition and trade between Member States, and secondly must play an effective part in such trade.

It is a matter for the court dealing with the main action to assess in each case whether the economic activity under review relates to such a product which, by virtue of its nature and the technical or international conditions to which it is subject, is capable of playing an effective part in imports or exports between nationals of the Member States.

On those grounds, the court ruling upon the plea of inadmissibility based on Article 177 hereby declares:

As a subsequent unilateral measure cannot take precedence over Community law, the questions put by the Giudice Conciliatore, Milan, are admissible in so far as they relate in this case to the interpretation of provisions of the EEC Treaty; and also rules:

1. Article 102 contains no provisions which are capable of creating individual rights which national courts must protect.
2. Those individual portions of Article 93 to which the question relates equally contain no such provisions.
3. Article 53 constitutes a Community rule capable of creating individual rights which national courts must protect. It prohibits any new measure which subjects the establishment of nationals of other Member States to more severe rules than those prescribed for nationals of the country of establishment, whatever the legal system governing the undertakings.
4. Article 37(2) is in all its provisions a rule of Community law capable of creating individual rights which national courts must protect. In so far as the question put to the Court is concerned, it prohibits the introduction of any new measure contrary to the principles of Article 37(1), that is, any measure having as its object or effect a new discrimination between nationals of Member States regarding the conditions in which goods are procured and marketed, by means of monopolies of bodies which must, first, have as their object transactions regarding a commercial product capable of being the subject of competition and trade between Member States, and secondly must play an effective part in such trade.

COMMENTS

1. The reader will have noticed that the ECJ—admittedly in rather colourless language—employs consequentialist reasoning in saying that the force of Community law cannot vary from one State to another in deference to subsequent domestic laws without jeopardizing the Treaty. The Advocate-General uses the same method when he points out that, if one Member State's courts held that subsequent national law prevailed, that would produce a chain reaction in the other countries.

2. Until this decision, several Member States may have considered that Case 26/62 *Van Gend en Loos* was an isolated aberration, and that most of the Treaty was not directly effective, so that their infringements could be tested only under EEC 169 and 170. Their view rested on two arguments. The first was that few articles of the Treaty apply expressly to individuals (as do EEC 7, 85, and 86); on the contrary, most of them impose obligations only on Member States, which—in terms of classical international law—would mean that only other States could enforce them. The second was the Treaty itself, which attributes direct applicability only to Regulations (EEC 189) and not to itself; and the enactment of regulations requires the consent of the national governments in the Council.

After this decision, however, it must have been evident that the Court was beginning to find much of the Treaty similar in effect to EEC 12.

3. In terms of substantive law, the case lays the foundation for later developments. Firstly, it shows that other Treaty articles have direct effect and must be enforced by domestic courts. Consider, for instance, EEC 37. Its first sentence, obliging Member States to eliminate discrimination in the activities of State commercial monopolies, is not a conspicuously clear provision. Nonetheless, EEC 37(2) forbids new contrary practices, and the ECJ holds this directly effective; from which it follows that 37(1) must at least have a kernel of clarity which the Court identifies as covering those State bodies which deal in commercial products (the provision says 'goods') capable of being the subject of competition. This enabled the ECJ to hold that State television does not fall within the provision in Case 155/73 *Sacchi*. The Court also emphasizes that monopolies are not forbidden, only their discriminatory trade practices, a view developed in Cases 59/75 *Manghera* and 91/75 *Miritz*.

Secondly, by holding EEC 53 directly effective, the ECJ paved the way for its later innovations in the whole field of freedom of establishment (Case 2/74 *Reyners*, below, extract no. 10). In fact much of the Community achievement in the free movement of goods and people, and in promoting equal pay for men and women, has been effected by what has been called negative integration. Seizing on the Treaty provisions which forbid new obstacles, and holding others, despite legislative inaction, to have become directly effective after the transitional period, the Court has made the Treaty do what the Commission cannot and the Council will not.

4. In terms of what might be called the 'constitutional law' of the Community, the ECJ's judgment is laconic but crucial:

By contrast with ordinary international treaties, the EEC Treaty has created *its own legal system* which ... became an *integral part* of the legal systems of the Member States and which their courts are *bound* to apply ... Member States have created a body of law which binds both their nationals *and themselves* ... [T]he law stemming from the Treaty, an *independent* source of law, could not, because of its special and *original* nature, be over-ridden by domestic legal provisions *however framed*...

Thus the Court affirms that Community law is like Frankenstein's monster: independent of its creator, imbued with a life of its own, supreme throughout the States' territories, and immune from attack by their laws and constitutions.

5. Case 6/64 *Costa* v. *ENEL* broaches, but does not have to resolve, one very difficult problem. Let us suppose that the national court loyally accepts some earlier ruling that a particular Treaty provision directly confers rights on an individual, that it wishes to obey its Community duty to protect them, and has at hand the appropriate remedy. If, however, there is in force a conflicting

national statute, what is the court to do, not about the individual, but about the statute itself? It can hardly repeal an Act of Parliament; it cannot declare the legislation unconstitutional, unless it is the appropriate Constitutional Court. A useful solution might be simply to hold the statute 'inapplicable', thus reserving its normative force for those cases with no conflicting Community element; but this is difficult if the Act explicitly sets out to cover situations which are also governed by Community law.

The problem is even greater for the judge of those countries whose legal system tells him simply to stay proceedings and to send the problem to some higher court. Meanwhile, the party with the Community right which the judge is supposed to protect, is left in suspense. The next case grapples with this issue.

4 Case 106/77 *Simmenthal*

1. *The action.* Under EEC 177, an Italian court asked the ECJ for help; the main point of the question put was to secure guidance as to what a court should do when faced, not just with conflicting national legislation, but with a domestic rule, that in such a situation, it should stay proceedings and ask the highest Italian (Constitutional) Court to rule on the national law. What the judge wanted was to be told how he should protect the community rights of a litigant but, in order to frame this as a request for interpretation of the Treaty, he asked about the meaning of the words 'directly applicable' in EEC 189. Briefs were filed by the firm involved, the Commission, and the Italian Government.

2. *The salient, simplified facts*

2.1 Simmenthal imported beef from France.

2.2 Under Italian legislation, culminating in a 1970 statute, veterinary and public health checks, for which the importer had to pay, were made at the frontier.

2.3 In Case 35/76 *Simmenthal S.p.A.* v. *Italian Minister of Finance*, the firm had sued for the return of their money in the Italian court. In that court's EEC 177 reference, the ECJ had held that the inspections were contrary to EEC 30, being equivalent to quotas, and the fees were contrary to EEC 12, as they were equivalent to customs duties. Moreover, the whole field of the relevant imports had been governed by Regulations of 1964 and 1968 from the date of their entry into force.

2.4 On receipt of this answer, the national court ordered the Finance Ministry to repay the fees charged.

2.5 The Ministry, however, pleaded the 1970 Italian statute and argued that, under the Italian Constitution, this bound them until set aside by the Constitutional Court.

3. *The legal issues*

3.1 The Italian Parliament is not 'sovereign' in the British sense. Under the Italian Constitution it is possible for a statute to be set aside if it conflicts with a Treaty, because Article 11 provides that Italy 'agrees ... to such limitations of sovereignty as may be necessary for a system calculated to ensure peace and justice between nations.'

3.2 However, such a step may not be taken by any court save one. The Constitution sets up a special Constitutional Court which, under Article 134, 'decides controversies concerning the constitutional legitimacy of statutes'. Furthermore, Article 136 says that when the Court declares a statute unconstitutional, it ceases to have effect on the following day.

3.3 Further, in earlier decisions, the Constitutional Court had reminded lower courts that it alone could annul statutes, and had told them to refer such problems to it. Its decisions, says the Constitution (Article 137) 'may not be contested'.

3.4 The firm, not unnaturally, did not want the question so referred. It had paid the charges five years previously, and had already waited patiently while the ECJ decided, indirectly, in its favour by its interpretation of EEC 12 and 30; a reference within the Italian legal system would take another three years. Meanwhile the firm, and all similar importers, would not know where they stood.

3.5 Moreover, even if the Constitutional Court eventually ruled that the 1970 statute was void, the Constitution itself laid down that the statute died only on the morrow of the judgment. So charges already paid would, under Italian law, have been lawfully exacted, had not the Constitutional Court earlier held that, on its death, an unconstitutional statute ceased to govern earlier situations which were still contested. This rule may be benevolent, but it is still a rule of Italian, not of Community, law.

3.6 Consequently, in its pleadings, the firm cited the ECJ's own words in Case 26/62 *Van Gend en Loos* and argued that they meant that Community law is uniform and mandatory, imposing on all national courts the duty to protect Community rights by, if necessary, ignoring their own constitutions.

3.7 In reply, the Italian Government loyally accepts that its courts cannot *apply* domestic legal rules which conflict with Community law. There is, however, a great difference between not applying a law and declaring it void; if the latter can be done at all (which is certainly not the case in all Member States), it can be done only by the body so empowered under the national constitution.

3.8 Further, the Government argued, a decision of the Constitutional Court is a much tidier way of removing conflicts; the alternative is to leave their resolution to the accidents of litigation.

3.9 The Commission argues that the Italian process is cumbersome and lengthy and that in effect it will mean common Community rules will come into force at different times in different countries.

3.10 Finally, there is the now familiar argument as to whether the Italian court needed to make the reference in order to dispose of the case. It was given a new twist by the fact that, between the time the request was filed and the oral hearing, a 1977 Italian statute had abolished the fees and, in the same year, the Constitutional Court had held the old system unconstitutional. Consequently, the Italian Government argued that the reference request was now moot. In reply, the Advocate-General adverts to the general importance of the issue and to the fact that it was likely to be raised again in the future.

TEXT

OPINION OF MR ADVOCATE-GENERAL REISCHL

1. In my view it would be appropriate to start the observations which have to be made in this matter with a comprehensive account of the relevant decided cases of the Court on the nature of Community law and on its effectiveness for citizens of the Common Market as well as on the relationship between Community and national law. I think it right to remind the Court of this case-law not only because this will make apparent the spirit and basic attitude adopted by the Court in dealing with such problems, but also because the cases hitherto decided give a definite indication of the solution of the problem before us.

In the first place emphasis must be laid on a ruling of a fundamental nature which was to some extent made in a very early case. This is that the Community constitutes a new legal order of international law and that Community law is independent of the legislation of Member States (Case 26/62 *Van Gend en Loos*). Similarly in Case 6/64 *Costa* v. ENEL it is stated that the EEC Treaty has created its own legal system which, on the entry into force of the Treaty, became an integral part of the legal systems of the Member States. It is of the essence of these findings that the Member States have limited their sovereign rights, albeit within limited fields (Case 26/62) or—as is stated in Case 6/64—that the Member States' sovereign powers have been transferred to the Community.

Furthermore an important feature of Community law is that the subjects of this law include the nationals of the Member States (Case 26/62). A whole host of provisions of Community law—there is an extensive case-law on this point—have direct effect in the national law of all Member States, that is to say that they confer upon individuals rights which they may invoke before their national courts (Case 26/62) and which national courts are bound to apply (Case 6/64).

As far as the relationship between Community law and national law in general is concerned the findings of the Court—for example in Case 6/64—mean that Community law takes precedence over national provisions. In other cases these findings are defined as meaning that this precedence applies as against national provisions of every kind.

DECISION

By an order of 28 July 1977, received at the Court on 29 August 1977, the Pretore di Susa referred to the Court for a ruling pursuant to Article 177 of the EEC Treaty, two questions relating to the principle of the direct applicability of Community law as set out in Article 189 of the Treaty for the purpose of determining the effects of that principle when a rule of Community law conflicts with a subsequent provision of national law.

It is appropriate to draw attention to the fact that at a previous stage of the proceedings the Pretore referred to the Court for a preliminary ruling questions designed to enable him to determine whether veterinary and public health fees levied on imports of beef and veal under the consolidated text of the Italian veterinary and public health laws, were compatible with the Treaty and with certain regulations. Having regard to the answers given by the Court in its judgment of 15 December 1976 in Case 35/76 (*Simmenthal S.p.A.* v.

Italian Minister for Finance) the Pretore held that the levying of the fees in question was incompatible with the provisions of Community law and ordered the Amministrazione delle Finanze dello Stato (Italian Finance Administration) to repay the fees unlawfully charged, together with interest. The Amministrazione appealed against that order.

The Pretore, taking into account the arguments put forward by the parties during the proceedings arising out of this appeal, held that the issue before him involved a conflict between certain rules of Community law and a subsequent national law. He pointed out that to resolve an issue of this kind, according to recently decided cases of the Italian Constitutional Court, the question whether the law in question was unconstitutional under Article 11 of the Constitution must be referred to the Constitutional Court itself.

The Pretore, having regard, on the one hand, to the well-established case-law of the Court of Justice relating to the applicability of Community law in the legal systems of the Member States and, on the other hand, to the disadvantages which might arise if the national court, instead of declaring of its own motion that a law impeding the full force and effect of Community law was inapplicable, were required to raise the issue of constitutionality, referred to the Court two questions framed as follows:

(*a*) Since, in accordance with Article 189 of the EEC Treaty and the established case-law of the Court of Justice of the European Communities, directly applicable Community provisions must, notwithstanding any internal rule or practice whatsoever of the Member States, have full, complete, and uniform effect in their legal systems in order to protect subjective legal rights created in favour of individuals, is the scope of the said provisions to be interpreted to the effect that any subsequent national measures which conflict with those provisions must be forthwith disregarded without waiting until those measures have been eliminated by action on the part of the national legislature concerned (repeal) or of other constitutional authorities (declaration that they are unconstitutional) especially, in the case of the latter alternative, where, since the national law continues to be fully effective pending such declaration, it is impossible to apply the Community provisions and, in consequence, to ensure that they are fully, completely, and uniformly applied and to protect the legal rights created in favour of individuals?

(*b*) Arising out of the previous question, in circumstances where Community law recognizes that the protection of subjective legal rights created as a result of 'directly applicable' Community provisions may be suspended until any conflicting national measures are actually repealed by the competent national authorities, is such repeal in all cases to have a wholly retroactive effect so as to avoid any adverse effects on those subjective legal rights?

The reference to the Court

The Agent of the Italian Government in his oral observations drew the attention of the Court to a judgment of the Italian Constitutional Court no. 163/77 of 22 December 1977 the provisions at issue in the action pending before the Pretore di Susa, were unconstitutional.

It was suggested that since the disputed provisions have been set aside by the declaration that they are unconstitutional, the questions raised by the Pretore no longer have relevance so that it is no longer necessary to answer them.

On this issue it should be borne in mind that in accordance with its unvarying practice the Court of Justice considers a reference for a preliminary ruling, pursuant to Article 177 of the Treaty, as having been validly brought before it so long as the reference has not been withdrawn by the court from which it emanates or has not been quashed on appeal by a superior court.

The judgment referred to, which was delivered in proceedings in no way connected with the action giving rise to the reference to this Court, cannot have such a result and the Court cannot determine its effect on third parties.

The preliminary objection raised by the Italian Government must therefore be overruled.

The substance of the case

The main purpose of the first question is to ascertain what consequences flow from the direct applicability of a provision of Community law in the event of incompatibility with a subsequent legislative provision of a Member State.

Direct applicability in such circumstances means that rules of Community law must be fully and uniformly applied in all the Member States from the date of their entry into force and for so long as they continue in force.

These provisions are therefore a direct source of rights and duties for all those affected thereby, whether Member States or individuals, who are parties to legal relationships under Community law.

This consequence also concerns any national court whose task it is as an organ of a Member State to protect, in a case within its jurisdiction, the rights conferred upon individuals by Community law.

Furthermore, in accordance with the principle of the precedence of Community law, the relationship between provisions of the Treaty and directly applicable measures of the institutions on the one hand and the national law of the Member States on the other is such that those provisions and measures not only by their entry into force render automatically inapplicable any conflicting provision of current national law but—in so far as they are an integral part of, and take precedence in, the legal order applicable in the territory of each of the Member States—also preclude the valid adoption of new national legislative measures to the extent to which they would be incompatible with Community provisions.

Indeed any recognition that national legislative measures which encroach upon the field within which the Community exercises its legislative power or which are otherwise incompatible with the provisions of Community law had any legal effect would amount to a corresponding denial of the effectiveness of obligations undertaken unconditionally and irrevocably by Member States pursuant to the Treaty and would thus imperil the very foundations of the Community.

The same conclusion emerges from the structure of Article 177 of the Treaty which provides that any court or tribunal of a Member State is entitled to make a reference to the Court whenever it considers that a preliminary ruling on a question of interpretation or validity relating to Community law is necessary to enable it to give judgment.

The effectiveness of that provision would be impaired if the national court were prevented from forthwith applying Community law in accordance with the decision or the case-law of the Court.

It follows from the foregoing that every national court must, in a case within its jurisdiction, apply Community law in its entirety and protect rights which the latter confers on individuals and must accordingly set aside any provision of national law which may conflict with it, whether prior or subsequent to the Community rule.

Accordingly any provision of a national legal system and any legislative, administrative, or judicial practice which might impair the effectiveness of Community law by withholding from the national court having jurisdiction to apply such law the power to do everything necessary at the moment of its application to set aside national legislative provisions which might prevent Community rules from having full force and effect are incompatible with those requirements which are the very essence of Community law.

This would be the case in the event of a conflict between a provision of Community law and a subsequent national law if the solution of the conflict were to be reserved for an authority with a discretion of its own, other than the court called upon to apply Community law, even if such an impediment to the full effectiveness of Community law were only temporary.

The first question should therefore be answered to the effect that a national court which is called upon, within the limits of its jurisdiction, to apply provisions of Community law is under a duty to give full effect to those provisions, if necessary refusing of its own motion to apply any conflicting provision of national legislation, even if adopted subsequently, and it is not necessary for the court to request or await the prior setting aside of such provision by legislation or other constitutional means.

The essential point of the second question is whether—assuming it to be accepted that the protection of rights conferred by provisions of Community law can be suspended until any national provisions which might conflict with them have been in fact set aside by the competent national authorities—such setting aside must in every case have unrestricted retroactive effect so as to prevent the rights in question from being in any way adversely affected.

It follows from the answer to the first question that national courts must protect rights conferred by provisions of the Community legal order and that it is not necessary for such courts to request or await the actual setting aside by the national authorities empowered so to act or any national measures which might impede the direct and immediate application of Community rules.

The second question therefore appears to have no purpose.

On those grounds the court hereby rules:

A national court which is called upon, within the limits of its jurisdiction, to apply provisions of Community law is under a duty to give full effect to those provisions, if necessary refusing of its own motion to apply any conflicting provisions of national legislation, even if adopted subsequently, and it is not necessary for the court to request or await the prior setting aside of such provisions by legislative or other constitutional means.

COMMENTS

1. The precedence of Community law has now become, in the ECJ's words, a 'principle'. Developing the language of the cases extracted earlier, the Court emphasizes that the entry into force of a Community law not only makes automatically inapplicable any existing incompatible national rule but, since the new Community rule is an integral part of, and takes precedence in, the domestic legal system, it precludes the enactment of later conflicting legislation. Thus it seems as if directly effective Community norms (such as, say, those in a new Regulation) become both integrated and entrenched in the national law.

2. The ECJ goes on to instruct national courts to set aside, where necessary, the law of their own country. This does not mean that the conflicting national law is necessarily void, for, as the Advocate-General points out, it may well have a role to play in cases with no Community element.

3. Since the conflicting incompatible law can be set aside by any domestic court, it follows that a second-order national norm confining this power to some higher court is itself incompatible with Community law, and can also be ignored by the lower court.

4. The Advocate-General's submissions on the main question review the ECJ's case-law and start, of course, with the 'ruling of a fundamental nature'—Case 26/62 *Van Gend en Loos*.

5. The conflict in this case was between Community law and national constitutional provisions of second order; that is to say, norms dealing with the question of who decides issues of constitutionality. But conflict may arise with much more fundamental provisions of a Member State's constitution—with its Bill of Rights. This more basic topic is the subject of the last extract in this section.

5 Case 11/70 *Internationale Handelsgesellschaft*

1. *The action.* Under EEC 177, the Frankfurt Administrative Court asked for the interpretation of parts of two agricultural regulations. In formal terms, the request was unremarkable, but it was accompanied by a powerful statement that the reason for the reference was the German court's belief that the regulations conflicted with elementary human rights guaranteed by entrenched provisions of the German Constitution. Moreover, the Frankfurt court had earlier tested the Community provisions against this Bill of Rights, had found them wanting, and had held them void. Briefs were filed by the firm involved, by the national cereals intervention agency, by the Commission, and by the Dutch and German Governments.

2. *The salient, simplified facts*

2.1 In order to export cornflour, the firm had, under Community law, to obtain a licence. The relevant Regulation provided for a performance deposit, payable on application and forfeit if the exports were not effected within the licence period. The only saving was for *force majeure*.

2.2 The firm paid such a deposit, obtained a licence, but managed only partial exports during the time allowed. They sued the cereals intervention agency for the return of all the deposit, whereupon the court made a reference to the ECJ.

3. *The legal issues*

3.1 There is no Bill of Rights in the Treaty of Rome to protect citizens against bad Community regulations and the like. The only possible reference to basic human rights has to be read into EEC 164 which enjoins the ECJ to ensure that 'in the interpretation and application of this Treaty *the law* is observed', and into EEC 173 which gives as one ground for judicial review of Community acts the fact that they infringe 'this Treaty or *any rule of law* relating to its exercise'.

3.2 In stark contrast, the Constitution of the Federal Republic of Germany begins with a detailed list of basic rights which are stated to 'bind the *legislature*, the executive, and the judiciary as directly enforceable law' (Article 1(3)). So, if the deposit system infringes these basic rights, not even the German Parliament could enact it.

3.3 Article 24(1) allows Germany by legislation to transfer sovereign powers to international institutions. But it can hardly transfer to the EEC a power which it does not possess, namely to enact rules which violate human rights.

3.4 It must be said that it is difficult for an outsider to see how the deposit system might offend in this way. Nonetheless, the Frankfurt court deduced from its Constitution, Articles 2 (everyone has the right to the free development of his personality) and 14 (no expropriation save for good public reason and with compensation), the principle of freedom of trade and the requirement that no rule be stricter than is necessary to safeguard the interest protected by its imposition (the principle of 'proportionality'—no sledgehammer to crack a nut).

3.5 These, it thought, were infringed by the deposit system. The aim of the system was to enable the Community to obtain the information needed to operate the common agricultural policy; indeed the Regulation's preamble recited only the statistical purposes it was to serve. Such an aim could be achieved by measures much less harsh. Furthermore, by allowing recovery of the deposit only where export was prevented by *force majeure*, the money was forfeit if the trader decided not to proceed for the best of all possible reasons—that prices had dropped. So the permission to export was turned into an obligation, and the free market became a planned economy.

3.6 Interesting as these objections are, they skirt the basic issue. The crucial Community problem is not whether the scheme is good or bad, but *who decides* that question: for if it can be reviewed against the constitution of one country, then it can be tested against those of all the Member States and ceases to be common Community law.

TEXT

GROUNDS OF JUDGMENT

1. By order of 18 March 1970 received at the Court on 26 March 1970, the Verwaltungsgericht Frankfurt-am-Main, pursuant to Article 177 of the EEC Treaty, has referred to the Court of Justice two questions on the validity of the system of export licences and of the deposit attaching to them—hereinafter referred to as 'the system of deposits'—provided for by Regulation no. 120/67/EEC of the Council on the common organization of the market in cereals and Regulation no. 473/67/EEC of the Commission on import and export licences.

2. It appears from the grounds of the order referring the matter that the Verwaltungsgericht has until now refused to accept the validity of the provisions in question and that for this reason it considers it to be essential to put an end to the existing legal uncertainty. According to the evaluation of the Verwaltungsgericht, the system of deposits is contrary to certain structural principles of national constitutional law which must be protected within the framework of Community law, with the result that the primacy of supranational law must yield before the principles of the German Basic Law. More particularly, the system of deposits runs counter to the principles of freedom of action and of disposition, of economic liberty, and of proportionality arising in particular from Articles 2(1) and 14 of the Basic Law. The obli-

gation to import or export resulting from the issue of the licences, together with the deposit attaching thereto, constitutes an excessive intervention in the freedom of disposition in trade, as the objective of the regulations could have been attained by methods of intervention having less serious consequences.

The protection of fundamental rights in the Community legal system

3. Recourse to the legal rules of concepts of national law in order to judge the validity of measures adopted by the institutions of the Community would have an adverse effect on the uniformity and efficacy of Community law. The validity of such measures can only be judged in the light of Community law. In fact, the law stemming from the Treaty, an independent source of law, cannot because of its very nature be overridden by rules of national law, however framed, without being deprived of its character as Community law and without the legal basis of the Community itself being called in question. Therefore the validity of a Community measure or its effect within a Member State cannot be affected by allegations that its runs counter to either fundamental rights as formulated by the constitution of that State or the principle of a national constitutional structure.

4. However, an examination should be made as to whether or not any analogous guarantee inherent in Community law has been disregarded. In fact, respect for fundamental rights forms an integral part of the general principles of law protected by the Court of Justice. The protection of such rights, whilst inspired by the constitutional traditions common to the Member States, must be ensured within the framework of the structure and objectives of the Community. It must therefore be ascertained, in the light of the doubts expressed by the Verwaltungsgericht, whether the system of deposits has infringed rights of a fundamental nature, respect for which must be ensured in the Community legal system.

The first question (legality of the system of deposits)

5. By the first question the Verwaltungsgericht asks whether the undertaking to export, the lodging of a deposit which accompanies that undertaking, and forfeiture of the deposit should exportation not occur during the period of validity of the export licence comply with the law.

6. According to the terms of the thirteenth recital of the preamble to Regulation no. 120/67, 'the competent authorities must be in a position constantly to follow trade movements in order to assess market trends and to apply the measures ... as necessary' and 'to that end, provision should be made for the issue of import and export licences accompanied by the lodging of a deposit guaranteeing that the transactions for which such licences are requested are

effected'. It follows from these considerations and from the general scheme of the regulation that the system of deposits is intended to guarantee that the imports and exports for which the licences are requested are actually effected in order to ensure both for the Community and for the Member States precise knowledge of the intended transactions.

7. This knowledge, together with other available information on the state of the market, is essential to enable the competent authorities to make judicious use of the instruments of intervention, both ordinary and exceptional, which are at their disposal for guaranteeing the functioning of the system of prices instituted by the regulation, such as purchasing, storing and distributing, fixing denaturing premiums and export refunds, applying protective measures, and choosing measures intended to avoid deflections of trade. This is all the more imperative in that the implementation of the common agricultural policy involves heavy financial responsibilities for the Community and the Member States.

8. It is necessary, therefore, for the competent authorities to have available not only statistical information on the state of the market but also precise forecasts on future imports and exports. Since the Member States are obliged to issue import and export licences to any applicant, a forecast would lose all significance if the licences did not involve the recipients in an undertaking to act on them. And the undertaking would be ineffectual if observance of it were not ensured by appropriate means.

9. The choice for that purpose by the Community legislature of the deposit cannot be criticized in view of the fact that that machinery is adapted to the voluntary nature of requests for licences and that it has the dual advantage over other possible systems of simplicity and efficacy.

10. A system of mere declaration of exports effected and of unused licences, as proposed by the plaintiff in the main action, would, by reason of its retrospective nature and lack of any guarantee of application, be incapable of providing the competent authorities with sure data on trends in the movement of goods.

11. Likewise, a system of fines imposed a posteriori would involve considerable administrative and legal complications at the stage of decision and of execution, aggravated by the fact that the traders concerned may be beyond the reach of the intervention agencies by reason of their residence in another Member State, since the regulation imposes on Member States the obligation to issue the licences to any applicant 'irrespective of the place of his establishment in the Community.'

12. It therefore appears that the requirement of import and export licences involving for the licensees an undertaking to effect the proposed transactions under the guarantee of a deposit constitutes a method which is both necessary

and appropriate to enable the competent authorities to determine in the most effective manner their interventions on the market in cereals.

13. The principle of the system of deposits cannot therefore be disputed.

14. However, examination should be made as to whether or not certain detailed rules of the system of deposits might be contested in the light of the principles enounced by the Verwaltungsgericht, especially in view of the allegation of the plaintiff in the main action that the burden of the deposit is excessive for trade, to the extent of violating fundamental rights.

15. In order to assess the real burden of the deposit on trade, account should be taken not so much of the amount of the deposit which is repayable—namely 0.5 unit of account per 1,000 kg—as of the costs and charges involved in lodging it. In assessing this burden, account cannot be taken of forfeiture of the deposit itself, since traders are adequately protected by the provisions of the regulation relating to circumstances recognized as constituting *force majeure*.

16. The costs involved in the deposit do not constitute an amount disproportionate to the total value of the goods in question and of the other trading costs. It appears therefore that the burdens resulting from the system of deposits are not excessive and are the normal consequence of a system of organization of the markets conceived to meet the requirements of the general interest, defined in Article 39 of the Treaty, which aims at ensuring a fair standard of living for the agricultural community while ensuring that supplies reach consumers at reasonable prices.

17. The plaintiff in the main action also points out that forfeiture of the deposit in the event of the undertaking to import or export not being fulfilled really constitutes a fine or a penalty which the Treaty has not authorized the Council and the Commission to institute.

18. This argument is based on a false analysis of the system of deposits which cannot be equated with a penal sanction, since it is merely the guarantee that an undertaking voluntarily assumed will be carried out.

19. Finally, the arguments relied upon by the plaintiff in the main action based first on the fact that the departments of the Commission are not technically in a position to exploit the information supplied by the system criticized, so that it is devoid of all practical usefulness, and secondly on the fact that the goods with which the dispute is concerned are subject to the system of inward processing are irrelevant. These arguments cannot put in issue the actual principle of the system of deposits.

20. It follows from all these considerations that the fact that the system of licences involving an undertaking, by those who apply for them, to import or export, guaranteed by a deposit, does not violate any right of a fundamental nature. The machinery of deposits constitutes an appropriate method, for

the purposes of Article 40(3) of the Treaty, for carrying out the common organization of the agricultural markets and also conforms to the requirements of Article 43.

21. The second question asks whether Article 9 of Regulation no. 473/67 of the Commission, adopted in implementation of the first regulation, is in conformity with the law, in that it only excludes forfeiture of the deposit in cases of *force majeure*.

22. It appears from the grounds of the order referring the matter that the court considers excessive and contrary to the above-mentioned principles the provision, the effect of which is to limit the cancellation of the obligation to import or export and release of the deposit only to 'circumstances which may be considered to be a case of *force majeure*'. In the light of its experience, the Verwaltungsgericht considers that provision to be too narrow, leaving exporters open to forfeiture of the deposit in circumstances in which exportation would not have taken place for reasons which were justifiable but not assimilable to a case of *force majeure* in the strict meaning of the term. For its part, the plaintiff in the main action considers this provision to be too severe because it limits the release of the deposit to cases of *force majeure* without taking into account the arrangements of importers or exporters which are justified by considerations of a commercial nature.

23. The concept of *force majeure* adopted by the agricultural regulations takes into account the particular nature of the relationships in public law between traders and the national administration, as well as the objectives of those regulations. It follows from those objectives as well as from the positive provisions of the regulations in question that the concept of *force majeure* is not limited to absolute impossibility but must be understood in the sense of unusual circumstances, outside the control of the importer or exporter, the consequences of which, in spite of the exercise of all due care, could not have been avoided except at the cost of excessive sacrifice. This concept implies a sufficient flexibility regarding not only the nature of the occurrence relied upon but also the care which the exporter should have exercised in order to meet it and the extent of the sacrifices which he should have accepted to that end.

24. The cases of forfeiture cited by the court as imposing an unjustified and excessive burden on the exporter appear to concern situations in which exportation has not taken place either through the fault of the exporter himself or as a result of an error on his part or for purely commercial considerations.

25. It therefore appears that by limiting the cancellation of the undertaking to export and the release of the deposit to cases of *force majeure* the Community legislature adopted a provision which, without imposing an undue burden

on importers or exporters, is appropriate for ensuring the normal functioning of the organization of the market in cereals, in the general interest as defined in Article 39 of the Treaty. It follows that no argument against the validity of the system of deposits can be based on the provisions limiting release of the deposit to cases of *force majeure*.

COMMENTS

1. The ECJ declares, in forthright terms, that Community law must not be tested by national courts against their own Bill of Rights, else it loses its character as law common to the Community.

2. National courts are not to worry, however, since respect for human rights is part of 'the law' which the European Court administers and, in framing its Community Bill of Rights, it is inspired by national constitutional traditions. Applying this Community version of a Bill of Rights, the Court approved the disputed provisions. It should be added, however, first, that certain fundamental rights are already recognized by the Treaty: EEC 7 (no discrimination on grounds of nationality); EEC 119 (equal remuneration for men and women); and EEC 222 (property ownership). Secondly, other such basic principles have been used by the ECJ to test Community regulations and decisions and sometimes, if found in breach, to annul them. Examples include: Cases 7/72 *Quinine*—double jeopardy; 17/74 *Transocean Paint*—*audi alteram partem*; 74/74 *CNTA*—legitimate reliance; and 29/69 *Stauder* v. *Ulm*—human dignity. Some slight textual remedy for the gap in the Treaty is to be found in the 1977 Joint Declaration on Fundamental Rights, made by the Parliament, Council, and Commission, and in the Preamble to the 1986 Single European Act. Both of these refer to the European Convention for the Protection of Human Rights (see Rudden and Wyatt, *BCL*, 138, 147).

3. In the case under discussion, the Frankfurt court was most dissatisfied with the ECJ's reply. It noted that the Community has no written Bill of Rights and no Parliament with powers to enact one, and it found in the ECJ's approval of what it continued to regard as the iniquitous deposit system a powerful confirmation of its deepest suspicions about the 'legal vacuum' of Community law.

4. Consequently, it referred the issue to its own Constitutional Court. That court unanimously approved the deposit scheme, but this is trivial beside the fact that, by a majority of 5 : 3, it refused to bow to the ECJ and held that, so long as there was no Parliamentary Bill of Rights in Community law, it would continue to accept references from lower German courts asking it to review Community regulations against the German Constitution. (An English translation of the Frankfurt and Constitutional Court decisions will be found at [1972] CMLR 177 and [1974] 2 CMLR 540.) The only consolation is that,

so far, no Community law has actually been held inapplicable in Germany for conflict with the Constitution; and there are some signs of a withdrawal from the proposition that the Constitutional Court reserves the right to test Community laws against its Bill of Rights (see Hartley, *FCL*, 230).

5. The ECJ has since found the deposit system for export licences to breach the principle of proportionality where the scheme imposed a forfeiture of the same sum both for major non-compliance and for minor infringements involving only brief delays: Case 181/84 *Man* (*Sugar*) *Ltd*.

II
The Development of Community Law

The extracts selected above have shown the ECJ laying the foundations of a common law of the Community: a 'legal order' which is independent in its creation, yet plays an integral part in the law to be administered by the national courts and, furthermore, is to prevail over any incompatible domestic norm, whatever its date and however august its source. All this is true, of course, only within an apparently limited area. The limits are twofold: firstly there must be some *Community* element, so that problems arising out of purely national matters—for instance an agreement not to compete concluded between two small shops in the same street—fall entirely under domestic law. Secondly, even if there be a wider, cross-border connection, there can be no Community law purporting to deal with matters outside the scope of the Treaties—for instance, divorce, succession, or the rule against perpetuities.

It seems to be the case, however, that almost any activity can fall within a Treaty whose title includes the word 'economic'. A glance at the history of the USA shows the gradual revelation of just how much of life, and how much of the *federal* power, were latent in the Constitutional grant to Congress of the right 'to regulate Commerce with foreign Nations, and among the several States, and with the Indian Tribes' (art. 1.8).

The European Community has not, of course, developed federalism to anything like, or even resembling, the American pattern. Nonetheless, the ECJ has been called upon to do two things, the first affecting ordinary trade and ordinary people, the second dealing with the constitutional balance of the other three institutions. As to the first, in many important areas of commercial life, the Treaty of Rome laid on the Council the duty to implement its basic rules within the transitional period. The Council, however, did not comply, and so the Court has used the Treaty itself to strengthen the fundamental freedoms of the internal market. As to the second, the growth of real power in the European Parliament has been fostered and controlled by the Court's bold interpretation of the Treaty so as to enable the Parliament both to sue and be sued.

This Part is therefore divided into two sections, the first illustrating the growth of the internal market as it relates to trade in goods and to the free movement of people, the second dealing with the development of constitutional checks and balances. In both areas, the Court wields powers which, one may think, could hardly have been foreseen by the signatories to the Treaty of Rome.

A The Internal Market

(1) *Goods*

The free flow of goods across borders can be hindered in many ways. Among those devised by States, the most obvious—customs duties and quotas—are prohibited clearly by the Treaty, and Case 26/62 *Van Gend en Loos* (above, extract no. 1) shows how the benefit of this prohibition protects individual traders.

These obvious obstacles are fairly easily dealt with. More elusive are the 'non-tariff' barriers resulting from national laws inspired by differing notions of the public interest, ranging from the mundane to the moral. As to the first, the manufacturer of electrical equipment who hopes to sell throughout the Community will find that (apart from voltage differences) his plugs may need three prongs, two prongs, straight or angled, rectangular, fat, thin, and sheathed, and his plug faces will have to be squares, circles, pentagons, or hexagons. As to the second, the Irish view of what sex-books may be sold is not the same as that of the Danes.

Many of these problems can be solved by directives issued under EEC 100, and the Single European Act of February 1986 promises more rapid progress towards a true internal market (see Rudden and Wyatt, *BCL*, 147). But it would not be enough to remove barriers or to harmonize technical requirements imposed by States if private cartels can still carve up the market. The three cases which follow illustrate some achievements of the Court in the struggle for a true common market in goods.

6 Case 120/78 *Cassis de Dijon*

1. *The action.* Under EEC 177, a German court asked for an interpretation of EEC 30 and 37. Briefs were filed by the firm involved, the Commission, and the Danish and German Governments.

2. *The salient, simplified facts*

2.1 The firm wanted to import a French liqueur called Cassis de Dijon. Its maximum strength is 20 per cent alcohol by volume.

2.2 The German authorities decided that the drink could be imported but not sold, because a German law forbade the marketing of liqueurs of so small an alcohol content.

2.3 The firm brought an action against that decision, and a national court made the reference.

3. *The legal issues*

3.1 Germany was not imposing a quota on, or in any other way, preventing the import. EEC 30, however, forbids 'measures having equivalent effect' to quotas.

3.2 Member States have traditionally laid down their own rules as to the minimum alcohol content of beverages of different types such as wine-spirits, or grain-spirits. The French requirements for the latter category were less strict than those of Germany. The German law did not directly discriminate against the French, but its effect was, in fact, to keep French spirits out of the German market.

3.3 Germany, however, argued that, if its own rules were held inapplicable to the import, then the much milder French law would, in fact, cover drink sold in Germany; as a result of this, German producers would have to be treated in the same way. It would then follow that any relaxation of the French law would automatically apply, so that, in the end, the law with the lowest standards would prevail throughout the Community.

3.4 The question at once arises, why not? To answer this, Germany is forced to plead EEC 36 which subjects the free market in goods to national measures justified on various grounds of public policy. With every appearance of sincerity, the Government argued that its minimum standard law was inspired by the wish to protect the consumer from alcoholism. Capotorti A-G confessed to having great difficulty in sharing this view.

3.5 The national court's question on EEC 37 was found irrelevant, and is not included in the following extract.

TEXT

DECISION

1. The Hessisches Finanzgericht referred two questions to the Court under Article 177 of the EEC Treaty for a preliminary ruling on the interpretation of Articles 30 and 37 of the EEC Treaty, for the purpose of assessing the compatibility with Community law of a provision of the German rules relating to the marketing of alcoholic beverages fixing a minimum alcoholic strength for various categories of alcoholic products.

2. It appears from the order making the reference that the plaintiff in the main action intends to import a consignment of 'Cassis de Dijon' originating in France for the purpose of marketing it in the Federal Republic of Germany.

The plaintiff applied to the Bundesmonopolverwaltung für Branntwein (Federal Monopoly Administration for Spirits) for authorization to import the product in question and the monopoly administration informed it that because of its insufficient alcoholic strength the said product does not have the characteristics required in order to be marketed within the Federal Republic of Germany.

3. The Monopoly Administration's attitude is based on Article 100 of the Branntweinmonopolgesetz and on the rules drawn up by the Monopoly Administration pursuant to that provision, the effect of which is to fix the minimum alcoholic content of specified categories of liqueurs and other potable spirits.

Those provisions lay down that the marketing of fruit liqueurs, such as 'Cassis de Dijon', is conditional upon a minimum alcohol content of 25 per cent, whereas the alcohol content of the product in question, which is freely marketed as such in France, is between 15 and 20 per cent.

4. The plaintiff takes the view that the fixing by the German rules of a minimum alcohol content leads to the result that well-known spirits products from other Member States cannot be sold in the Federal Republic of Germany and that the said provision therefore constitutes a restriction on the free movement of goods between Member States which exceeds the bounds of the trade rules reserved to the latter.

In its view it is a measure having an effect equivalent to a quantitative restriction on imports contrary to Article 30 of the EEC Treaty.

5. In order to reach a decision on this dispute the Hessisches Finanzgericht has referred [a] question to the Court, worded as follows:

Must the concept of measures having an effect equivalent to quantitative restrictions on imports contained in Article 30 of the EEC Treaty be understood as meaning that the fixing of a minimum wine-spirit content for potable spirits laid down in the German Branntweinmonopolgesetz, the result of which is that traditional products of other Member States whose wine-spirit is below the fixed limit cannot be put into circulation in the Federal Republic of Germany, also comes within the concept?

6. The national court is thereby asking for assistance in the matter of interpretation in order to enable it to assess whether the requirement of a minimum alcohol content may be covered by the prohibition on all measures having an effect equivalent to quantitative restrictions in trade between Member States contained in Article 30 of the Treaty.

7. [The Court finds the other question irrelevant.]

8. In the absence of common rules relating to the production and marketing of alcohol, it is for the Member States to regulate. Obstacles to movement within the Community resulting from disparities between the national laws relating to the marketing of the products in question must be accepted in so far as those provisions may be recognized as being necessary in order to satisfy mandatory requirements relating in particular to the effectiveness of fiscal supervision, the protection of public health, the fairness of commercial transactions, and the defence of the consumer.

9. The Government of the Federal Republic of Germany put forward various arguments, adducing considerations relating on the one hand to the protection of public health and on the other to the protection of the consumer against unfair commercial practices.

10. As regards the protection of public health the German Government states that the purpose of the fixing of minimum alcohol contents by national legislation is to avoid the proliferation of alcoholic beverages on the national market, in particular alcoholic beverages with a low alcohol content, since, in its view, such products may more easily induce a tolerance towards alcohol than more highly alcoholic beverages.

11. Such considerations are not decisive since the consumer can obtain on the market an extremely wide range of weakly or moderately alcoholic products and furthermore a large proportion of alcoholic beverages with a high alcohol content freely sold on the German market is generally consumed in a diluted form.

12. The German Government also claims that the fixing of a lower limit for the alcohol content of certain liqueurs is designed to protect the consumer against unfair practices. This argument is based on the consideration that the lowering of the alcohol content secures a competitive advantage since alcohol constitutes by far the most expensive constituent of beverages by reason of the high rate of tax to which it is subject.

Furthermore, according to the German Government, to allow alcoholic products into free circulation wherever, as regards their alcohol content, they comply with the rules laid down in the country of production would have the effect of imposing as a common standard within the Community the lowest alcohol content permitted in any of the Member States, and even of rendering any requirements in this field inoperative since a lower limit of this nature is foreign to the rules of several Member States.

13. As the Commission rightly observed, the fixing of limits in relation to the alcohol content of beverages may lead to the standardization of products placed on the market and of their designations, in the interests of a greater transparency of commercial transactions and offers for sale to the public.

However, this line of argument cannot be taken so far as to regard the mandatory fixing of minimum alcohol contents as being an essential guarantee of the fairness of commercial transactions, since it is a simple matter to ensure that suitable information is conveyed to the purchaser by requiring the display of an indication of origin and of the alcohol content on the packaging of products.

14. It is clear from the foregoing that the requirements relating to the minimum alcohol content of alcoholic beverages do not serve a purpose which is in the general interest and such as to take precedence over the requirement of the free movement of goods, which constitutes one of the fundamental rules of the Community.

In practice, the principal effect of requirements of this nature is to promote alcoholic beverages having a high alcohol content by excluding from the national market products of other Member States which do not answer that description.

It therefore appears that the unilateral requirements imposed by the rules of a Member State of a minimum alcohol content for the purposes of the sale of alcoholic beverages constitute an obstacle to trade which is incompatible with the provisions of Article 30 of the Treaty.

There is therefore no valid reason why, provided they have been lawfully produced and marketed in one of the Member States, alcoholic beverages should not be introduced into any other Member States; the sale of such products may not be subject to a legal prohibition on the marketing of beverages with an alcohol content lower than the limit set by the national rules.

On these grounds, the Court, in answer to the questions referred to it, hereby rules:

> The concept of 'measures having an effect equivalent to quantitative restrictions on imports' contained in Article 30 of the EEC Treaty is to be understood to mean that the fixing of a minimum alcohol content for alcoholic beverages intended for human consumption by the legislation of a Member State also falls within the prohibition laid down in that provision where the importation of alcoholic beverages lawfully produced and marketed in another Member State is concerned.

COMMENTS

1. The importance of EEC 30's prohibition on measures whose effect is similar to quotas was appreciated only gradually. In fact its width was first pointed out in 1967 in an article (in Dutch) by P. VerLoren van Themaat, now Advocate-General. The Commission, under EEC 37(7), had issued partial directives, but it was not until Directive 70/50 that the general scope began to emerge (see Rudden and Wyatt, *BCL*, 205). Even that measure, however, did not wholeheartedly cover national rules which, in formal terms, applied equally to home and foreign products, even though their effect might be to hinder imports.

2. The above case is merely one in a series clarifying the scope of EEC 30. The phrase 'measures having equivalent effect' was held applicable to agricultural products in Case 48/74 *Charmasson*, and in the same year the ECJ defined its general meaning as covering measures 'capable of hindering, directly or indirectly, actually or potentially intra-Community trade' (Case 8/74 *Dassonville*).

3. After the *Cassis de Dijon* judgment, the Commission sent a circular to the Member States spelling out its consequences. The Commission deduced from the case that one Member State could not forbid the home sale of imports lawfully marketed in another Member State, even if they complied with quite different technical or quality requirements. The Commission promised to tackle the vast work of harmonizing the innumerable technical and commercial rules in force in the different countries (OJ 1980 C 256/2).

4. The exact relationship between restrictions forbidden to States by EEC 30 and those permitted on various grounds of public policy by EEC 36 is not easy to define. In the case above, para. 8, the Court recognizes that within EEC 36 may fall national laws concerned with public health, fair trading, and consumer protection. The Article itself, however, ends by saying that it may not be used as a means of disguised restrictions on trade. More recent cases have seen the gradual shrinking of national discretion in this field. Indeed in one the ECJ has apparently had second thoughts, saying 'public policy cannot be extended so as to include considerations of consumer protection' (Case 177/83 *Kohl*); and, in a preliminary ruling requested by an English court, the ECJ has held that foreign indecent products may not be refused entry if similar material is available here (Case 121/85 *Conegate Ltd. v. HM Customs and Excise*).

5. Even where national measures are inspired by considerations of fair trading, the ECJ rules in Case 120/78 *Cassis de Dijon* that the restrictions must be proportionate to the aim to be achieved: thus, on the facts, information on the label would suffice to warn the potential buyer that the spirit was not strong.

7 Case 249/81 *Commission* v. *Ireland*

1. *The action.* Under EEC 169, the Commission brought an action against Ireland for breach of EEC 30.

2. *The salient facts*

   2.1 In 1978 the Irish Government announced a programme to create jobs in Ireland's manufacturing and service industries by persuading people to purchase Irish goods. A 'Buy Irish' campaign was launched, supported by public funds, involving the Irish Goods Council, advertising, and the use of a 'Guaranteed Irish' symbol.

   2.2 During the first three years of the campaign, the proportion of Irish goods to all goods sold fell considerably.

   2.3 In 1981, the Commission delivered its reasoned opinion that the campaign was equivalent to a quantitative restriction on imports, and so in breach of EEC 30.

3. *The legal issues*

   3.1 The campaign was not introduced by any law or delegated legislation; consequently, Ireland argued that it had not passed *measures* equivalent to quotas.

   3.2 The campaign failed.

   3.3 Commission Directive 70/50 expressly forbids measures which encourage the purchase of domestic products (art. 2(3)(k); see Rudden and Wyatt, *BCL*, 205). Further, its preamble defines 'measure' as including recommendations; however, an implementation measure can only clarify, not extend, a Treaty prohibition. Consequently, the main thrust of the decision concerns EEC 30 itself.

   3.4 The Irish Government also argued that the financial aid given was compatible with EEC 92, which permits State aids to industry for such purposes as to combat unemployment. The ECJ holds, however, that EEC 30 still applies to the particular grant-aided programme. Consequently, the extract below gives only the heart of the judgment on EEC 30.

TEXT

DECISION

20. The Commission maintains that the 'Buy Irish' campaign and the measures taken to prosecute the campaign must be regarded, as a whole, as measures encouraging the purchase of domestic products only. Such measures are said to be contrary to the obligations imposed on Member States by Article 30.

21. The Irish Government maintains that the prohibition is concerned only with 'measures', that is to say binding provisions emanating from a public authority. However, no such provision has been adopted by the Irish Government, which has confined itself to giving moral support and financial aid to the activities pursued by the Irish industries.

22. The Irish Government goes on to emphasize that the campaign has had no restrictive effect since the proportion of Irish goods to all goods sold on the Irish market fell from 49.2 per cent in 1977 to 43.4 per cent in 1980.

23. The first observation to be made is that the campaign cannot be likened to advertising by private or public undertakings to encourage people to buy [their] goods. Regardless of the means used to implement it, the campaign is a reflection of the Irish Government's considered intention to substitute domestic products for imported products on the Irish market and thereby to check the flow of imports from other Member States.

24. It must be remembered here that a representative of the Irish Government stated when the campaign was launched that it was a carefully thought-out set of initiatives constituting an integrated programme for promoting domestic products.

25. Whilst it may be true that two elements of the programme, namely the advertising campaign and the use of the 'Guaranteed Irish' symbol, have not had any significant success, it is not possible to overlook the fact that, regardless of their efficacy, those two activities form part of a government programme which is designed to achieve the substitution of domestic products for imported products and is liable to affect the volume of trade between Member States.

26. The advertising campaign cannot be divorced from its origin as part of the Government programme. The establishment of a system for investigating complaints about Irish products provides adequate confirmation of the degree of organization of the 'Buy Irish' campaign and of the discriminatory nature of the campaign.

27. In the circumstances, the two activities in question amount to the establishment of a national practice, introduced by the Irish Government and prosecuted with its assistance, the potential effect of which on imports from other member States is comparable to that resulting from government measures of a binding nature.

28. Such a nature cannot escape the prohibition laid down by Article 30 of the Treaty solely because it is not based on decisions which are binding on undertakings. Even measures which do not have binding effect may be capable of influencing the conduct of traders and consumers and thus of frustrating the aims of the Community as set out in Article 2 and enlarged upon in Article 3 of the Treaty.

29. That is the case where, as in this instance, such a restrictive practice represents the implementation of a programme defined by the Government which affects the national economy as a whole and which is designed to check the flow of trade between Member States by encouraging the purchase of domestic products, by means of an advertising campaign on a national scale and the organization of special procedures applicable solely to domestic products, and where those activities are attributable to domestic products, and where those activities are attributable as a whole to the Government and are pursued in an organized fashion throughout the whole of the national territory.

30. Ireland has therefore failed to fulfil its obligations under the Treaty by organizing a campaign to promote the sale and purchase of Irish goods within its territory.

COMMENTS

1. The campaign in question did receive support from public funds, and so the State was directly involved. If a private person, or firm, financed such a campaign, two questions would seem to arise. Firstly, EEC 30 has direct effect in giving rights to individuals; does it also impose duties on them? If that were so, the person concerned could not be sued by anyone before the ECJ for breach of EEC 30; but it is faintly possible that he might be sued in a national court, either by the Commission or by a foreign importer. Secondly, would the Government which stood by and watched such a private campaign without trying to prevent it, be in breach of its obligation to 'abstain from measures which could jeopardize the attainment of the objectives of this Treaty' (EEC 5(2))?

2. In Case 113/80 *Commission* v. *Ireland*, Ireland was held to have broken EEC 30 by imposing a legal requirement that imported 'souvenirs of Ireland' bear either the name of their country of origin of the word 'foreign'. Yet the tourist who buys a shillelagh or a statue of Our Lady of Knock is likely to be gravely disappointed if close inspection reveals that it was made in Birmingham.

3. The 'Buy Irish' campaign did not have the effect intended. But a State measure may be contrary to EEC 30 if it tries to infringe the prohibition or if, even without trying, it manages to do so. The ECJ actually uses the phrase 'restrictive practice', thus recalling the two distinct criteria under EEC 85 which forbids agreements and the like whose object *or* effect is the restriction of competition. The next case deals with this Article.

8 Joined Cases 56 and 58/64
Consten and Grundig v. *Commission*

Judging by the amount of case-law and commentary, the efforts of private traders to carve up the internal market are even more strenuous than those of Member States. The following makes no attempt whatever to provide a comprehensive account of Community competition law. Instead, it presents extracts from one basic case, selected only to demonstrate the range of the prohibition against restrictive practices contained in the first sentence of EEC 85.

1. *The action.* Consten (a French firm) and Grundig (a German firm) each brought an action against a decision addressed to them. Their cases were joined. The Italian and German Governments intervened to file briefs in support of the plaintiffs, and two rival companies supported the Commission.

2. *The salient, simplified facts*

2.1 Grundig made radios, television sets, tape recorders, and the like in Germany; Consten were French wholesalers. In 1957, the two firms made an exclusive distributorship contract, the point of which was to ensure that the French could buy Grundig products only through Consten. Grundig promised not to deliver to any other French distributor, and to include in their contracts with firms elsewhere a clause preventing Grundig goods from being shipped to France. In return, Consten promised to buy Grundig's products, not to deal in those of competitors, and not to deliver outside France.

2.2 The products all carried the trade mark GINT, from the words Grundig International. With Grundig's consent, Consten registered in France the mark in its own name; the point of this was to enable Consten to use French trade-mark law against other importers of Grundig goods.

2.3 The Treaty of Rome came into force in 1958, and in 1962 Regulation 17 required such agreements to be notified to the Commission (see Rudden and Wyatt, *BCL*, 291). Grundig did so.

2.4 Meanwhile, French competitors were getting Grundig products into France, were selling them at lower prices, and were being sued by Consten in the French courts for unfair competition and infringement of their trade mark.

2.5 In 1964, acting under Articles 3, 6 and 7 of Regulation 17/62, the Commission took a decision addressed to the two firms holding their contract to be a breach of EEC 85, refusing to lift the prohibition imposed by EEC 85 (1), and forbidding the firms to hinder the acquisition by competitors, for resale in France, of the goods covered by the contract. The firms brought suit under EEC 173.

3. *The legal issues.* The firms raised several relatively technical points concerning the form of the decision itself, and the Commission's refusal to clear the particular contract. What follows, however, concerns only the main issues.

3.1 EEC 85 begins by prohibiting (*inter alia*) agreements 'which may affect trade between Member States and which have as their object or effect the prevention, restriction, or distortion of competition within the common market'. EEC 85 (2) says that such agreements are 'automatically void'. This provision would be virtually meaningless if it had no direct effect.

3.2 Grundig and Consten were not competitors—one made things, the other sold them—and so never promised not to compete with each other. Their contract was designed to stop *other* French firms competing with Consten. Consequently, they and the Italian Government argued that the word 'agreement' in EEC 85 covers only contracts between competitors at the same level—two manufacturers, or two distributors; the judgment called this type 'horizontal'.

3.3 The point of the contract was to prevent other firms from selling Grundig products in France; it could not limit their sale of other firms' goods, and in fact there was fierce competition between different manufacturers. Consequently, the Court had to decide whether a restriction of competition in only one brand was prohibited by EEC 85.

3.4 The Community element in EEC 85 is shown by its prohibition of restrictive agreements only if they may affect trade between Member States. The firms argued that this must mean 'affect for the worse' and that therefore the Commission had to show that this contract in fact cut down trade between France and Germany.

3.5 Even if the contract had as its object the restriction of competition, the firms argued that this was not its effect; on the contrary, by strengthening Grundig, it intensified competition between them and rival manufacturers. EEC 85, however, is deliberately disjunctive and very wide, forbidding arrangements whose object *or* effect is the prevention, restriction, *or* distortion of competition.

3.6 Consten owned the trade mark in France, and EEC 222 says that the Treaty 'shall in no way prejudice the rules in Member States governing the system of property ownership'. The Commission's decision had held against Consten's use of its trade mark protection to prevent parallel imports of Grundig products. But the decision did not seek to stop Consten from owning the trade mark; it merely forbade its use against importers of Grundig products from other Community countries.

3.7 Finally, the decision annulled the entire contract, although not all its provisions broke EEC 85. The ECJ was prepared to quash this over-wide use of the Commission's power.

TEXT

DECISION

The complaints concerning the applicability of Article 85 (1) to sole distribution agreements

The applicants submit that the prohibition in Article 85(1) applies only to so-called horizontal agreements. The Italian Government submits furthermore that sole distributorship contracts do not constitute 'agreements between undertakings' within the meaning of the provision, since the parties are not on a footing of equality. With regard to these contracts, freedom of competition may be protected only by virtue of Article 86 of the Treaty.

Neither the wording of Article 85 nor that of Article 86 gives any ground for holding that distinct areas of application are to be assigned to each of the two articles according to the level of the economy in which all the contracting parties operate. Article 85 refers in a general way to all agreements which distort competition within the common market and does not lay down any distinction between these agreements based on whether they are made between competitors operating on the same level in the economic process or between non-competing persons operating at different levels. In principle, no distinction can be made where the Treaty does not make any distinction.

Furthermore, the possible application of Article 85 to a sole distributorship contract cannot be excluded merely because the grantor and the concessionaire are not competitors *inter se* and not on a footing of equality. Competition may be distorted within the meaning of Article 85(1) not only by agreements which limit it as between the parties, but also by agreements which prevent or restrict the competition which might take place between one of them and third parties. For this purpose, it is irrelevant whether the parties to the agreement are or are not on a footing of equality as regards their position and function in the economy. This applies all the more since, by such an agreement, the parties might seek, by preventing or limiting the competition of third parties in respect of the products, to create or guarantee for their benefit an unjustified advantage at the expense of consumers, contrary to the general aims of Article 85(1).

Finally, an agreement between producer and distributor which might tend to restore the national divisions in trade between Member States might be such as to frustrate the most fundamental objectives of the Community. The Treaty, whose preamble and content aim at abolishing the barriers between States, and which in several provisions gives evidence of a stern attitude to their reappearance, could not allow undertakings to reconstruct such barriers.

The submissions set out above are consequently unfounded.

The complaints relating to the concepts of 'agreements ... which may affect trade between Member States'

The applicants and the German Government maintain that the Commission has relied on a mistaken interpretation of the concept of an agreement which may affect trade between Member States and has not shown that such trade would have been greater without the agreement in dispute.

The defendant replies that this requirement in Article 85(1) is fulfilled once trade between Member States develops, as a result of the agreement, differently from ways in which it would have done without the restriction resulting from the agreement, and once the influence of the agreement on market conditions reaches a certain degree. Such is the case here, according to the defendant, particularly in view of the impediments resulting within the Common Market from the disputed agreement as regards the exporting and importing of Grundig products to and from France.

The concept of an agreement 'which may affect trade between Member States' is intended to define, in the law governing cartels, the boundary between the areas respectively covered by Community law and national law. It is only to the extent to which the agreement may affect trade between Member States that the deterioration in competition falls under the prohibition of Community law contained in Article 85; otherwise it escapes the prohibition.

In this connection, what is particularly important is whether the agreement is capable of constituting a threat, either direct or indirect, actual or potential, to freedom of trade between Member States in a manner which might harm the attainment of the objectives of a single market between States. Thus the fact that the agreement encourages an increase, even a large one, in the volume of trade between States is not sufficient to exclude the possibility that the agreement may 'affect' such trade in the above-mentioned manner. In the present case, the contract between Grundig and Consten, on the one hand by preventing undertakings other than Consten from importing Grundig products into France, and on the other hand by prohibiting Consten from re-exporting those products to other countries of the Common Market, indisputably affects trade between Member States. These limitations on the freedom of trade, as well as those which might ensue for third parties from the registration in France by Consten of the GINT trade mark which Grundig places on all its products, are enough to satisfy the requirement in question.

Consequently, the complaints raised in this respect must be dismissed.

The complaints concerning the criterion of restriction on competition

The applicants and the German Government maintain that, since the Commission restricted its examination solely to Grundig products, the decision was based upon a false concept of competition, since this applies particularly to competition between similar products of different makes; the Commission, before declaring Article 85 (1) to be applicable, should, by basing itself upon the 'rule of reason', have considered the economic effects of the disputed contract upon competition between the different makes. There is a presumption that vertical sole-distribution agreements are not harmful to competition, and in the present case there is nothing to invalidate that presumption. On the contrary, the contract in question has increased the competition between similar products of different makes.

The principle of freedom of competition concerns the various stages and manifestations of competition. Although competition between producers is generally more noticeable than between distributors of products of the same make, it does not thereby follow than an agreement tending to restrict the latter kind of competition should escape the prohibition of Article 85 (1) merely because it might increase the former.

Besides, for the purpose of applying Article 85 (1), there is no need to take account of the concrete effects of an agreement once it appears that it has as its object the prevention, restriction, or distortion of competition.

The complaints relating to the extent of the prohibition

The applicant Grundig and the German Government complain that the Commission did not exclude from the prohibition, in the operative part of the disputed decision, those clauses of the contract in respect of which there was found no effect capable of restricting competition, and that it thereby failed to define the infringement.

It is apparent from the statement of the reasons for the contested decision that the infringement is not to be found in the undertaking by Grundig not to make direct deliveries in France except to Consten. That infringement arises from the clauses which, added to this grant of exclusive rights, are intended to impede, relying upon national law, parallel imports of Grundig products into France by establishing absolute territorial protection in favour of the sole concessionaire.

The provision in Article 85 (2) that agreements prohibited pursuant to Article 85 (1) shall be automatically void applies only to those parts of the agreement which are subject to the prohibition, or to the agreement as a whole if those parts do not appear to be severable. The Commission should, therefore, either have confined itself to declaring that an infringement lay in parts only of the agreement, or else it should have set out the reason why those parts did not appear to be severable.

Article 1 of the contested decision must therefore be annulled, in so far as it renders void, without any valid reason, all the clauses of the agreement.

The submissions concerning the finding of an infringement in respect of the agreement on the GINT trade mark

The applicants complain that the Commission infringed Article 222 of the EEC Treaty and furthermore exceeded the limits of its powers by excluding, in its decision, any possibility of Consten's asserting its rights under national trade-mark law to oppose parallel imports.

Consten's right under the contract to be the exclusive user of the GINT trade mark is intended to make it possible to place an obstacle in the way of parallel imports. Thus the agreement tends to restrict competition.

That agreement therefore is one which may be caught by the prohibition in Article 85(1). The prohibition would be ineffective if Consten could continue to use the trade mark to achieve the same object as that pursued by the agreement which has been held to be unlawful.

Article 222 confines itself to stating that the 'Treaty shall in no way prejudice the rules in Member States governing the system of property ownership'. The injunction contained in the contested decision to refrain from using rights under national trade-mark law in order to set an obstacle in the way of parallel imports does not affect the grant of those rights but only limits their exercise to the extent necessary to give effect to Article 85(1). The power of the Commission to issue such an injunction is in harmony with the nature of the Community rules on competition which have immediate effect and are binding on individuals.

Such a body of rules, by reason of its nature described above and its function, does not allow the improper use of rights under any national trade-mark law in order to frustrate the Community's law on cartels.

The above-mentioned submissions are therefore unfounded.

COMMENTS

1. The novice reader may imagine that one way in which the firms could achieve the desired result would be to amalgamate: the whole network would then be run by one firm and there would be no 'agreement between undertakings' to be caught by EEC 85. EEC 86, however, deals with the single firm which abuses its dominance in the market.

2. Exclusive distribution agreements are now governed by Regulation 1983/83 (see Rudden and Wyatt, *BCL*, 315).

(2) *People*

9 Case 41/74 *Van Duyn*

1. *The action.* This was a reference under EEC 177 made by an English court (Pennycuick V-C) asking whether EEC 48 and Directive 64/221, art. 3 were 'directly applicable so as to confer on individuals rights enforceable by them in the courts of a Member State'. The Commission, the plaintiff, and the UK filed briefs. (For the text of the legal provisions, see Rudden and Wyatt, *BCL*, 39, 265).

2. *The facts.* The salient facts are clearly set out in the extracts printed below.

3. *The legal issues*

3.1 No domestic legislation outlawed scientology, and UK citizens could freely accept employment at its Church in East Grinstead. Nationals of other Member States, however, although offered similar jobs, were not allowed in to take them up. The result looks like discrimination on the grounds of nationality, forbidden in principle by EEC 7 and in detail by EEC 48.

3.2 *EEC 48*. Article EEC 48 considered as a norm, does not resemble EEC 12 or the other standstill articles. First, it is not expressly addressed to Member States; it begins in the abstract by saying 'freedom of movement for workers shall be secured'. Secondly, the Member States' obligations implied by this abstract affirmation are to act positively: EEC 48 (2) spells out the consequence that this freedom 'shall entail the abolition of any discrimination based on nationality'. Thirdly, it is not an absolute, unqualified, norm: EEC 48(3) makes the rights 'subject to limitations justified on the grounds of public policy, public security, or public health'; and 48 (4) says that the rest of the Article does not 'apply to employment in the public service'.

3.3 Given that the transitional period had elapsed, the issue is thus whether this kind of article is going to be directly effective. The Commission, Ms Van Duyn, and the Advocate-General all submitted that it was, and the UK did not argue against this view.

3.4 However, if, in principle, it were held directly effective, the problem of the public policy and public service exceptions remains. Once again it raises the issue of 'who decides' the public policy of a country—the Member State itself, the Community, or the former, subject (as the Commission argued) to some sort of supervision by the latter, based on the text of EEC 48 (3) which permits limitations *justified* on such grounds: justified by whom, and to whom? Can a Member State genuinely plead public policy when it permits

its own citizens to work as scientologists? May it argue that the cult is tolerated but not facilitated by its policy of excluding foreign employees?

3.5 *Directive 64/221* This was an attempt to resolve some of these difficulties by co-ordinating national rules on public policy and the like, so that even if the source of the rules was still domestic law, their ambit and effect were similar.

3.6 Article 3.1 attempts to remove guilt by association, to deal that is with the situation where the traditional public policy of a country holds that all Xenubians are criminals, therefore no Xenubian should be allowed in. It says that public policy measures 'shall be based exclusively on the personal conduct of the individual concerned'. This raises several issues: does it directly give rights to Ms Van Duyn; if so, has not her personal conduct been blameless, save that she believes in scientology; and who decides whether that belief suffices to stain her? Do her beliefs amount to 'conduct'? Does her acceptance of an offer of employment by the Church?

3.7 The question of whether a directive can have direct effect is clearly posed. EEC 189 says that regulations are directly applicable, but appears to contrast them with directives which bind Member States only as to the end to be achieved, leaving them to select the most appropriate means. It does not need to be decided, however, whether an entire directive has direct effect; the reference concerned only one article.

3.8 Although, grammatically, Article 3 is positive, its implication is negative: that is, it forbids the use of others as a criterion for judging the individual. Read like this, it resembles Treaty Articles such as EEC 12 in the sense that it restricts Member States and does so absolutely; it does not merely require them to try not to take the conduct of others into account.

TEXT

OPINION OF MR ADVOCATE-GENERAL MAYRAS

Introduction

Mr President, members of the court, this preliminary reference is of special interest for two reasons. It is the first time that a court of the United Kingdom, the High Court of Justice in London, has made a reference to the Court of Justice for interpretation of Community rules under Article 177 of the EEC Treaty. This is also the first time that the Court has been called on to decide the important problem raised by the limitations, expressed in Article 48 of the EEC Treaty, to the principle of freedom of movement for workers within the Community imposed by considerations of public policy and public security.

Consequently, you will have to examine, in this connection, the extent to which the power of the Member States to assess the essential requirements of national public policy can be reconciled with a uniform application of Community law and in particular with the application of the principle of non-discrimination between migrant and national workers. You will also have to make a ruling as to the direct effect of a directive of the Council, or at least of a particular provision of a directive. The case-law of this Court does however already indicate the reply to be given to that question.

I The facts

The facts giving rise to the main action are straightforward. Ms Yvonne Van Duyn, a Dutch national, arrived at Gatwick Airport in England on 9 May 1973. She declared that her purpose in coming to the United Kingdom was to take up an offer of employment as a secretary, made to her a few days earlier by the Church of Scientology of California, the headquarters of which are at Saint Hill Manor, East Grinstead, in the county of Sussex. After an interview with the immigration authorities, she was sent back to the Netherlands that same day.

The ground of refusal of leave to enter the United Kingdom is stated in the document handed to her by the immigation officer. It reads:

You have asked for leave to enter the United Kingdom in order to take employment with the Church of Scientology but the Secretary of State considers it undesirable to give anyone leave to enter the United Kingdom on the business of or in the employment of that organisation.

This decision was taken in accordance with the policy adopted, in 1968, by the Government of the United Kingdom which considered—and still considers—the activities of the Church of Scientology to be socially harmful.

I must however re-examine the grounds of the decision to exclude Ms Van Duyn when I come to consider the question whether the decision taken by the immigration authorities was based on the 'personal conduct' of Miss Van Duyn, within the meaning of Article 3(1) of EEC Directive 64/221, a provision which the Court is asked to interpret.

In her action in the Chancery Division against the Home Office, Ms Van Duyn sought, in fact, to rely on Article 48 of the EEC Treaty and on Article 3 of EEC Directive 64/221, adopted for the purpose of co-ordinating special measures concerning the movement and residence of foreign nationals which are justified on grounds of public policy, public security, or public health.

After examining the motion made by Ms Van Duyn in the main action and on hearing counsel for the Home Office, Pennycuick V-C decided to stay the proceedings and to refer three preliminary questions to the court.

The first question concerns the direct effect of Article 48 of the EEC Treaty. Under the second, the Court is asked whether EEC Directive 64/221 is also directly applicable so as to confer on individuals rights enforceable by them in the courts of the member states. The third question concerns the interpretation of Article 48 of the EEC Treaty and of Article 3 of the directive. The High Court asks you whether, when the competent authorities of a Member State decide, on grounds of public policy, to refuse a Community national leave to enter the State on the basis of the personal conduct of the individual concerned, those authorities are entitled to take into account, as being matters of personal conduct: (a) the fact that the individual is or has been associated with an organization the activities of which the government of the Member State considers to be contrary to the public good but which are not unlawful in that State; (b) the fact that the individual intends to take up employment in the Member State with such an organization, it being the case however that no restrictions are placed on nationals of the Member State who take up similar employment. These three questions are clearly framed and follow a logical order.

II Discussion

1. DIRECT EFFECT OF ARTICLE 48 OF THE EEC TREATY

My Lords, the first question need not long detain us. The criteria which the Court has evolved over the past years for the purpose of determining whether a provision of Community law and, in particular, a rule set out in the EEC Treaty, is directly applicable so as to confer on individuals rights enforceable by them in the national courts, are clearly laid down: the provision must impose a clear and precise obligation on Member States; it must be unconditional, in other words subject to no limitation; if, however, a provision is subject to certain limitations, their nature and extent must be exactly defined; finally, the implementation of a Community rule must not be subject to the adoption of any subsequent rules or regulations on the part either of the Community institutions or of the Member States, so that, in particular, Member States must not be left any real discretion with regard to the application of the rule in question.

2. DIRECT EFFECT OF EEC DIRECTIVE 64/221

There is less certainty regarding the solution of the second question which, as has been seen, is concerned with the direct applicability of the Council directive of 25 February 1964.

Article 189 of the EEC Treaty distinguishes in fact between regulations, which are not only binding but also directly applicable in the Member States, and directives, which are also binding on the States but which have, in principle, no direct effect inasmuch as they leave to the States the choice of methods for their implementation.

When faced with a directive, it is therefore necessary to examine, in each case, whether the wording, nature, and general scheme of the provisions in question are capable of producing direct effects between the Member States to which the directive is addressed and their subjects.

What is the position as regards EEC Directive 64/221? The purpose of this act is to co-ordinate, in the Member States, measures concerning the movement and residence of foreign nationals which are justified on the grounds on public policy, public security, or public health. It was adopted on the basis of Article 48—and in fact it refers expressly to the rules applicable at that time to freedom of movement for workers—and of Article 56, on the right of establishment. The directive is intended to limit the powers which the States have undeniably retained to ensure, within the area of their competence, the safeguarding of their public policy and, in particular, of public security within their territory. As the Court knows, Article 3(1) of the directive provides: 'Measures taken on grounds of public policy or of public security shall be based exclusively on the personal conduct of the individual concerned.'

For the purpose of giving a practical answer to the question put by the High Court there is in fact no need to examine whether all the rules fixed by the directive have direct effect or not. Only Article 3(1) is relevant in this case. It seems that the Council thereby wished to prevent Member States from taking general measures relating to whole categories of person and, were seeking, in particular, to prohibit collective exclusions and expulsions.

The Council has, in any case, imposed on Member States a clear and precise obligation. The first condition for direct effect is satisfied. The second is also. The rule is sufficient in itself. It is not subject either to the adoption of subsequent acts on the part either of the Community authority or of Member States. The fact that the latter have, in accordance with the principle relating to directives, the choice of form and methods which accord with their national law does not imply that the Community rule is not directly applicable. On the contrary, it is so closely linked to the implementation of Article 48, as regards employed persons, that it seems to me to be inseparable from and of the same nature as the provision of the EEC Treaty.

Finally, it is clear that even though the states have retained their competence in the field of public security, Article 3(1) of the directive imposes a specific limitation on that competence, in the exercise of which they cannot act in a discretionary manner towards Community nationals.

These considerations lead me to conclude that the provision in question confers on Community nationals rights which are enforceable by them in the national courts and which the latter must protect.

3. PUBLIC SECURITY AND THE CONCEPT OF PERSONAL CONDUCT

I now come to the third question. What is meant by 'personal conduct' which is such as to justify refusal of leave to enter a Member State? How should this concept be defined? Looking beyond a commentary on the words themselves, the solution seems to me to be governed by two prime considerations: Firstly, freedom of movement for workers is one of the fundamental principles of the Treaty and the prohibition of any discrimination on grounds of nationality between workers of the Member States is not subject to any other limitations than those provided for, in restrictive terms, in para. 3 of Article 48, relating to public policy, public security, and public health. Secondly, if a 'Community public policy' exists in areas where the Treaty has the aim or the effect of transferring directly to Community institutions powers previously exercised by Member States, it can only be an economic public policy relating for example to Community organizations of the agricultural market, to trade, to the Common Customs Tariff, or to the rules on competition. On the other hand, it seems to me that, under present conditions and given the present position of the law, Member States have sole power, given the exceptions expressed in certain Community provisions such as EEC Directive 64/221, to take measures for the safeguarding of public security within their territory and to decide the circumstances under which that security may be endangered.

In other words, even though the general proviso relating to public policy, which is found both in Article 48 and in Article 56, is a limited exception to the principles of the EEC Treaty concerning freedom of movement and freedom of establishment, and one which must be restrictively construed, I do not think, contrary to the opinion of the Commission, that it is possible to deduce a Community concept of public security. This concept remains, at least for the present, national, and this conforms with reality inasmuch as the requirements of public security vary, in time and in space, from one State to another.

In my opinion, the third question must be decided in accordance with the above considerations. First of all, to what extent can the concept 'personal conduct' be applied to the facts provided by the national court, namely that a Community national is associated with an organization, the activities of which are considered to be contrary to public policy, without however being illegal, and that she intends to take up employment with that organization, it being the case that nationals are not subject, in similar circumstances, to any restriction? In truth, the question, expressed in those terms led me to examine the file received from the High Court for evidence permitting a clearer understanding of the facts which warranted the exclusion of Ms Van Duyn in the main action. It is clear from the file that not only did Ms Van Duyn go to England with the avowed intention of taking up employment as a secretary with the Church of Scientology, but that she had already worked in a scientology establishment in the Netherlands for six months prior to her arrival in England and that she had taken a course in scientology and was a practising scientologist. It is clearly on the basis of these facts as a whole, the accuracy of which it is obviously not for the Court to judge, that the British immigration authorities decided to refuse her leave to enter.

It also emerges from the file that in 1968 the United Kingdom Minister of Health made a statement in Parliament in which he expressed the opinion that: 'Scientology is a pseudo-philosophical cult' of which the principles and practice were, in the opinion of the British Government, a danger both to public security and to the health of those who submitted to it. The Minister announced, on that occasion, the decision of the government to take all steps within its power to curb the activity of the organization. He stated that although there was no power under national law to prohibit the practice of scientology, the Government could at least refuse entry to foreign nationals intending to work at the headquarters of the Church of Scientology in England.

It seems that it was on the basis of this policy that Ms Van Duyn was refused leave to enter the United Kingdom by reason as much of the links which she had already had in the past with that 'Church' in the Netherlands as of the fact that she was herself a practising scientologist and, finally, by reason of her intention to take up employment at Saints Hill Manor.

DECISION

1. By order of Pennycuick V-C of 1 March 1974, lodged at the court on 13 June, the Chancery Division of the High Court of Justice of England referred to the Court, under Article 177 of the EEC Treaty, three questions relating to the interpretation of certain provisions of Community law concerning freedom of movement for workers.

2. These questions arise out of an action brought against the Home Office by a woman of Dutch nationality who was refused leave to enter the United Kingdom to take up employment as a secretary with the 'Church of Scientology'.

3. Leave to enter was refused in accordance with the policy of the Government of the United Kingdom in relation to that organization, the activities of which it considers to be socially harmful.

First question

4. By the first question, the Court is asked to say whether Article 48 of the EEC Treaty is directly applicable so as to confer on individuals rights enforceable by them in the courts of a Member State.

5. It is provided, in Article 48 (1) and (2), that freedom of movement for workers shall be secured by the end of the transitional period and that such freedom 'shall entail the abolition of any discrimination based on nationality between workers of the Member States as regards employment, remuneration, and other conditions of work and employment'.

6. These provisions impose on Member States a precise obligation which does not require the adoption of any further measure on the part either of the Community institutions or of the Member States and which leaves them, in relation to its implementation, no discretionary power.

7. Paragraph 3, which defines the rights implied by the principle of freedom of movement for workers, subjects them to limitations justified on grounds of public policy, public security, or public health. The application of these limitations is, however, subject to judicial controls, so that a Member State's right to invoke the limitations does not prevent the provisions of Article 48, which enshrine the principle of freedom of movement for workers, from conferring on individuals rights which are enforceable by them and which the national courts must protect.

8. The reply to the first question must therefore be in the affirmative.

Second question

9. The second question asks the Court to say whether EEC Directive 64/221 of 25 February 1964 on the co-ordination of special measures concerning the movement and residence of foreign nationals which are justified on grounds of public policy, public security, or public health is directly applicable so as to confer on individuals rights enforceable by them in the courts of a Member State.

10. It emerges from the order making the reference that the only provision of the directive which is relevant is that contained in Article 3(1) which provides: 'Measures taken on grounds of public policy or public security shall be based exclusively on the personal conduct of the individual concerned.'

11. The United Kingdom observes that, since Article 189 of the EEC Treaty distinguishes between the effects ascribed to regulations, directives, and

decisions, it must therefore be presumed that the Council, in issuing a directive rather than making a regulation, must have intended that the directive should have an effect other than that of a regulation and accordingly that the former should not be directly applicable.

12. If, however, by virtue of the provisions of Article 189 regulations are directly applicable and, consequently, may by their very nature have direct effects, it does not follow from this that other categories of act mentioned in that article can never have similar effects. It would be incompatible with the binding effect attributed to a directive by Article 189 to exclude, in principle, the possibility that the obligation which it imposes may be invoked by those concerned. In particular, where the Community authorities have, by directive, imposed on Member States the obligation to pursue a particular course of conduct, the useful effect of such an act would be weakened if individuals were prevented from relying on it before their national courts and if the latter were prevented from taking it into consideration as an element of Community law. Article 177, which empowers national courts to refer to the Court questions concerning the validity and interpretation of all acts of the Community institutions, without distinction, implies furthermore that these acts may be invoked by individuals in the national courts. It is necessary to examine, in every case, whether the nature, general scheme, and wording of the provision in question are capable of having direct effects on the relations between Member States and individuals.

13. By providing that measures taken on grounds of public policy shall be based exclusively on the personal conduct of the individual concerned, Article 3(1) of EEC Directive 64/221 is intended to limit the discretionary power which national laws generally confer on the authorities responsible for the entry and expulsion of foreign nationals. First, the provision lays down an obligation which is not subject to any exception or condition and which, by its very nature, does not require the intervention of any act on the part either of the institutions of the Community or of Member States. Secondly, because Member States are thereby obliged, in implementing a clause which derogates from one of the fundamental principles of the EEC Treaty in favour of individuals, not to take account of factors extraneous to personal conduct, legal certainty for the persons concerned requires that they should be able to rely on this obligation even though it has been laid down in a legislative act which has no automatic direct effect in its entirety.

14. If the meaning and exact scope of the provision raise questions of interpretation, these questions can be resolved by the courts, taking into account also the procedure under Article 177 of the EEC Treaty.

15. Accordingly, in reply to the second question, Article 3(1) of EEC Directive 64/221 of 25 February 1964 confers on individuals rights which are

enforceable by them in the courts of a Member State and which the national courts must protect.

Third question

16. By the third question the Court is asked to rule whether Article 48 of the EEC Treaty and Article 3 of EEC Directive 64/221 must be interpreted as meaning that:

a Member State in the performance of its duty to base a measure taken on grounds of public policy exclusively on the personal conduct of the individual concerned is entitled to take into account as matters of personal conduct (*a*) the fact that the individual is or has been associated with some body or organization the activities of which the Member State considers contrary to the public good but which are not unlawful in that state (*b*) the fact that the individual intends to take employment in the Member State with such a body or organization it being the case that no restrictions are place upon nationals of the Member State who wish to take similar employment with such a body or organization.

17. It is necessary, first to consider whether association with a body or an organization can in itself constitute personal conduct within the meaning of Article 3 of EEC Directive 64/221. Although a person's past association cannot, in general, justify a decision refusing him the right to move freely within the Community, it is nevertheless the case that present association, which reflects participation in the activities of the body or of the organization as well as identification with its aims and its designs, may be considered a voluntary act of the person concerned and, consequently, as part of his personal conduct within the meaning of the provision cited.

18. This third question further raises the problem of what importance must be attributed to the fact that the activities of the organization in question which are considered by the Member State as contrary to the public good are not however prohibited by national law. It should be emphasized that the concept of public policy in the context of the Community and where, in particular, it is used as a justification for derogating from the fundamental principle of freedom of movement for workers, must be interpreted strictly, so that its scope cannot be determined unilaterally by each Member State without being subject to control by the institutions of the Community. Nevertheless, the particular circumstances justifying recourse to the concept of public policy may vary from one country to another and from one period to another, and it is therefore necessary in this matter to allow the competent national authorities an area of discretion within the limits imposed by the EEC Treaty.

19. It follows from the above that where the competent authorities of a Member State have clearly defined their standpoint as regard the activities

of a particular organization and where, considering it to be socially harmful, they have taken administrative measures to counteract these activities, the Member State cannot be required, before it can rely on the concept of public policy, to make such activities unlawful, if recourse to such a measure is not thought appropriate in the circumstances.

20. The question raises finally the problem of whether a Member State is entitled, on grounds on public policy, to prevent a national of another Member State from taking gainful employment within its territory with a body or organization, it being the case that no similar restriction is placed on its own nationals.

21. In this connection, the EEC Treaty, while enshrining the principle of freedom of movement for workers without any discrimination on grounds of nationality, admits, in Article 48 (3), limitations justified on grounds of public policy, public security, or public health to the rights deriving from this principle. Under the terms of the provision cited above, the right to accept offers of employment actually made, the right to move freely within the territory of Member States for this purpose, and the right to stay in a Member State for the purpose of employment are, among others, all subject to such limitations. Consequently, the effect of such limitations, when they apply, is that leave to enter the territory of a Member State and the right to reside there may be refused to a national of another Member State.

22. Furthermore, it is a principle of international law, which the EEC Treaty cannot be assumed to disregard in the relations between Member States, that a state is precluded from refusing its own nationals the right of entry or residence.

23. It follows that a Member State, for reasons of public policy, can, where it deems necessary, refuse a national of another Member State the benefit of the principle of freedom of movement for workers in a case where such a national proposes to take up a particular offer of employment even though the Member State does not place a similar restriction on its own nationals.

24. Accordingly, the reply to the third question must be that Article 48 of the EEC Treaty and Article 3 (1) of EEC Directive 64/221 are to be interpreted as meaning that a Member State, in imposing restrictions justified on grounds of public policy, is entitled to take into account, as a matter of personal conduct of the individual concerned, the fact that the individual is associated with some body or organization the activities of which the Member State considers socially harmful but which are not unlawful in that state, despite the fact that no restriction is placed on nationals of the Member State who wish to take similar employment with these same bodies or organizations.

On those grounds, the Court, in answer to the questions referred to it by the High Court of Justice, by order of that court dated 1 March 1974, hereby rules:

1. Article 48 of the EEC Treaty has a direct effect in the legal orders of the Member States and confers on individuals rights which the national courts must protect.
2. Article 3(1) of EEC Directive 64/221 of 25 February 1964 on the co-ordination of special measures concerning the movement and residence of foreign nationals which are justified on grounds of public policy, public security, or public health confers on individuals rights which are enforceable by them in the national courts of a Member State and which the national courts must protect.
3. Article 48 of the EEC Treaty and Article 3(1) of EEC Directive 64/221 must be interpreted as meaning that a Member State, in imposing restrictions justified on grounds of public policy, is entitled to take into account as a matter of personal conduct of the individual concerned, the fact that the individual is associated with some body or organization the activities of which the Member State considers socially harmful but which are not unlawful in that state, despite the fact that no restriction is placed on nationals of the Member State who wish to take similar employment with the same body or organization.

COMMENTS

1. This was the first use of EEC 177 by an English court. The proceedings which preceded the reference by the English court are reported at [1974] 3 All ER 178 and [1974] 1 WLR 1107. They are worth reading as an example of the sort of case where there is a dispute as to both the applicability of Community law and the need for a reference. The Home Office defended Ms Van Duyn's action for a declaration of entitlement to enter by denying that EEC 48 and Directive 64/221, art. 3 directly gave her rights, and by asserting that this view was so obvious that no reference was necessary; counsel also cautioned the Vice-Chancellor against overburdening the ECJ. The plaintiff, of course, took the other view on the effect of the Articles but was quite happy to accede to a reference. The Vice-Chancellor found himself faced with a question of interpretation, resolution of which was necessary to enable him to dispose of the action.

2. The ECJ points out that the public policy limitation is a derogation from the general principle of free movement. It must, therefore, be construed strictly and the views of Member States—while of course not all necessarily the same—must be subject to Community control.

3. This public policy exception is a means of derogating from the free movement of goods (EEC 36) and of limiting the right of establishment and

freedom to provide services (EEC 56 and 66). It has been pleaded in numerous cases, including 67/74 *Bonsignore*, 36/75 *Rutili*, and 48/75 *Royer*. Furthermore, more recent decisions suggest that the Court may have been very indulgent towards the UK in the extract above: Case 30/77 *Bouchereau*, and Joined Cases 115 and 116/81 *Adoui and Cornuaille*.

4 Member States are also prone to use the concept to block harmonization measures, and the Treaty amendments of the 1986 Single European Act include a procedure (EEC 100A(4)) whereby a Member State making improper use of the notion in this context may be sued immediately without the delays involved in EEC 169 and 170.

5. The issue of the direct effect of part of a directive had come before the Court in previous lawsuits (Case 9/70 *Grad*; Case 33/70 *SACE*) but the present action is much a clearer decision. Nonetheless, at the stage of Community law by then reached, all the provisions of directives held to be directly effective were themselves tied to, and in implementation of, Treaty Articles which are in themselves directly effective: this case is a simple example. But many hundreds of directives are issued under EEC 100 (harmonization) and EEC 235 (extending Community powers) and these Treaty Articles are not directly effective. Are the directives? Or will one have to distinguish: to say that they are directly effective as against the Member State, but not as against other individuals. These points occur in Case 148/78 *Ratti*; Case 271/82 *Auer*; Case 152/84 *Marshall* below, extract no. 14).

6. In Case 41/74 *Van Duyn*, the negative obligation imposed by Article 3 of the Directive bore directly on the Member State. Can a provision which gives rights impose correlative duties on individuals? And is this question to be answered differently depending on whether the provision is in the Treaty or in a directive? The next extract gives a partial answer.

10 Case 2/74 *Reyners*

1. *The action.* Under EEC 177, the highest Belgian public-law court (Conseil d'Etat) asked whether EEC 52 (on the right of establishment) became directly applicable at the end of the transitional period; and whether the 'official authority' exception of EEC 55 applied to advocates. The importance of the reference is shown by the fact that briefs were filed, not only by Reyners and the Commission, but by six Governments: Belgium, Germany, Luxemburg, Ireland, the Netherlands, and the UK. In addition, the Belgian Bar made submissions at the oral stage.

2. *The salient, simplified facts*

   2.1 Although born and bred in Belgium, Reyners was of Dutch nationality.

   2.2 Having successfully completed the normal Belgian legal education he applied to be called to the Bar, in order to set up in practice. Domestic laws closed the profession to all save Belgian nationals.

   2.3 Applications for dispensation from the nationality provision were provided for by a Decree of 1970. They were limited to the nationals of countries which themselves admitted Belgians to the profession, but the Netherlands Bar was open only to the Dutch.

   2.4 Reyners brought an action in the Conseil d'Etat to have this provision of the Decree quashed on the grounds of its incompatibility with EEC 52. To enable it to decide the question, that court made the reference.

3. *The legal issues*

   3.1 *EEC 52*. The Belgian nationality limitation was not a new provision; consequently the ECJ was not asked to rule on the effect of the 'standstill' clause (EEC 53) which is, in normative structure, similar to EEC 12.

   3.2 By contrast, EEC 52 follows the pattern of those Treaty articles which provide for the gradual dismantling of existing restrictions. It begins: 'Within the framework of the provisions set out below, restrictions on the freedom of establishment of nationals of a Member State in the territory of another Member State shall be abolished by progressive stages in the course of the transitional period'. Thus the norm does not forbid, it enjoins a course of action.

   3.3 The framework referred to is provided by EEC 54 which tells the law-making institutions to draw up a general programme and to proceed by issuing directives to the Member States. The Article goes on to provide general guidance; for instance, priority is generally to be given to activities of particular importance to production and trade. At the expiry of the transitional period, a programme had been drawn up, but few directives had been issued (see Rudden and Wyatt, *BCL*, 246).

   3.4 In this state of affairs, the Governments were divided as to the direct effect of EEC 52. While the German Government thought that its main provision was clear and capable of operating directly, without being dependent on Community or national measures, the Belgian, Irish, Luxemburg, and UK Governments disagreed. They relied on the fact that the Article covered 'restrictions' and was thus wider and vaguer than the prohibition of non-discrimination on the grounds of nationality; and on the fact that it was to be enforced, not by directly applicable regulations, but by directives which leave to Member States the choice of the appropriate means of implementation (EEC 189). The Commission was in some doubt, but argued that the balance was in favour of direct effect at least as regards those restrictions that are simply and solely defined in terms of nationality. Since the rules which Member States apply to their own nationals when practising a profession will be clear enough, EEC 52 at least prevents them imposing different requirements on other Community nationals. The ECJ accepts this as part of its reasoning, although its actual decision goes further.

3.5 *EEC 55*. This Article derogates from the freedoms of establishment and services (EEC 66) by saying that their provisions do not apply, so far as any given Member State is concerned, to activities which in that State are connected, even occasionally with the exercise of official authority. In Belgium (as in several other countries) a barrister may be called upon to sit as a judge in a particular case; and a judge clearly exercises official authority.

3.6 Consequently, the Belgian Bar and Luxemburg Government argued that the whole profession of advocate was excluded from EEC 52. Everyone else (though with different emphases) contended that the derogation applied only to particular, and separate, activities open to the Bar.

TEXT

LAW

1. By judgment dated 21 December 1973, filed at the Registry on 9 January 1974, the Conseil d'Etat of Belgium raised two questions under Article 177 of the EEC Treaty on the interpretation of Articles 52 and 55 of the EEC Treaty relating to the rights of establishment in relation to the practice of the profession of *avocat*.

2. These questions had been raised in the context of an action brought by a Dutch national, the holder of the legal diploma giving the right to take up the profession of *avocat* in Belgium, who has been excluded from that profession by reason of his nationality as a result of the Royal Decree of 24 August 1972 relating to the title and exercise of the profession of *avocat*.

On the interpretation of Article 52 of the EEC Treaty

3. The Conseil d'Etat enquires whether Article 52 of the EEC Treaty is, since the end of the transitional period, a 'directly applicable provision' despite the absence of directives as prescribed by Articles 54 (2) and 57 (1) of the Treaty.

4. The Belgian and Irish Governments have argued, for reasons largely in agreement, that Article 52 does not have such an effect.

5. Taken in the context of the chapter on the right of establishment, to which reference is expressly made by the wording 'within the framework of the provisions set out below', this Article, in view of the complexity of the subject, is said to constitute only the expression of a simple principle, the implementation of which is necessarily subject to a set of complementary provisions, both Community and national, provided for by Articles 54 and 57.

6. The form chosen by the Treaty for these implementing acts—the establishment of a 'general programme', implemented in turn by a set of directives—confirms, it is argued, that Article 52 does not have a direct effect.

7. It is not for the courts to exercise a discretionary power reserved to the legislative institutions of the Community and the Member States.

8. This argument is supported in substance by the British and Luxemburg Governments, as well as by the Ordre national des avocats de Belgique, the intervening party in the main action.

9. The plaintiff in the main action, for his part, states that all that is in question in his case is a discrimination based on nationality by reason of the fact that he is subject to conditions of admission to the profession of *avocat* which are not applicable to Belgian nationals.

10. In this respect (he submits) Article 52 is a clear and complete provision, capable of producing a direct effect.

11. The German Government, supported in substance by the Dutch Government, considers that the provisions which impose on Member States an obligation which they have to fulfil within a particular period, become directly applicable when, on the expiration of this period, the obligation has not been fulfilled.

12. At the end of the transitional period, the Member States no longer have the possibility of maintaining restrictions on the freedom of establishment, since Article 52 has, as from this period, the character of a provision which is complete in itself and legally perfect.

13. In these circumstances the 'general programme' and the directives provided for by Article 54 were of significance only during the transitional period, since the freedom of establishment was fully attained at the end of it.

14. The Commission, in spite of doubts which it experiences on the subject of the direct effect of the provision to be interpreted—both in view of the reference by the Treaty to the 'general programme' and to the implementing directives and by reason of the tenor of certain liberalizing directives already taken, which do not attain in every respect perfect equality of treatment—considers, however, that Article 52 has at least a partial direct effect in so far as it specifically prohibits discrimination on grounds of nationality.

15. Article 7 of the Treaty, which forms part of the 'principles' of the Community, provides that within the scope of application of the Treaty and without prejudice to any special provisions contained therein, 'any discrimination on grounds of nationality shall be prohibited'.

16. Article 52 provides for the implementation of this general provision in the special sphere of the right of establishment.

17. The words 'within the framework of the provisions set out below' refer to the chapter relating to the right of establishment taken as a whole and require, in consequence, to be interpreted in this general context.

18. After having stated that 'restrictions on the freedom of establishment of nationals of a Member State in the territory of another Member State shall be abolished by progressive stages in the course of the transitional period', Article 52 expresses the guiding principle in the matter by providing that freedom of establishment shall include the right to take up and pursue activities as self-employed persons 'under the conditions laid down for its own nationals by the law of the country where such establishment is effected'.

19. For the purpose of achieving this objective by progressive stages during the transitional period Article 54 provides for the drawing up by the Council of a 'general programme' and, for the implementation of this programme, directives intended to attain freedom of establishment in respect of the various activities in question.

20. Besides these liberalizing measures, Article 57 provides for directives intended to ensure mutual recognition of diplomas, certificates, and other evidence of formal qualifications and in a general way for the co-ordination of laws with regard to establishment and the pursuit of activities as self-employed persons.

21. It appears from the above that in the system of the chapter on the right of establishment the 'general programme' and the directives provided for by the Treaty are intended to accomplish two functions, the first being to eliminate obstacles in the way of attaining freedom of establishment during the transitional period, the second being to introduce into the law of Member States a set of provisions intended to facilitate the effective exercise of this freedom for the purpose of assisting economic and social interpenetration within the Community in the sphere of activities as self-employed persons.

22. This second objective is the one referred to, first, by certain provisions of Article 54 (3), relating in particular to co-operation between the competent authorities in the Member States and adjustment of administrative procedures and practices, and, secondly, by the set of provisions in Article 57.

23. The effect of the provisions of Article 52 must be decided within the framework of this system.

24. The rule on equal treatment with nationals is one of the fundamental legal provisions of the Community.

25. As a reference to a set of legislative provisions effectively applied by the country of establishment to its own nationals, this rule is, by its essence, capable of being directly invoked by nationals of all the other Member States.

26. In laying down that freedom of establishment shall be attained at the end of the transitional period, Article 52 thus imposes an obligation to attain a precise result, the fulfilment of which had to be made easier by, but not made dependent on, the implementation of a programme of progressive measures.

27. The fact that this progression has not been adhered to leaves the obligation itself intact beyond the end of the period provided for its fulfilment.

28. This interpretation is in accordance with Article 8 (7) of the Treaty, according to which the expiry of the transitional period shall constitute the latest date by which all the rules laid down must enter into force and all the measures required for establishing the common market must be implemented.

29. It is not possible to invoke against such an effect the fact that the Council has failed to issue the directives provided for by Articles 54 and 57 or the fact that certain of the directives actually issued have not fully attained the objective of non-discrimination required by Article 52.

30. After the expiry of the transitional period the directives provided for by the chapter on the right of establishment have become superfluous with regard to implementing the rule on nationality, since this is henceforth sanctioned by the Treaty itself with direct effect.

31. These directives have however not lost all interest since they preserve an important scope in the field of measures intended to make easier the effective exercise of the right of freedom of establishment.

32. It is right therefore to reply to the question raised that, since the end of the transitional period, Article 52 of the Treaty is a directly applicable provision despite the absence in a particular sphere of the directives prescribed by Articles 54 (2) and 57 (1) of the Treaty.

On the interpretation of Article 55 of the EEC Treaty

33. The Conseil d'Etat has also requested a definition of what is meant in the first paragraph of Article 55 by 'activities which in that State are connected, even occasionally, with the exercise of official authority'.

34. More precisely, the question is whether, within a profession such as that of *avocat*, only those activities inherent in this profession which are connected with the exercise of official authority are expected from the application of the chapter on the right of establishment, or whether the whole of this profession is expected by reason of the fact that it comprises activities connected with the exercise of this authority.

35. The Luxemburg Government and the Ordre national des avocats de Belgique consider that the whole profession of *avocat* is exonerated from the rules in the Treaty on the right of establishment by the fact that it is connected organically with the functioning of the public service of the administration of justice.

36. This situation (it is argued) results both from the legal organization of the Bar, involving a set of strict conditions for admission and discipline, and from the functions performed by the *avocat* in the context of judicial procedure where his participation is largely obligatory.

37. These activities, which make the *avocat* an indispensable auxiliary of the administration of justice, form a coherent whole, the parts of which cannot be separated.

38. The plaintiff in the main action, for his part contends that at most only certain activities of the profession of *avocat* are connected with the exercise of official authority and that they alone therefore come within the exception created by Article 55 to the principle of free establishment.

39. The German, Belgian, British, Irish, and Dutch Governments, as well as the Commission, regard the exception contained in Article 55 as limited to those activities alone within the various professions concerned which are actually connected with the exercise of official authority, subject to their being separable from the normal practice of the profession.

40. Differences exist, however, between the Governments referred to as regards the nature of the activities which are thus excepted from the principle of the freedom of establishment, taking into account the different organization of the professions corresponding to that of *avocat* from one Member State to another.

41. The German Government in particular considers that by reason of the compulsory connection of the Rechtsanwalt with certain judicial processes, especially as regards criminal or public law, there are such close connections between the profession of Rechtsanwalt and the exercise of judicial authority

that large sectors of this profession, at least, should be excepted from freedom of establishment.

42. Under the terms of the first paragraph of Article 55 the provisions of the chapter on the right of establishment shall not apply 'so far as any given Member State is concerned, to activities which in that State are connected, even occasionally, with the exercise of official authority'.

43. Having regard to the fundamental character of freedom of establishment and the rule on equal treatment with nationals in the system of the Treaty, the exceptions allowed by the first paragraph of Article 55 cannot be given a scope which would exceed the objective for which this exemption clause was inserted.

44. The first paragraph of Article 55 must enable Member States to exclude non-nationals from taking up functions involving the exercise of official authority which are connected with one of the activities of self-employed persons provided for in Article 52.

45. This need is fully satisfied when the exclusion of nationals is limited to those activities which, taken on their own, constitute a direct and specific connection with the exercise of official authority.

46. An extension of the exception allowed by Article 55 to a whole profession would be possible only in cases where such activities were linked with that profession in such a way that freedom of establishment would result in imposing on the Member State concerned the obligation to allow the exercise, even occasionally, by non-nationals of functions appertaining to official authority.

47. This extension is on the other hand not possible when, within the framework of an independent profession, the activities connected with the exercise of official authority are separable from the professional activity in question taken as a whole.

48. In the absence of any directive issued under Article 57 for the purpose of harmonizing the national provisions relating, in particular, to professions such as that of *avocat*, the practice of such professions remains governed by the law of the various Member States.

49. The possible application of the restrictions on freedom of establishment provided for by the first paragraph of Article 55 must therefore be considered separately in connection with each Member State having regard to the national provisions applicable to the organization and the practice of this profession.

56. This consideration must however take into account the Community character of the limits imposed by Article 55 on the exceptions permitted to

the principle of freedom of establishment in order to avoid the effectiveness of the Treaty being defeated by unilateral provisions of Member States.

57. Professional activities involving contacts, even regular and organic, with the courts, including even compulsory co-operation in their functioning, do not constitute, as such, connection with the exercise of official authority.

52. The most typical activities of the profession of *avocat*, in particular, such as consultation and legal assistance and also representation and the defence of parties in court, even when the intervention or assistance of the *avocat* is compulsory or is a legal monopoly, cannot be considered as connected with the exercise of official authority.

53. The exercise of these activities leaves the discretion of judicial authority and the free exercise of judicial power intact.

54. It is therefore right to reply to the question raised that the exception to freedom of establishment provided for by the first paragraph of Article 55 must be restricted to those of the activities referred to in Article 52 which in themselves involve a direct and specific connection with the exercise of official authority.

55. In any case it is not possible to give this description, in the context of a profession such as that of *avocat*, to activities such as consultation and legal assistance or the representation and defence of parties in court, even if the performance of these activities is compulsory or there is a legal monopoly in respect of it.

On those grounds, the Court hereby rules:

1. Since the end of the transitional period, Article 52 of the Treaty is a directly applicable provision, despite the absence, in a particular sphere, of the directives prescribed by Articles 54(2) and 57(1) of the Treaty.

2. The exception to freedom of establishment provided for by the first paragraph of Article 55 must be restricted to those of the activities referred to in Article 52 which in themselves involve a direct and specific connection with the exercise of official authority; it is not possible to give this description, in the context of a profession such as that of *avocat*, to activities such as consultation and legal assistance or the representation and defence of parties in court, even if the performance of these activities is compulsory or there is a legal monopoly in respect of it.

COMMENTS

1. Once this judgment was delivered, numerous draft directives were withdrawn.

2. On the first accession of new Member States, a British architect, whose

professional qualifications were recognized under French law, was, on the grounds of his nationality, refused permission to set up in practice in France. The ECJ held that, as regards the new Member States, EEC 52 was directly effective on accession: Case 11/77 *Patrick*.

3. The decision in Case 2/74 *Reyners* does not, of course, mean that any citizen of a Member State can simply move to another and set up in business or a profession. The host state may well subject its own nationals to some kind of qualification requirements—the practice of medicine is an obvious example. Consequently, the relevant issue will be the recognition by the host State of the qualifications which enable the newcomer to practise in some other Member State. This requires legislation by way of directive: see, for instance Directive 75/362/ECC (OJ 1975 L 167/1).

4. If, however, the professional or other qualification is already recognized in the host country as being equivalent, EEC 52 forbids the requirement that the arrival obtain the national qualification: Case 71/76 *Thieffry*.

11 Case 33/74 *Van Binsbergen*

1. *The action.* Under EEC 177, a Netherlands social security court asked the ECJ to rule on two simple questions: the transitional period having expired, are EEC 59 and EEC 60 (freedom to provide services) directly applicable to create individual rights which national courts must protect; and, if so, what do they mean. Briefs were filed by the Commission and by the Irish and UK Governments; and, at the hearing, the individual concerned, the Commission, and the German Government made submissions.

2. *The salient, simplified facts*

2.1 A Dutch citizen practised in his own country as legal adviser and representative in social security matters. During a case, he moved his home to Belgium, and it was from there that he corresponded with the Dutch court, so it seems as if he was practising from ('established in') Belgium.

2.2 He was then told by the Court registrar that he could no longer act, since a Netherlands statute on the procedure in social security cases allowed legal representation to be furnished only by persons established in the Netherlands.

2.3 He came before the court to plead EEC 59 and EEC 60, and the reference was made.

3. *The legal issues*

3.1 Like the provisions on freedom of establishment, litigated in the preceding case, EEC 59 is a dismantling provision to be implemented by a programme and directives (EEC 63).

3.2 Its first paragraph says:

Within the framework of the provisions set out below, restrictions on freedom to provide services within the Community shall be progressively abolished during the transitional period in respect of nationals of Member States who are established in a State of the Community other than that of the person for whom the services are intended.

3.3 Like EEC 48 and 52, it contains a clear cross-border element. It does not, apparently, require the two persons involved to be of different nationalities, merely to be in different States, so that the service crosses a border. The legal adviser and his client were both Dutch, but the former was practising from Belgium.

3.4 EEC 60 shows that the provisions on services are meant to catch anything normally done for money which does not fall within the sections on goods, capital, and persons. That clearly covers legal representation.

3.5 Most of the submissions (including that of the UK Government) accepted that, after Case 2/74 *Reyners*, the ECJ could hold EEC 59 and 60 to have become directly effective after the expiry of the transitional period at least as regards discrimination on the grounds of nationality.

3.6 The difficulty was that the legal adviser was obviously not suffering from that sort of discrimination: he, his client, the social security court, and the domestic law in question, were all Dutch. Nor did the last mention nationality: it disqualified any legal adviser of any country who was not established in the Netherlands.

3.7 Consequently, given that the establishment requirement is a *restriction* within EEC 59, the question still remains as to whether the article has now become effective to forbid it, or whether directives are still needed.

3.8 A domestic law which says that legal representatives must be established in the country of the court is in fact forbidding the provision of cross-border services. To appear in the court, the advisers must move their practices to the country.

3.9 Nonetheless, some impartial territorial restriction may be justified. Frequently, in Continental countries, only the Supreme Court has nation-wide jurisdiction; courts of appeal and of first instance sit for a particular locality. And in these countries it is common to find a rule that any lawyer licensed at the bar of such a court must have his or her practice within that locality. This is thought to assist the administration of justice.

TEXT

DECISION

1. By order of 18 April 1974, lodged at the Registry of the Court on 15 May, the Centrale Raad van Beroep put to the Court, under Article 177 of the EEC Treaty, questions relating to the interpretation of Articles 59 and 60 of the Treaty establishing the European Economic Community concerning freedom to provide services within the Community.

2. These questions arose incidentally, during the course of an action before the said court, and are concerned with the admission before that court of the person whom the appellant in the main action chose to act as his legal representative.

3. It appears from the file that the appellant had entrusted the defence of his interests to a legal representative of Netherlands nationality entitled to act for parties before courts and tribunals where representation by an *advocaat* is not obligatory.

4. Since this legal representative had, during the course of the proceedings, transferred his residence from the Netherlands to Belgium, his capacity to represent the party in question before the Centrale Raad van Beroep was contested on the basis of a provision of Netherlands law under which only

persons established in the Netherlands may act as legal representatives before that court.

5. In support of his claim the person concerned invoked the provisions of the Treaty relating to freedom to provide services within the Community, and the Centrale Raad van Beroep referred to the Court two questions relating to the interpretation of Articles 59 and 60 of the Treaty.

The actual scope of Articles 59 and 60

6. The Court is requested to interpret Articles 59 and 60 in relation to a provision of national law whereby only persons established in the territory of the State concerned are entitled to act as legal representatives before certain courts or tribunals.

7. Article 59, the first paragraph of which is the only provision in question in this connection, provides that:

Within the framework of the provisions set out below, restrictions on freedom to provide services within the Community shall be progressively abolished during the transitional period in respect of nationals of Member States who are established in a State of the Community other than that of the person for whom the services are intended.

8. Having defined the concept 'services' within the meaning of the Treaty in its first and second paragraphs, Article 60 lays down in the third paragraph that, without prejudice to the provisions of the chapter relating to the right of establishment, the person providing a service may, in order to provide that service, temporarily pursue his activity in the State where the service is provided, under the same conditions as are imposed by that State on its own nationals.

9. The question put by the national court therefore seeks to determine whether the requirement that legal representatives be permanently established within the territory of the State where the service is to be provided can be reconciled with the prohibition, under Articles 59 and 60, on all restrictions on freedom to provide services within the Community.

10. The restrictions to be abolished pursuant to Articles 59 and 60 include all requirements imposed on the person providing the service by reason in particular of his nationality or of the fact that he does not habitually reside in the State where the service is provided, which do not apply to persons established within the national territory or which may prevent or otherwise obstruct the activities of the person providing the service.

11. In particular, a requirement that the person providing the service must be habitually resident within the territory of the State where the service is to be provided may, according to the circumstances, have the result of depriving

Article 59 of all useful effect, in view of the fact that the precise object of that Article is to abolish restrictions on freedom to provide services imposed on persons who are not established in the State where the service is to be provided.

12. However, taking into account the particular nature of the services to be provided, specific requirements imposed on the person providing the service cannot be considered incompatible with the Treaty where they have as their purpose the application of professional rules justified by the general good—in particular rules relating to organization, qualifications, professional ethics, supervision and liability—which are binding upon any person established in the State in which the service is provided, where the person providing the service would escape from the ambit of those rules being established in another Member State.

13. Likewise, a Member State cannot be denied the right to take measures to prevent the exercise by a person providing services whose activity is entirely or principally directed towards its territory of the freedom guaranteed by Article 59 for the purpose of avoiding the professional rules of conduct which would be applicable to him if he were established within that State; such a situation may be subject to judicial control under the provisions of the chapter relating to the right of establishment and not of that on the provision of services.

14. In accordance with these principles, the requirement that persons whose functions are to assist the administration of justice must be permanently established for professional purposes within the jurisidiction of certain courts or tribunals cannot be considered incompatible with the provisions of Articles 59 and 60, where such requirement is objectively justified by the need to ensure observance of professional rules of conduct connected, in particular, with the administration of justice and with respect for professional ethics.

15. That cannot, however, be the case when the provision of certain services in a Member State is not subject to any sort of qualification or professional regulation and when the requirement of habitual residence is fixed by reference to the territory of the State in question.

16. In relation to a professional activity the exercise of which is similarly unrestricted within the territory of a particular Member State, the requirement of residence within the State constitutes a restriction which is incompatible with Articles 59 and 60 of the Treaty if the administration of justice can satisfactorily be ensured by measures which are less restrictive, such as the choosing of an address for service.

17. It must therefore be stated in reply to the question put to the Court that the first paragraph of Article 59 and the third paragraph of Article 60 of the EEC Treaty must be interpreted as meaning that the national law of a

Member State cannot, by imposing a requirement as to habitual residence within that State, deny persons established in another Member State the right to provide services, where the provision of services is not subject to any special condition under the national law applicable.

The question of the direct applicability of Articles 59 and 60

18. The Court is also asked whether the first paragraph of Article 59 and the third paragraph of Article 60 of the EEC Treaty are directly applicable and create individual rights which national courts must protect.

19. This question must be resolved with reference to the whole of the chapter relating to services, taking account, moreover, of the provisions relating to the right of establishment to which reference is made in Article 66.

20. With a view to the progressive abolition during the transitional period of the restrictions referred to in Article 59, Article 63 has provided for the drawing up of a 'general programme'—laid down by Council Decision of 18 December 1961—to be implemented by a series of directives.

21. Within the scheme of the chapter relating to the provision of services, these directives are intended to accomplish different functions, the first being to abolish, during the transitional period, restrictions on freedom to provide services, the second being to introduce into the law of Member States a set of provisions intended to facilitate the effective exercise of this freedom, in particular by the mutual recognition of professional qualifications and the co-ordination of laws with regard to the pursuit of activities as self-employed persons.

22. These directives also have the task of resolving the specific problems resulting from the fact that where the person providing the service is not established on a habitual basis, in the State where the service is performed he may not be fully subject to the professional rules of conduct in force in that State.

23. As regards the phased implementation of the chapter relating to services, Article 59, interpreted in the light of the general provisions of Article 8(7) of the Treaty, expresses the intention to abolish restrictions on freedom to provide services by the end of the transitional period, the latest date for the entry into force of all the rules laid down by the Treaty.

24. The provisions of Article 59, the application of which was to be prepared by directives issued during the transitional period, therefore became unconditional on the expiry of that period.

25. The provisions of that article abolish all discrimination against the person providing the service by reason of his nationality or the fact that he is

established in a Member State other than that in which the service is to be provided.

26. Therefore, as regards at least the specific requirement of nationality or of residence, Articles 59 and 60 impose a well-defined obligation, the fulfilment of which by the Member States cannot be delayed or jeopardized by the absence of provisions which were to be adopted in pursuance of powers conferred under Articles 63 and 66.

27. Accordingly, the reply should be that the first paragraph of Article 59 and the third paragraph of Article 60 have direct effect and may therefore be relief on before national courts, at least in so far as they seek to abolish any discrimination against a person providing a service by reason of his nationality or of the fact that he resides in a Member State other than that in which the service is to be provided. On those grounds, the Court hereby rules:

1. The first paragraph of Article 59 and the third paragraph of Article 60 of the EEC Treaty must be interpreted as meaning that the national law of a Member State cannot, by imposing a requirement as to habitual residence within that State, deny persons established in another Member State the right to provide services, where the provision of services is not subject to any special condition under the national law applicable.
2. The first paragraph of Article 59 and the third paragraph of Article 60 have direct effect and may therefore be relied on before national courts, at least in so far as they seek to abolish any discrimination against a person providing a service by reason of his nationality or of the fact that he resides in a Member State other than that in which the service is to be provided.

COMMENTS

1. It is worth repeating that this was an action by a Dutchman prevented by Dutch law from appearing for a Dutch client before the courts of his own country by the fact that he lived and had his office in another. It shows how a Treaty provision aimed principally at safeguarding the interests of foreigners may serve to protect a citizen against his own State.

2. In one respect, EEC 59 is not very happily drafted. Its condition of applicability is that the provider of the service be *established* in a Member State other than that of the person for whom the service is intended. If the word emphasized means the same as it does in EEC 52, then the clear freedom to provide services is given only to the self-employed. The university professor asked to give expert advice in another country is not established in his own; he is a worker. The retired judge invited to perform an arbitration is neither a worker nor established; he is retired. Presumably, however, both are 'established' for the purposes of EEC 59.

Similarly, the condition quoted above envisages the normal situation, that is where the service is provided directly to someone in another Member State. The article does not clearly cover the case where both parties live in the same State but the service relates to another—as where a surveyor is hired to report on the condition of a building abroad.

3. The particular details of freedom to provide legal services are now governed by Directive 77/249 (see Rudden and Wyatt, *BCL*, 261).

4. It may seem that Case 33/74 *Van Binsbergen* follows inexorably from Case 2/74 *Reyners*. Its importance, however, lies in two things. Firstly, it shows the ECJ carefully delimiting an area within which EEC 59 works directly—that of restrictions based on nationality and residence. Yet it would seem that there must be restrictions not covered by these factors, for EEC 65 provides that, during the period while there are restrictions within the meaning of EEC 59, they shall be applied without distinction on grounds of nationality or residence. So these other restrictions have to go sometime—which looks like a firm commitment to the creation of a free internal market within the Community. The Court says that the article prohibits not merely discrimination on the grounds of nationality or location but 'all requirements which may prevent or otherwise obstruct the activities of the person providing the service'.

5. The second important consequence of this case follows from the foregoing: there is an almost limitless number of activities which may count as 'services' within the meaning of the Treaty; and, if the customers cannot come to the provider, that is a restriction. Once this is granted, tourism and perhaps even education seem to fall within EEC 59. The next extract provides an example.

12 Case 293/83 *Gravier* v. *Liège*

1. *The action.* A Belgian First Instance Court, in a dispute concerning vocational training, asked whether the Treaty of Rome applied to learning the art of strip-cartoons, and requested an interpretation of EEC 7, the first sentence of which says: 'Within the scope of application of this Treaty, and without prejudice to any special provisions contained therein, any discrimination on grounds of nationality shall be prohibited.'

Briefs were filed by Ms Gravier, the art education authority, the Commission, and the Governments of Denmark, Belgium, and the UK.

2. *The salient, simplified facts*

2.1 A French national, whose parents lived in France, came to Belgium to do a four-year course on strip-cartoons.

2.2 Alone among EEC countries, Belgium exacted an enrolment fee from non-nationals. It was not based on residence, since, although resident non-nationals were excused the fee, no Belgian citizen, wherever resident, was required to pay it.

2.3 On declining to pay the fee, she was refused enrolment.

2.4 She began an action against the Art College in the Belgian court which made the reference. The exact terms of its questions appear in the extract below.

3. *The legal issues*

3.1 *Direct effect.* Although the phrase 'direct effect' is not used, clearly the Belgian court needs to know whether EEC 7 gives rights to the student. After the statement of principle quoted in 1 above, the article goes on to provide for implementing measures to be taken. There have been no such measures based solely on EEC 7. The Governments argued that it was too general, standing alone, to create direct rights. It may be added that, if it does, the correlative obligation would not be limited to the Member State but, in the proper case, would seem to fall on individuals.

3.2 *The scope of the Treaty.* EEC 7's first words naturally limit its application to the scope of application of the Treaty. Remembering that the Treaty creates an *economic* community, the first relevant question is whether it covers education in general. Here one can distinguish, as does the ECJ, educational policy (what subjects are to be taught, at what level, and so on), which is outside the Treaty, from questions of access to the system so created.

3.3 *Vocational training.* In any event, the Court did not have to rule on access to education in general, because the course involved prepared its students for the job of strip-cartoonist. That vocational training is within the Treaty is demonstrated by the provisions of EEC 128 which tells the Council to lay down general principles for a common policy thereon; see also EEC 118, 125.

3.4 *EEC 48–9.* EEC 7 is explicitly without prejudice to any special Treaty provisions: some apply the principle of non-discrimination on the grounds of nationality, others, in more general terms, outlaw 'restrictions'. In the first category come EEC 48–9 and measures taken thereunder which open all educational facilities to the children of migrant workers: see, for instance, Regulation no. 1612/68, art. 12 (Rudden and Wyatt, *BCL*, 228). Ms Gravier was not covered by these.

3.5 *EEC 52.* It is also possible to argue, as did the Commission, that since EEC 52 gives the citizen of one Member State the right to set up in business as a strip-cartoonist in another, it also covers learning the job. The ECJ does not rule on this, as it is able to define the problems more narrowly.

3.6 *EEC 59–62.* The provisions on services are potentially the most dynamic because of the width of what they prohibit and the range of activity which they cover. As to the first, they deal with 'restrictions on freedom to provide [cross-border] services within the Community' (EEC 59) and '*any* new restrictions' (EEC 62). The ECJ has held that this is wider than discrimination on the grounds of nationality or residence; Case 33/74 *Van Binsbergen* (above, extract no. 11). As to the second, they cover not just narrowly 'economic' activities, such as those of craftsmen and the professions, but extend to the fields of literature, art, music, sport, the press, and broadcasting.

Consequently, a case was made by Ms Gravier and the Commission, and discussed by the Advocate-General, on the freedom to provide services. Although the Treaty does not expressly cover the recipient of services, the argument may be greatly simplified as follows. If the art teacher who crosses a border to give lessons is providing a service covered by the Treaty, then he or she is expressly protected under EEC 59–62. Therefore, the student who comes to the teacher is crossing a border to receive a service and the Articles must similarly apply. In Joined Cases 286/82 and 26/83 *Luisi and Carbone*, the ECJ held this result to be the necessary corollary of the express provisions of the Articles, whose purpose it said was to 'liberalize all gainful activity not covered by the free movement of goods, persons, and capital'. Although the cases concerned medical services and tourism, the Court said, *obiter*, 'the freedom to provide services includes the freedom for the recipients to go to another Member State ... and tourists, persons receiving medical treatment, and persons travelling for the purpose of education or business are to be regarded as recipients of services.'

3.7 *Education and gain.* But this brings us back to the fundamental question on the scope of the Treaty raised in 3.2 above: giving lessons is providing a service, but is it a service within the meaning of the crucial word *economic*? EEC 60 foresees the general problem and includes within the range of the

Community rules only those services 'normally provided for remuneration'. Teachers are paid, of course, but usually not by the pupil; their salaries come out of public funds raised from all taxpayers. If, however, we still classify them as remunerated, it seems to follow that virtually all—medical, or even religious—services are within the Treaty. If, on the other hand, we conclude that public education is not a service within the Treaty it seems to follow that such services are not *'normally* provided for remuneration' as required by EEC 60, and so private education is similarly excluded. This leads to the bizarre result that the private art teacher who wishes to cross a border to give a lesson to a fee-paying pupil cannot plead EEC 59 and 60. It is possibly from a sense of these complexities that the Court's judgment is confined to the effect of EEC 7.

3.8 *The policy arguments.* The Governments argued a wider case. States, they said, have special responsibilities to their own young nationals. Education is largely financed from taxes paid by citizens and residents, so in a sense the parents of young nationals are paying for their teaching; and this point is reinforced by the fact that it is accepted Community law that the children of a non-national who is actually working in a host State are treated exactly like those of nationals (see 3.4 above).

Other views put forward by the Governments were that the State provides education as a matter of social policy, at prices which, even if any are charged, bear no relation to its cost. If non-national students have equal access to institutions whose places are limited, then those admitted exclude nationals.

3.9 In the face of these, and the other problems outlined above, the ECJ carefully limits ruling to the problem of the discrimination on the grounds of nationality in access to vocational training.

TEXT

DECISION

[The Court summarized the facts and proceedings and continued:]

11. That is the background to the questions referred; it must therefore first be considered whether or not the establishment of a fee such as that which is the subject of the order making the reference constitutes 'discrimination on grounds of nationality' within the meaning of Article 7 of the Treaty.

12. The Belgian State and the Communauté Française argued before the Court that the reason why foreign students in Belgium are required to contribute to the financing of education is the imbalance which has existed since 1976 between the number of foreign students studying in Belgium and the number of Belgian students living abroad. Since that imbalance had serious consequences for the national education budget the Belgian Government was compelled to ask students who are nationals of other Member

States and who normally do not pay taxes in Belgium to make a proportional contribution to the cost of education. Far from being discriminatory, such a contribution puts foreign students on the same footing as Belgian nationals.

13. The Commission provided the Court with figures showing that the mobility of students within the Community is limited in scope but that Belgium is the Member State in which the percentage of students who are nationals of other Member States, in relation to the total number of students, is the highest. The information provided also shows that Belgium is the only Member State which requires foreign students to pay an enrolment fee, although Greece requires an identical payment, for reasons of reciprocity, from Belgian students enrolled in Greek universities. The Commission considers, moreover, that the imposition of the fee establishes a difference in treatment between students of Belgian nationality, whether or not their parents or they themselves pay taxes in Belgium, and nationals of other Member States, a difference which is based on the nationality of the students.

14. In that regard it is clear from the content of the Belgian legislation and from the practice followed in relation to the fee, as summarized above, that the cost of higher art education is not borne by students of Belgian nationality, whereas foreign students must bear part of that cost. The inequality of treatment is therefore based on nationality, and that finding is not affected by the mere fact that there are certain exceptions to the distinction made between Belgian and foreign students, some based on nationality, such as the special situation of Luxembourg students, and some on other criteria such as the residence in Belgium of parents who pay taxes in that country.

15. Such unequal treatment based on nationality must be regarded as discrimination prohibited by Article 7 of the Treaty if it falls within the scope of the Treaty.

16. The Danish Government and the United Kingdom expressed concern on that point. They consider that this case raises problems of principle whose importance goes beyond the questions referred by the Belgian court. After challenging the argument that anyone wishing to study in another Member State may be regarded as a person to whom services are provided, they argue that Article 7 of the Treaty does not prevent a Member State from treating its own nationals more favourably in the area of education, particularly as regards access to education, scholarships, and grants, other social facilities provided for students, and the contribution by students to the cost of education. On those points each Member State has special responsibilities towards its own nationals.

17. For its part the Commission argues principally that the imposition of the fee on students who are nationals of other Member States is contrary to Article 59 of the Treaty, in so far as students who are nationals of the State

in question are not obliged to pay it. It is only in the alternative that the Commission contends that such a requirement amounts to discrimination on grounds of nationality contrary to Article 7 of the Treaty. Participation in vocational training is, it maintains, covered by the provisions of Articles 48, 52, 59, and 128 of the Treaty, and therefore falls within the scope of the Treaty.

18. In view of this difference of opinion it is first necessary to define precisely the nature of the problem. In the first place, the questions referred concern neither the organization of education nor even its financing, but rather the establishment of a financial barrier to access to education for foreign students only. Secondly, they concern a particular type of education, referred to as 'vocational training' in the first question and as 'a course in strip cartoon art' in the second question.

19. The first remark which must be made in that regard is that although educational organization and policy are not as such included in the spheres which the Treaty has entrusted to the Community institutions, access to and participation in courses of instruction and apprenticeship, in particular vocational training, are not unconnected with Community law.

20. Article 7 of Regulation no. 1612/68 of the Council on freedom of movement for workers within the Community provides that a worker who is a national of a Member State and who is employed in another Member State is to have access to training in vocational schools and retraining centres in that country by virtue of the same right and under the same conditions as national workers. Article 12 of the regulation provides that the children of such workers are to be admitted to that State's general educational apprenticeship and vocational training courses under the same conditions as the nationals of that State.

21. With regard more particularly to vocational training, Article 128 of the Treaty provides that the Council is to lay down general principles for implementing a common vocational training policy capable of contributing to the harmonious development both of the national economies and of the Common Market ...

23. The common vocational training policy referred to in Article 128 of the Treaty is gradually being established. It constitutes, moreover, an indispensable element of the activities of the Community, whose objectives include *inter alia* the free movement of persons, the mobility of labour and the improvement of the living standards of workers.

24. Access to vocational training is in particular likely to promote free movement of persons throughout the Community, by enabling them to obtain a qualification in the Member State where they intend to work and by enabling them to complete their training and develop their particular talents

in the Member State whose vocational training programmes include the special subject desired.

25. It follows from all the foregoing that the conditions of access to vocational training fall within the scope of the Treaty.

26. The answer to the first question must therefore be that the imposition on students who are nationals of other Member States, of a charge, a registration fee or the so-called 'minerval' as a condition of access to vocational training, where the same fee is not imposed on students who are nationals of the host Member State, constitutes discrimination on grounds of nationality contrary to Article 7 of the Treaty.

27. In its second question the national court wishes to know what criteria must be used in deciding whether courses in strip-cartoon art constitute vocational training....

29. The general guidelines laid down by the Council in 1971 state that 'in view of the constantly changing needs of the economy the aim' of vocational training 'should be to offer everyone the opportunity of basic and advanced training and a continuity of in-service training designed, from a general and vocational point of view, to enable the individual to develop his personality and to take up a career'.

30. It follows from those statements that any form of education which prepares for a qualification for a particular profession, trade, or employment or which provides the necessary training and skills for such a profession, trade, or employment is vocational training, whatever the age and the level of training of the pupils or students, and even if the training programme includes an element of general education.

31. The answer to the second question must consequently be that the term 'vocational training' includes courses in strip-cartoon art provided by an institution of higher art education where that institution prepares students for a qualification for a particular profession, trade, or employment or provides them with the skills necessary for such a profession, trade, or employment.

On those grounds the court in answer to the questions referred to it hereby rules:

1. The imposition on students who are nationals of other Member States of a charge, a registration fee, or the so-called 'minerval' as a condition of access to vocational training, where the same fee is not imposed on students who are nationals of the host Member State, constitutes discrimination on grounds of nationality contrary to Article 7 of the Treaty.

2. The term 'vocational training' includes courses in strip-cartoon art provided by an institution of higher art education where that institution

prepares students for a qualification for a particular profession, trade, or employment or provides them with the skills necessary for such a profession, trade, or employment.

COMMENTS

1. Some States subsidize higher education directly, and students pay low fees. Others do so indirectly: high fees are charged, but national and resident students obtain public funds to cover them, through State or local authority awards. Will the result of this decision be an increase in the number of non-nationals applying to study in countries of the first category? Belgium has the highest number of such students.

2. The problem of identifying those services which fall within the Treaty has arisen in litigation involving sport: see Case 36/74 *Walrave*; Case 13/76 *Donà v. Mantero*; broadcasting: see Case 155/73 *Sacchi*; Case 52/79 *Debauve*; Case 62/79 *Coditel*; and entertainment: Joined Cases 110 and 111/78 *Van Wesemael*. The place of education within the Treaty is also considered in Case 152/82 *Forcheri* and Case 9/74 *Casagrande*.

13 Case 43/75 *Defrenne 2*

1. *The action.* This was a request under EEC 177 made by a Belgian Labour Court for an interpretation of the effect of EEC 119. Briefs were filed by Ms Defrenne, the Commission, and the UK and Irish Governments. In addition, the last three complied with the Court's request to file written answers to certain questions.

2. *The salient facts.* These are simple and are clearly set out in the extracts printed below, but a few points should be emphasized.

2.1 Ms Defrenne was not employed by the Belgian State: the airline is a separate legal entity.

2.2 It was conceded that she did the same job as did male cabin stewards.

2.3 Until 1966 she was paid less than them, under the terms of a collective agreement negotiated between the airline and the unions.

2.4 Her Belgian action was begun in 1968, claiming (*inter alia*) the difference between her remuneration and that of men from 1963 to 1966. The reason for the first date is the Belgian five-year limitation rule—an example of how the right may be conferred by Community, but the remedy is governed by national law.

2.5 EEC 119 provides that equal pay will be ensured during the first stage. Although this expired at the end of 1961, neither the Member States nor the Commission considered that the Article then became directly effective. On the contrary, the Commission made a mere recommendation, whereupon the States adopted a Resolution purporting to give themselves more time. Even on the expiry of this period, the Commission did not bring actions under EEC 169 against defaulting Member States.

3. *The legal issues*

3.1 *EEC 119.* It will be evident at a glance that the structure of EEC 119 as a norm is entirely different from that of EEC 12 and the other standstill clauses. First, they impose obligations to refrain, so that States which do nothing, comply; by contrast, EEC 119 enjoins States 'to ensure and subsequently maintain' the equal-pay principle. The State which does nothing is in breach, but it does not follow that therefore EEC 119 has direct effect.

3.2 Secondly, the article has no necessary 'transnational' element: it applies to citizens who never leave their home, whereas, by contrast, the standstill Articles and those on the free movement of persons are framed to take effect only when something (goods, persons, services) crosses a border.

3.3 Thirdly, EEC 48 forbids discrimination on the grounds of nationality in the matters of pay, working conditions, and so on, and was held to be directly effective in Case 41/74 *Van Duyn* (above, extract no. 9). Yet EEC

119 stipulates 'equal pay for equal work' and, as national experience amply demonstrates, it is far from simple to determine what the last two words mean.

3.4 Fourthly, the standstill clauses and those on free movement give rights to individuals by imposing obligations on States. Does EEC 119 do only the same (as the Commission argued), so that public-sector workers have the right to equal pay, whereas others do not. If so, it produces distinctions where there is no real difference.

3.5 If not, however, and if it applies to all employers it has the consequence that an individual may become burdened with an obligation (for which he is liable to suit in his own courts by his employee) contained, not in his own law, but in a Treaty which he may never have heard of, let alone read, and which both his own government and the Treaty's watch-dog thought did not directly affect him. And this would apply to the small shopkeeper as well as to the large industry; furthermore it would seem to mean that the employer who, out of kindness, paid more to a widow with young children than to a single man doing the same job, would be liable to the latter for the difference.

3.6 In short, the normative structure of EEC 119 resembles that of the typical directive which sets out Community aims to be implemented by Member States. And it is only the relatively rare provision of a directive which could produce direct effect, and then only against a Member State and its public authorities.

3.7 *The effective date.* If EEC 119 has direct effect then this ought to be from the end of, in its own words, 'the first stage'—that is from the beginning of 1962. This would mean that, depending on the periods of limitation in the various legal systems, underpaid employees could bring actions for several years back pay against their public or private employers; many of the latter would go bankrupt. The Court specifically asked the Governments to file briefs on this problem. The UK stressed the factual difficulties in such fields as the already vulnerable textile and clothing industry; Ireland pointed out that in numerous important economic sectors the majority of the work-force would have a claim for equal pay, and bitingly observed that EEC 6 (2), which tells Community institutions to take care not to prejudice the financial stability of Member States, applied equally to the Court of Justice. Although the Advocate-General argued for complete retroactivity, the Court was more prudent.

TEXT

OPINION OF MR ADVOCATE-GENERAL TRABUCCHI

Mr President, Members of the Court, after the solemn declarations made by the heads of state and of government in Paris in 1972 on the importance of the social aspects of European integration, here we have a private individual, a female worker, who succeeds in obtaining from her national court a reference for a preliminary ruling on the interpretation of the provision in the EEC Treaty which establishes the principle of equal treatment for men and women in the field of employment. A reference which in itself is of very modest financial importance provides an opportunity for this court to clarify certain aspects of the protection which fundamental rights are entitled to receive within the framework of the Community structure.

Miss Defrenne brought proceedings against Sabena before the Tribunal du travail, Brussels, claiming compensation for the injury she alleged she had suffered owing to the fact that the salary paid to her during the period between 15 February 1963 and 1 February 1966 was less than that to which a male 'steward' with the same seniority would have been entitled. The questions referred to the Court are in the following terms: (1) does Article 119 of the EEC Treaty introduce directly into the national law of each Member State of the European Community the principle that men and women should receive equal pay for equal work and does it therefore, independently of any national provision, entitle workers to institute proceedings before national courts in order to ensure its observance, and if so as from what date? (2) has Article 119 become applicable in the internal law of the Member States by virtue of measures adopted by the authorities of the European Economic Community (if so, which, and as from what date?) or must the national legislature be regarded as alone competent in this matter?

This brings us to the wording of Article 199. The first paragraph reads as follows: 'Each Member State shall during the first stage ensure and subsequently maintain the application of the principle that men and women should receive equal pay for equal work.' The principle quoted was, therefore, due to be put into operation before the end of the first stage, namely before 1 January 1962.

Under the criteria established by the case-law of this Court, a Community provision produces direct effects so as to confer on individuals the right to enforce it in the courts, provided that it is clear and sufficiently precise in its content, does not contain any reservation and is complete in itself in the sense that its application by national courts does not require the adoption of any subsequent measure of implementation either by the States or the Community.

Let us consider whether, viewed in the light of the context and spirit of the treaty, the character and content of Article 119 satisfy these conditions.

The provision in question places every Member State under the unconditional obligation to ensure during the first stage, and subsequently to maintain, the application of the principle that men and women should receive equal pay for equal work. Although the form of words used, 'Principle that men and women should receive equal pay', may seem too vague and the meaning of the word 'principle' itself not to be very specific, the purpose of the rule is nevertheless clear: to prohibit any discrimination to the detriment of women with regard to pay.

It can be argued that, even though Article 119 defines the concept of pay for the purposes of equality, the definition given of it is not so complete as to exclude all doubts about the precise meaning of the rule. Under the case-law of the Court, however, the fact that the concepts relied on in a provision require interpretation by the national court, which may, *inter alia*, avail itself of the procedure in Article 177 of the Treaty, constitutes no obstacle to recognition of its direct effect.

The conclusion may therefore be drawn that, as regards the abolition, in connection with pay, of all discrimination based on sex, Article 119 imposes an obligation which is clear, precise, and unconditional. It must, however, be emphasized that Article 119 does not provide for, or rather does not always necessarily provide for, all possible implications of the principle of equal pay for men and women in its fullest sense. The application of the principle to situations other than those referred to in the aforesaid article (cases where 'the same work', namely identical work, is performed) lies, without doubt, outside the context in which the question of the direct applicability of the rule can arise and more properly falls within the field of social policy the definition and application of which primarily depend on the initiative and co-ordinating action of the Community executive and of the Member States.

The obligation imposed on the Member States, to which the rule is formally addressed, consists of an obligation to act subject to a specific time limit (the end of the first stage). From the precedents established by this Court it is clear that an Article of the Treaty does not cease to have direct effect merely because it imposes on the States an obligation to act, provided that the obligation is expressed clearly and unconditionally, its tenor is precise and no real discretion is left to the Member States with respect to the application of the provision.

The decisive factor in determining what the effects of a Community provision are in national law is not the identity of those to whom it is addressed but its nature, which the Court defines on the basis of 'the spirit, the general scheme, and the wording' of the provision itself.

The object of Article 119 is, within a specified time, to abolish discrimination of any kind in fixing rates of pay and, moreover, not only discrimination created by the laws or regulations of the Member States but also discrimination produced by collective agreements or individual contracts of employment.

It follows that the obligation to observe the principle of equality is imposed not only on the States, inasmuch as the determination of the pay of government servants is concerned, but, provided that the requirement stated in the provision is sufficiently clear and precise in meaning to enable it to apply in relation to third parties, it also has effects in the field left to trade union organizations and individuals in which to conclude their collective or individual contracts. This is due entirely to the provision of the EEC Treaty, regardless of other implementing provisions adopted to this end by the State.

It is true that, in contrast to the free movement of persons, the principle of equal pay is not included amongst the fundamental objectives of the EEC Treaty but its attainment is of exceptional importance as a step towards 'economic and social progress' and in achieving the 'constant improvement of the living and working conditions ...' (see the preamble to the Treaty).

I therefore feel able to conclude that the principle of equal pay, which by its very nature is of direct concern to individuals, is, within the limits which I have indicated above, capable of producing direct effects in respect of such individuals and enables them to rely on it in the national courts without the need for it to be subject to adoption of relevant legislative measures by the States.

Of course, the adoption of administrative or even penal sanctions could only reinforce the direct effectiveness of Community laws and would for this reason be particularly favourable, but the main sanction is the inapplicability of national law or of any other kind of act, public or private, which conflicts with directly applicable Community law. Accordingly, for the purposes of Article 119, there is a very simple and effective method of moving against a discrimination; it is enough for the national courts to declare null and void any clause in an individual or collective contract which conflicts with that Article. Here again, however, we must define the precise meaning of the words 'null and void'. Notwithstanding the axiom 'no nullity save as provided for by the law', the nullity to which I refer is based on public policy and thus takes priority over any individual provision of the law. On the question of pay, nullity means that the rate of pay provided for by the clause which is void is automatically replaced by the higher rate of pay granted to male workers.

DECISION

1. By a judgment of 23 April 1975, received at the Court Registry on 2 May 1975, the Cour du travail, Brussels, referred to the Court under Article 177 of the EEC Treaty two questions concerning the effect and implementation of Article 119 of the Treaty regarding the principle that men and women should receive equal pay for equal work.

2. These questions arose within the context of an action between an air hostess and her employer, Sabena, concerning compensation claimed by the applicant in the main action on the ground that, between 15 February 1963 and 1 February 1966, she suffered as a female worker discrimination in terms of pay as compared with male colleagues who were doing the same work as 'cabin steward'.

3. According to the judgment containing the reference, the parties agree that the work of an air hostess is identical to that of a cabin steward and in these circumstances the existence of discrimination in pay to the detriment of the air hostess during the period in question is not disputed.

The first question (*direct effect of Article 119*)

4. The first question asks whether Article 119 of the EEC Treaty introduces

directly into the national law of each Member State of the European Community the principle that men and women should receive equal pay for equal work and does it therefore, independently of any national provision, entitle workers to institute proceedings before national courts in order to ensure its observance.

5. If the answer to this question is in the affirmative, the question further inquires as from what date this effect must be recognized.

6. The reply to the final part of the first question will therefore be given with the reply to the second question.

7. The question of the direct effect of Article 119 must be considered in the light of the nature of the principle of equal pay, the aim of this provision, and its place in the scheme of the EEC Treaty.

8. Article 119 pursues a double aim.

9. First, in the light of the different stages of the development of social legislation in the various Member States, the aim of Article 119 is to avoid a situation in which undertakings established in States which have actually implemented the principle of equal pay suffer a competitive disadvantage in intra-Community competition as compared with undertakings established in States which have not yet eliminated discrimination against women workers as regards pay.

10. Second, this provision forms part of the social objectives of the Community, which is not merely an economic union but is at the same time intended, by common action, to ensure social progress and seek the constant improvement of the living and working conditions of their peoples, as is emphasized by the preamble of the EEC Treaty.

11. This aim is accentuated by the insertion of Article 119 into the body of a chapter devoted to social policy whose preliminary provision, Article 117, marks 'the need to promote improved working conditions and an improved standard of living for workers, so as to make possible their harmonization while the improvement is being maintained'.

12. This double aim, which is at once economic and social, shows that the principle of equal pay forms part of the foundations of the Community.

13. Furthermore, this explains why the EEC Treaty has provided for the complete implementation of this principle by the end of the first stage of the transitional period.

14. Therefore, in interpreting this provision, it is impossible to base any argument on the dilatoriness and resistance which have delayed the actual implementation of this basic principle in certain Member States.

15. In particular, since Article 119 appears in the context of the harmonization of working conditions while the improvement is being maintained, the objection that the terms of this Article may be observed in other ways than by raising the lowest salaries may be set aside.

16. Under the terms of the first paragraph of Article 119, the Member States are bound to ensure and maintain 'the application of the principle that men and women should receive equal pay for equal work'.

17. The second and third paragraphs of the same article add a certain number of details concerning the concepts of pay and work referred to in the first paragraph.

18. For the purposes of the implementation of these provisions a distinction must be drawn within the whole area of application of Article 119 between, first, direct and overt discrimination which may be identified solely with the aid of the criteria based on equal work and equal pay referred to by the Article in question and, second, indirect and disguised discrimination which can only be identified by reference to more explicit implementing provisions of a Community or national character.

19. It is impossible not to recognize that the complete implementation of the aim pursued by Article 119, by means of the elimination of all discrimination, direct or indirect, between men and women workers, not only as regards individual undertakings but also entire branches of industry and even of the economic system as a whole, may in certain cases involve the elaboration of criteria whose implementation necessitates the taking of appropriate measures at Community and national level.

20. This view is all the more essential in the light of the fact that the Community measures on this question, to which reference will be made in answer to the second question, implement Article 119 from the point of view of extending the narrow criterion of 'equal work', in accordance in particular with the provisions of Convention no. 100 on equal pay concluded by the International Labour Organization in 1951, Article 2 of which establishes the principle of equal pay for work 'of equal value'.

21. Among the forms of direct discrimination which may be identified solely by reference to the criteria laid down by Article 119 must be included in particular those which have their origin in legislative provisions or in collective labour agreements and which may be detected on the basis of a purely legal analysis of the situation.

22. This applies even more in cases where men and women receive unequal pay for equal work carried out in the same establishment or service, whether public or private.

23. As is shown by the very findings of the judgment making the reference, in such a situation the Court is in a position to establish all the facts which enable it to decide whether a woman worker is receiving lower pay than a male worker performing the same tasks.

24. In such a situation, at least, Article 119 is directly applicable and may thus give rise to individual rights which the courts must protect.

25. Furthermore, as regards equal work, as a general rule, the national legislative provisions adopted for the implementation of the principle of equal

pay as a rule merely reproduce the substance of the terms of Article 119 as regards the direct forms of discrimination.

26. Belgian legislation provides a particularly apposite illustration of this point, since Article 14 of Royal Decree no. 40 of 24 October 1967 on the employment of women merely sets out the right of any female worker to institute proceedings before the relevant court for the application of the principle of equal pay set out in Article 119 and simply refers to that Article.

27. The terms of Article 119 cannot be relied on to invalidate this conclusion.

28. First of all, it is impossible to put forward an argument against its direct effect based on the use in this Article of the word 'principle', since, in the language of the Treaty, this term is specifically used in order to indicate the fundamental nature of certain provisions, as is shown, for example, by the heading of the first part of the Treaty which is devoted to 'Principles' and by Article 113, according to which the commercial policy of the Community is to be based on 'uniform principles'.

29. If this concept were to be attenuated to the point of reducing it to the level of a vague declaration, the very foundations of the Community and the coherence of its external relations would be indirectly affected.

30. It is also impossible to put forward arguments based on the fact that Article 119 only refers expressly to 'member states'.

31. Indeed, as the Court has already found in other contexts, the fact that certain provisions of the treaty are formally addressed to the Member States does not prevent rights from being conferred at the same time on any individual who has an interest in the performance of the duties thus laid down.

32. The very wording of Article 119 shows that it imposes on states a duty to bring about a specific result to be mandatorily achieved within a fixed period.

33. The effectiveness of this provision cannot be affected by the fact that the duty imposed by the Treaty has not been discharged by certain member States and that the joint institutions have not reacted sufficiently energetically against this failure to act.

34. To accept the contrary view would be to risk raising the violation of the right to the status of a principle of interpretation, a position the adoption of which would not be consistent with the task assigned to the Court of Justice by Article 164 of the Treaty.

35. Finally, in its reference to 'member states', Article 119 is alluding to those States in the exercise of all those of their functions which may usefully contribute to the implementation of the principle of equal pay.

36. Thus, contrary to the statements made in the course of the proceedings,

this provision is far from merely referring the matter to the powers of the national legislative authorities.

37. Therefore, the reference to 'member states' in Article 119 cannot be interpreted as excluding the intervention of the courts in direct application of the Treaty.

38. Furthermore, it is not possible to sustain any objection that the application by national courts of the principle of equal pay would amount to modifying independent agreements concluded privately or in the sphere of industrial relations such as individual contracts and collective labour agreements.

39. In fact, since Article 119 is mandatory in nature, the prohibition of discrimination between men and women not only applies to the action of public authorities, but also extends to all agreements which are intended to regulate paid labour collectively, as well as to contracts between individuals.

40. The reply to the first question must therefore be that the principle of equal pay contained in Article 119 may be relied on before the national courts and that these courts have a duty to ensure the protection of the rights which this provision vests in individuals, in particular as regards those types of discrimination arising directly from legislative provisions or collective labour agreements, as well as in cases in which men and women receive unequal pay for equal work which is carried out in the same establishment or service, whether private or public.

The second question (implementation of Article 119 and powers of the Community and of the Member States)

41. The second question asks whether Article 119 has become 'applicable in the internal law of the Member States by virtue of measures adopted by the authorities of the European Economic Community', or whether the national legislature must 'be regarded as alone competent in this matter'.

42. In accordance with what has been set out above, it is appropriate to join to this question the problem of the date from which Article 119 must be regarded as having direct effect.

43. In the light of all these problems it is first necessary to establish the chronological order of the measures taken on a Community level to ensure the implementation of the provision whose interpretation is requested.

44. Article 119 itself provides that the application of the principle of equal pay was to be uniformly ensured by the end of the first stage of the transitional period at the latest.

45. The information supplied by the Commission reveals the existence of

important differences and discrepancies between the various states in the implementation of this principle.

46. Although, in certain Member States, the principle had already largely been put into practice before the entry into force of the Treaty, either by means of express constitutional and legislative provisions or by social practices established by collective labour agreements, in other States its full implementation has suffered prolonged delays.

47. In the light of this situation, on 30 December 1961, the eve of the expiry of the time limit fixed by Article 119, the Member States adopted a resolution concerning the harmonization of rates of pay of men and women which was intended to provide further details concerning certain aspects of the material content of the principle of equal pay, while delaying its implementation according to a plan spread over a period of time.

48. Under the terms of that resolution all discrimination, both direct and indirect, was to have been completely eliminated by 31 December 1964.

49. The information provided by the Commission shows that several of the original Member States have failed to observe the terms of that resolution and that, for this reason, within the context of the tasks entrusted to it by Article 155 of the Treaty, the Commission was led to bring together the representatives of the governments and the two sides of industry in order to study the situation and to agree on the measures necessary to ensure progress towards the full attainment of the objective laid down in Article 119.

50. This led to the drawing up of successive reports on the situation in the original Member States, the most recent of which, dated 18 July 1973, recapitulates all the facts.

51. In the conclusion to that report the Commission announced its intention to initiate proceedings under Article 169 of the Treaty, for failure to take the requisite action, against those of the Member States who had not by that date discharged the obligations imposed by Article 119, although this warning was not followed by any further action.

52. After similar exchanges with the competent authorities in the new Member States the Commission stated in its report dated 17 July 1974 that, as regards those states, Article 119 had been fully applicable since 1 January 1973 and that from that date the position of those states was the same as that of the original Member States.

53. For its part, in order to hasten the full implementation of Article 119, the Council on 10 February 1975 adopted Directive 75/117 on the approximation of the laws of the Member States relating to the application of the principle of equal pay for men and women.

54. This directive provides further details regarding certain aspects of the

material scope of Article 119 and also adopts various provisions whose essential purpose is to improve the legal protection of workers who may be wronged by failure to apply the principle of equal pay laid down by Article 119.

55. Article 8 of this directive allows the Member States a period of one year to put into force the appropriate laws, regulations, and administrative provisions.

56. It follows from the express terms of Article 119 that the application of the principle that men and women should receive equal pay was to be fully secured and irreversible at the end of the first stage of the transitional period, that is, by 1 January 1962.

57. Without prejudice to its possible effects as regards encouraging and accelerating the full implementation of Article 119, the resolution of the Member States of 30 December 1961 was ineffective to make any valid modification of the time limit fixed by the Treaty.

58. In fact, apart from any specific provisions, the Treaty can only be modified by means of the amendment procedure carried out in accordance with Article 236.

59. Moreover, it follows from the foregoing that, in the absence of transitional provisions, the principle contained in Article 119 has been fully effective in the new Member States since the entry into force of the Treaty of Accession, that is, since 1 January 1973.

60. It was not possible for this legal situation to be modified by Directive 75/117, which was adopted on the basis of Article 100 dealing with the approximation of laws and was intended to encourage the proper implementation of Article 119 by means of a series of measures to be taken on the national level, in order, in particular, to eliminate indirect forms of discrimination, but was unable to reduce the effectiveness of that article or modify its temporal effect.

61. Although Article 119 is expressly addressed to the Member States in that it imposes on them a duty to ensure, within a given period, and subsequently to maintain the application of the principle of equal pay, that duty assumed by the States does not exclude competence in this matter on the part of the Community.

62. On the contrary, the existence of competence on the part of the Community is shown by the fact that Article 119 sets out one of the 'social policy' objectives of the Treaty which form the subject of Title III, which itself appears in Part Three of the Treaty dealing with the 'Policy of the Community'.

63. In the absence of any express reference in Article 119 to the possible

action to be taken by the Community for the purposes of implementing the social policy, it is appropriate to refer to the general scheme of the Treaty and to the courses of action for which it provided, such as those laid down in Articles 100, 155, and, where appropriate, 235.

64. As has been shown in the reply to the first question, no implementing provision, whether adopted by the institutions of the Community or by the national authorities, could adversely affect the direct effect of Article 119.

65. The reply to the second question should therefore be that the application of Article 119 was to have been fully secured by the original Member States as from 1 January 1962, the beginning of the second stage of the transitional period, and by the new Member States as from 1 January 1973, the date of entry into force of the Treaty of Accession.

66. The first of these time limits was not modified by the resolution of the Member States of 30 December 1961.

67. As indicated in reply to the first question, EEC Council Directive 75/117 does not prejudice the direct effect of Article 119 and the period fixed by that directive for compliance therewith does not affect the time limits laid down by Article 119 of the EEC Treaty and the Treaty of Accession.

68. Even in the areas in which Article 119 has no direct effect, that provision cannot be interpreted as reserving to the national legislature exclusive power to implement the principle of equal pay since, to the extent to which such implementation is necessary, it may be relieved by a combination of Community and national measures.

The temporal effect of this judgment

69. The Governments of Ireland and the United Kingdom have drawn the Court's attention to the possible economic consequences of attributing direct effect to the provisions of Article 119, on the ground that such a decision might, in many branches of economic life, result in the introduction of claims dating back to the time at which such effect came into existence.

70. In view of the large number of people concerned, such claims, which undertakings could not have foreseen, might seriously affect the financial situation of such undertakings and even drive some of them to bankruptcy.

71. Although the practical consequences of any judicial decision must be carefully taken into account, it would be impossible to go so far as to diminish the objectivity of the law and compromise its future application on the ground of the possible repercussions which might result, as regards the past, from such a judicial decision.

72. However, in the light of the conduct of several of the Member States and the views adopted by the Commission and repeatedly brought to the notice

of the circles concerned, it is appropriate to take exceptionally into account the fact that, over a prolonged period, the parties concerned have been led to continue with practices which were contrary to Article 119, although not yet prohibited under their national law.

73. The fact that, in spite of the warnings given, the Commission did not initiate proceedings under Article 169 against the Member States concerned on grounds of failure to fulfil an obligation was likely to consolidate the incorrect impression as to the effects of Article 119.

74. In these circumstances, it is appropriate to determine that, as the general level at which pay would have been fixed cannot be known, important considerations of legal certainty affecting all the interests involved, both public and private, make it impossible in principle to reopen the question as regards the past.

75. Therefore, the direct effect of Article 119 cannot be relied on in order to support claims concerning pay periods prior to the date of this judgment, except as regards those workers who have already brought legal proceedings or made an equivalent claim.

On those grounds, the Court, in answer to the questions referred to it hereby rules:

1. the principle that men and women should receive equal pay, which is laid down by Article 119, may be relied on before the national courts. These courts have a duty to ensure the protection of the rights which that provision vests in individuals, in particular in the case of those forms of discrimination which have their origin in legislative provisions or collective labour agreements, as well as where men and women receive unequal pay for equal work which is carried out in the same establishment or service, whether private or public.
2. The application of Article 119 was to have been fully secured by the original Member States as from 1 January 1962, the beginning of the second stage of the transitional period, and by the new Member States as from 1 January 1973, the date of entry into force of the Treaty of Accession. The first of these time limits was not modified by the resolution of the Member States of 30 December 1961.
3. EEC Council Directive 75/117 does not prejudice the direct effect of Article 119 and the period fixed by that directive for compliance therewith does not affect the time limits laid down by Article 119 of the EEC Treaty and the Treaty of Accession.
4. Even in the areas in which Article 119 has no direct effect, that provision cannot be interpreted as reserving to the national legislature exclusive power to implement the principle of equal pay since, to the extent to which such implementation is necessary, it may be achieved by a combination of Community and national provisions.

5. Except as regards those workers who have already brought legal proceedings or made an equivalent claim, the direct effect of Article 119 cannot be relied on in order to support claims concerning pay periods prior to the date of this judgment.

COMMENTS

1. It is worth repeating that EEC 119 has no intrinsic cross-border element. It is found in the Treaty Title III on social policy along with four other Articles, none of which has direct effect.

2. It may be thought, however, that the ECJ was hoist with its own petard. As we have seen, it has forcefully announced its role of guardian of the fundamental rights of Community citizens. Equal pay would seem to count as one such; it is recognized in the Constitutions of Germany (art. 3), Italy (art. 37), and France (preamble) and had been applied by the Court in actions by Community employees: Case 20/71 *Sabbatini* and Case 21/74 *Airola*.

3. The Court sees the rationale of EEC 119 as falling in two different areas. The first is economic—parity of overheads among competitors in different countries, thus introducing a clear Community element; the second is social.

4. The difference between the structure of EEC 119 and articles which had earlier been held directly effective is discussed in 3.1 above. In particular, the ECJ does not limit its scope to employment in the public service, so it follows that (quite apart from national legislation) one might say that every contract of employment now contains a term guaranteeing equal pay for equal work.

5. Numerous difficulties arise as to what this last phrase means: in particular, does it refer to the same work, to similar work, or to work which is of equal value to the employer. If the latter, how is the equality to be determined? As a result, much remains to be done by Member States, as is acknowledged in the preamble to Directive 75/117 (see Rudden and Wyatt, *BCL*, 385). That measure makes the principle of equal pay apply to work to which equal value is attributed (art. 1).

6. The ECJ, in effect, holds that its judgment applies only to pending and future claims. This is interesting, for several reasons. In the first place, the Court is supposed to be interpreting EEC 119, that is, telling the people what it means. Having divined that it means a direct right to equal pay, it seems difficult to avoid the one thing that is clear about the sentence: namely, that whatever effect it produces begins in 1962. It is hard to see that a ruling which, in defiance of the words used, postpones the coming into effect of a Treaty provision is merely an interpretation of that provision.

7. Nothing in the Treaty or Court Statute expressly empowers the ECJ to issue such a judgment, which recalls the 'prospective overruling' technique

of the US Supreme Court. Nonetheless, it is eminently sensible. The small shopkeeper, forced, by a provision of an international Treaty, into bankruptcy by claims for back pay for a period when discrimination between men and women was perfectly lawful under domestic law (and a part of many collective agreements between management and unions), would scarcely be grateful to the new guardian of his fundamental rights.

8. It was noted earlier, that one of the differences between actions under EEC 177 and those under EEC 169–70 was that the latter allowed the defendant Member States to adduce detailed factual argument. In Case 43/75 *Defrenne*, the ECJ itself asks for such evidence; it was, no doubt, this (together with the Commission's earlier attitude) which led it to ignore its Advocate-General's opinion and to postpone the operation of the equal pay principle.

9. EEC 119 deals only with pay. More recent lawsuits have seen the ECJ interpret this widely (e.g. Case 170/84 *Karin Weber von Hartz*) but inequalities may well exist in other features of employment—promotion prospects, training, working conditions, and the like. The Treaty does not confer specific legislative powers in this field, and the relevant rules were adopted under EEC 235: Directive 76/207 (see Rudden and Wyatt, *BCL*, 387). The same Article provided the power necessary to issue a directive on equal treatment in social security matters: Directive 79/7 (see Rudden and Wyatt, *BCL*, 390).

10. One field in which inequality persists is that of old-age pensions; in the UK, for instance, women are entitled at sixty, while men must wait until the age of sixty-five. So far, Community law has not sought to harmonize national old-age pension provisions, and the equal treatment social security Directive just mentioned, expressly excludes them from its scope (art. 7 (1) (*a*)). The ECJ has also held that the fact that access to voluntary redundancy is available only during the five years before the normal pensionable age—so that women may benefit earlier than men—is not forbidden by the equal treatment Directive 76/207: Case 19/81 *Burton*. Some employers, however, link their normal retirement age to that at which pensions are attained. The next extract deals with the problem, and is the first case selected dealing with the effect, not of the Treaty, but of a directive only.

14 Case 152/84 *Marshall*

1. *The action.* Under EEC 177, the English Court of Appeal sought a preliminary ruling on two questions concerning the meaning and the direct effect of Council Directive 76/207 on equal treatment (see Rudden and Wyatt, *BCL*, 387). Briefs were filed by the parties to the English lawsuit, by the Commission, and by the UK.

2. *The salient, simplified facts*
   2.1 An English woman worked under a contract of employment with a local Health Authority. The retiring age was that at which state pensions become payable, i.e. sixty for women, sixty-five for men.
   2.2 Her employment was terminated, on this ground, when she was over sixty but under sixty-five.
   2.3 She brought an action in the Industrial Tribunal contending that this was discriminatory conduct contrary to both national and Community law. After mixed success before the Employment Appeal Tribunal, she went to the Court of Appeal, which referred two questions. The first asks whether her dismissal was discrimination forbidden by the Directive, and—as usual—the ECJ replies with an interpretation of the law, not a decision about the individual. The second asks whether she may rely on a directive in an action against her employer.

3. *The legal issues*
   3.1 *The meaning of equal treatment.* The equal treatment Directive 76/207, art. 5 begins (emphasis added): 'Application of the principle of equal treatment with regard to working conditions, *including the conditions governing dismissal*, means that men and women shall be guaranteed the same conditions without discrimination on grounds of sex.'
   3.2 At this stage, therefore, the different retiring ages look like discrimination. The Directive, however, (art. 1 (2)) carefully excludes social security from its ambit by saying that provisions will later be adopted defining its substance, scope, and application.
   3.3 Now the different retiring ages were fixed by reference to national social security legislation. Consequently, the Court of Appeal needs to know first whether the general principle cited above (3.1) applies to the retiring age.
   3.4 On the one hand, presumably the reason for the difference was that women could leave work and collect the state pension five years earlier than men. On the other hand, however, the pensions legislation does not oblige recipients to stop work. Furthermore, the retiring ages were not tied to some extra benefit paid by the employer. Finally, the present favourable position of women in the field of state pension rights is clearly discriminatory, and so

its scope should be construed narrowly as a derogation from the principle of equal treatment.

3.5 *Direct effect.* If the equal treatment principle covers the case of different retirement ages, since it is spelled out only in a directive (and not by the Treaty or a regulation) Member States ought to adjust their law to comply. EEC 189 says that directives bind Member States as to the aims to be achieved, but leave to them the choice of form and methods.

3.6 Directive 76/207 gave Member States thirty months to carry out the necessary domestic measures of implementation. The period had long since expired, but the UK had enacted no law dealing with different retirement ages. Consequently, the Court of Appeal's second question was whether Article 5 (1) could by now be pleaded by individuals and enforced by national courts.

3.7 The Article seems clear enough, and gives Member States no measure of discretion in applying it. But conferring rights on an employee must impose correlative duties on the employer.

3.8 The problem of whether a directive can directly *improve* a person's legal position was settled in Case 41/74 *Van Duyn* (above, extract no. 9). But its application in the situation under review entails a direct worsening in the legal position of the employer, and an indirect threat to other employees. The employer could comply by fixing the retirement age for everyone at sixty-five, so that women would benefit and men would not lose; but could punctiliously comply by fixing it at sixty, so that women would not benefit and men would lose.

3.9 Furthermore, while there is no great problem in worsening the legal position of the employer when he is the State—since the State is the addressee of the Directive—it would be hard to impose directly on private employers an onerous obligation stemming from a directive which their own country has not implemented. It would certainly be hard to do this retroactively, which would in fact be the effect of any ruling in an individual case.

3.10 Consequently, the ECJ's ruling on direct effect applies only as against a *State* authority acting as employer.

TEXT

DECISION

12. The Court of Appeal referred the following questions to the Court of Justice for a preliminary ruling:

'1. Whether the respondent's dismissal of the appellant after she had passed her sixtieth birthday pursuant to the policy (followed by the respondent) and on the grounds only that she was a woman who has

passed the normal retiring age applicable to women was an act of discrimination prohibited by the Equal Treatment Directive.
2. If the answer to 1 above is in the affirmative, whether or not the Equal Treatment Directive can be relied upon by the appellant in the circumstances of the present case in national courts or tribunals notwithstanding the inconsistency (if any) between the directive and section 6 (4) of the Sex Discrimination Act.'

Relevant legal provisions

13. Article 1 (1) of Directive no. 76/207 provides as follows:

The purpose of this directive is to put into effect in the Member States the principle of equal treatment for men and women as regards access to employment, including promotion, and to vocational training and as regards working conditions and, on the conditions referred to in paragraph 2, social security. This principle is hereinafter referred to as 'the principle of equal treatment'.

14. Article 2 (1) of the Directive provides that:

... the principle of equal treatment shall mean that there shall be no discrimination whatsoever on grounds of sex either directly or indirectly by reference in particular to marital or family status.

15. Article 5 (1) of the Directive provides that:

Application of the principle of equal treatment with regard to working conditions, including the conditions governing dismissal, means that men and women shall be guaranteed the same conditions without discrimination on grounds of sex.

Article 5 (2) thereof provides that:

To this end, Member States shall take the measures necessary to ensure that:
(a) any laws, regulations, and administrative provisions contrary to the principle of equal treatment shall be abolished;
(b) any provisions contrary to the principle of equal treatment which are included in collective agreements, individual contracts of employment, internal rules of undertakings, or in rules governing the independent occupations and professions shall be, or may be declared, null and void or may be amended;
(c) those laws, regulations, and administrative provisions contrary to the principle of equal treatment when the concern for protection which originally inspired them is no longer well founded shall be revised; and that where similar provisions are included in collective agreements labour and management shall be requested to undertake the desired revision.

16. Article 1 (2) of the Directive provides that:

With a view to ensuring the progressive implementation of the principle of equal treatment in matters of social security, the Council, acting on a proposal from the Commission, will adopt provisions defining its substance, its scope, and the arrangements for its application.

17. Pursuant to the last-mentioned provision, the Council adopted Directive no. 79/7/EEC of 19 December 1978 on the progressive implementation of the principle of equal treatment for men and women in matters of social security, which the Member States were to transpose into national law, according to Article 8 (1) thereof, within six years of its notification. The Directive applies, according to Article 3 (1) thereof, to:

(*a*) statutory schemes which provide protection against the following risks:
   sickness,
   invalidity,
   old age,
   accidents at work and occupational diseases,
   unemployment;
(*b*) social assistance, in so far as it is intended to supplement or replace the schemes referred to in (*a*).

18. According to Article 7 (1) thereof, the directive is to be:

without prejudice to the right of Member States to exclude from its scope:
(*a*) the determination of pensionable age for the purposes of granting old-age and retirement pensions and the possible consequences thereof for other benefits.

19. With regard to occupational social security schemes, Article 3 (3) of the Directive provides that with a view to ensuring implementation of the principle of equal treatment in such schemes 'the Council, acting on a proposal from the Commission, will adopt provisions defining its substance, its scope, and the arrangements for its application.' ...

First question

32. The Court observes in the first place that the question of interpretation which has been referred to it does not concern access to a statutory or occupational retirement scheme, that is to say the conditions for payment of an old-age or retirement pension, but the fixing of an age limit with regard to the termination of employment pursuant to a general policy concerning dismissal. The question therefore relates to the conditions governing dismissal and falls to be considered under Directive no. 76/207.

33. Article 5 (1) of Directive no. 76/207 provides that application of the principle of equal treatment with regard to working conditions, including the conditions governing dismissal, means that men and women are to be guaranteed the same conditions without discrimination on grounds of sex.

34. In its judgment in the *Burton* case the Court has already stated that the term 'dismissal' contained in that provision must be given a wide meaning.

Consequently, an age limit for the compulsory dismissal of workers pursuant to an employer's general policy concerning retirement falls within the term 'dismissal' construed in that manner, even if the dismissal involves the grant of a retirement pension.

35. As the Court emphasized in its judgment in the *Burton* case, Article 7 of Directive no. 79/7 expressly provides that the directive does not prejudice the right of Member States to exclude from its scope the determination of pensionable age for the purposes of granting old-age and retirement pensions and the possible consequences thereof for other benefits falling within the statutory social security schemes. The Court thus acknowledged that benefits tied to a national scheme which lays down a different minimum pensionable age for men and women may lie outside the ambit of the aforementioned obligation.

36. However, in view of the fundamental importance of the principle of equality of treatment, which the Court has reaffirmed on numerous occasions, Article 1 (2) of Directive no. 76/207, which excludes social security matters from the scope of that Directive, must be interpreted strictly.

Consequently, the exception to the prohibition of discrimination on grounds of sex provided for in Article 7 (1) (*a*) of Directive no. 79/7 applies only to the determination of pensionable age for the purposes of granting old-age and retirement pensions and the possible consequences thereof for other benefits.

37. In that respect it must be emphasized that, whereas the exception contained in Article 7 of Directive no. 79/7 concerns the consequences which pensionable age has for social security benefits, this case is concerned with dismissal within the meaning of Article 5 of Directive no. 76/207.

38. Consequently, the answer to the first question referred to the Court by the Court of Appeal must be that Article 5 (1) of Directive no. 76/207 must be interpreted as meaning that a general policy concerning dismissal involving the dismissal of a woman solely because she has attained the qualifying age for a state pension, which age is different under national legislation for men and for women, constitutes discrimination on grounds of sex, contrary to that directive.

Second question

39. Since the first question has been answered in the affirmative, it is necessary to consider whether Article 5 (1) of Directive no. 76/207 may be relied upon by an individual before national courts and tribunals.

40. The appellant and the Commission consider that that question must be answered in the affirmative. They contend in particular, with regard to Articles 2 (1) and 5 (1) of Directive no. 76/207, that those provisions are

sufficiently clear to enable national courts to apply them without legislative intervention by the Member States, at least so far as overt discrimination is concerned.

41. In support of that view, the appellant points out that directives are capable of conferring rights on individuals which may be relied upon directly before the courts of the Member States; national courts are obliged by virtue of the binding nature of a directive, in conjunction with Article 5 of the EEC Treaty, to give effect to the provisions of directives where possible, in particular when construing or applying relevant provisions of national law. Where there is any inconsistency between national law and Community law which cannot be removed by means of such a construction, the appellant submits that a national court is obliged to declare that the provision of national law which is inconsistent with the Directive is inapplicable.

42. The Commission is of the opinion that the provisions of Article 5 (1) of Directive no. 76/207 are sufficiently clear and unconditional to be relied upon before a national court. They may therefore be set up against section 6 (4) of the Sex Discrimination Act, which, according to the decisions of the Court of Appeal, has been extended to the question of compulsory retirement and has therefore become ineffective to prevent dismissals based upon the difference in retirement ages for men and for women.

43. The respondent and the United Kingdom propose, conversely, that the second question should be answered in the negative. They admit that a directive may, in certain specific circumstances, have direct effect as against a Member State in so far as the latter may not rely on its failure to perform its obligations under the directive. However, they maintain that a directive can never impose obligations directly on individuals and that it can only have direct effect against a Member State *qua* public authority and not against a Member State *qua* employer. As an employer a State is no different from a private employer. It would not therefore be proper to put persons employed by the State in a better position than those who are employed by a private employer.

44. With regard to the legal position of the respondent's employees the United Kingdom states that they are in the same position as the employees of a private employer. Although according to United Kingdom constitutional law the health authorities, created by the National Health Service Act 1977, as amended by the Health Services Act 1980 and other legislation, are Crown bodies and their employees are Crown servants, nevertheless the administration of the National Health Service by the health authorities is regarded as being separate from the Government's central administration and its employees are not regarded as civil servants.

45. Finally, both the respondent and the United Kingdom take the view

that the provisions of Directive no. 76/207 are neither unconditional nor sufficiently clear and precise to give rise to direct effect. The directive provides for a number of possible exceptions, the details of which are to be laid down by the Member States. Furthermore, the wording of Article 5 is quite imprecise and requires the adoption of measures for its implementation.

46. It is necessary to recall that, according to a long line of decisions of the Court wherever the provisions of a directive appear, as far as their subject-matter is concerned, to be unconditional and sufficiently precise, those provisions may be relied upon by an individual against the State where that State fails to implement the Directive in national law by the end of the period prescribed or where it fails to implement the Directive correctly.

47. That view is based on the consideration that it would be incompatible with the binding nature which Article 189 confers on the Directive to hold as a matter of principle that the obligation imposed thereby cannot be relied on by those concerned. From that the Court deduced that a Member State which has not adopted the implementing measures required by the Directive within the prescribed period may not plead, as against individuals, its own failure to perform the obligations which the Directive entails.

48. With regard to the argument that a directive may not be relied upon against an individual, it must be emphasized that according to Article 189 of the EEC Treaty the binding nature of a directive, which constitutes the basis for the possibility of relying on the Directive before a national court, exists only in relation to 'each Member State to which it is addressed'. It follows that a directive may not *of itself* impose obligations on an individual and that a provision of a directive may not be relied upon as such against such a person. It must therefore be examined whether, in this case, the respondent must be regarded as having acted as an individual.

49. In that respect it must be pointed out that where a person involved in legal proceedings is able to rely on a directive as against the State he may do so regardless of the capacity in which the latter is acting, whether employer or public authority. In either case it is necessary to prevent the State from taking advantage of its own failure to comply with Community law.

50. It is for the national court to apply those considerations to the circumstances of each case; the Court of Appeal has, however, stated in the order for reference that the Health Authority is a public authority.

51. The argument submitted by the United Kingdom that the possibility of relying on provisions of the directive against the respondent *qua* organ of the State would give rise to an arbitrary and unfair distinction between the rights of State employees and those of private employees does not justify any other conclusion. Such a distinction may easily be avoided if the Member State concerned has correctly implemented the Directive in national law.

52. Finally, with regard to the question whether the provision contained in Article 5 (1) of Directive no. 76/207, which implements the principle of equality of treatment set out in Article 2 (1) of the Directive, may be considered, as far as its contents are concerned, to be unconditional and sufficiently precise to be relied upon by an individual as against the State, it must be stated that the provision, taken by itself, prohibits any discrimination on grounds of sex with regard to working conditions, including the conditions governing dismissal, in a general manner and in unequivocal terms. The provision is therefore sufficiently precise to be relied on by an individual and to be applied by the national courts.

53. It is necessary to consider next whether the prohibition of discrimination laid down by the Directive may be regarded as unconditional, in the light of the exceptions contained therein and of the fact that according to Article 5 (2) thereof the Member States are to make the measures necessary to ensure the application of the principle of equality of treatment in the context of national law.

54. With regard, in the first place, to the reservation contained in Article 1 (2) of Directive no. 76/207 concerning the application of the principle of equality of treatment in matters of social security, it must be observed that, although the reservation limits the scope of the Directive *ratione materiae*, it does not lay down any condition on the application of that principle in its field of operation and in particular in relation to Article 5 of the Directive. Similarly, the exceptions to Directive no. 76/207 provided for in Article 2 thereof are not relevant to this case.

55. It follows that Article 5 of Directive no. 76/207 does not confer on the Member States the right to limit the application of the principle of equality of treatment in its field of operation or to subject it to conditions and that that provision is sufficiently precise and unconditional to be capable of being relied upon by an individual before a national court in order to avoid the application of any national provision which does not conform to Article 5 (1).

56. Consequently, the answer to the second question must be that Article 5 (1) of Council Directive no. 76/207 of 9 February 1976, which prohibits any discrimination on grounds of sex with regard to working conditions, including the conditions governing dismissal, may be relied upon as against a State authority acting in its capacity as employer, in order to avoid the application of any national provision which dose not conform to Article 5 (1).

On those grounds, the Court, in answer to the questions referred to it, hereby rules:

1. Articles 5 (1) of Directive no. 76/207 must be interpreted as meaning that a general policy concerning dismissal involving the dismissal of a

woman solely because she has attained or passed the qualifying age for a State pension, which age is different under national legislation for men and for women, constitutes discrimination on grounds of sex, contrary to that directive.

2. Article 5 (1) of Council Directive no. 76/207 of 9 February 1976, which prohibits any discrimination on grounds of sex with regard to working conditions, including the conditions governing dismissal, may be relied upon as against a State authority acting in its capacity as employer, in order to avoid the application of any national provision which does not conform to Article 5 (1).

COMMENTS

1. The Directive discussed in Case 41/74 *Van Duyn* (above, extract no. 9) was tied to EEC 48 which is itself of direct effect. By contrast, the equal treatment Directive was adopted under EEC 235 which itself is clearly not of direct effect. Yet the ECJ holds that it may be relied upon by individuals.

2. In the notes to Case 43/75 *Defrenne 2* (above, extract no. 13) it was pointed out that EEC 119 contains no transnational element, but appears in the Treaty's Title III on social policy. Yet a Community element can be discerned in the need to equalize overheads among employers in different States. Presumably, although not spelled out by the Court, the same element can be found here.

3. The exact status of a given worker whose salary is paid from public funds may vary according to the national legal system involved. Thus in the UK, although health authorities are public ('Crown bodies'), they are not administered centrally, their workers are not civil servants, and the jobs that many of them do (for instance, cleaners) are identical with private sector employment. The arbitrary distinctions which may result from the decision can, says the Court, 'easily be avoided if the Member State concerned has correctly implemented the Directive'. See now the Sex Discrimination Act 1986, ss. 2 and 3.

B Constitutional Checks and Balances

15 Case 22/70 *ERTA*

1. *The action.* This was a suit by the Commission under EEC 173 seeking annulment of certain Council proceedings.

2. *The salient, simplified facts*

   2.1 The great lorries which transport products drive long distances to make a single delivery. It is clearly desirable that the countries through which they pass should agree on common rules concerning the composition of the crews, their rest periods, and the like.

   2.2 The 1962 European Road Transport Agreement (ERTA or, in French, AETR) was *not* a Community measure. It was signed by several European States, some being of Eastern Europe, and five being EEC Members, but, after several years, it had not been ratified by enough of them to come into force.

   2.3 Meanwhile, the EEC had acted for the six Member States by issuing a 1969 Regulation covering the same ground and including a provision that 'the Community shall enter into any necessary negotiations with third countries'.

   2.4 Attempts were being made to renegotiate ERTA and bring it into force, and a Community Council meeting in 1970 set out the common basis that each of the Six would (and later did) adopt in the negotiations which would (and did) lead to a new ERTA. It was the proceedings of this Council meeting that the Commission sought to have annulled.

3. *The legal issues*

   3.1 *Admissibility.* There is no problem about the Commission as plaintiff in an application for judicial review, for it is, of course, included in EEC 173. But how can it ask for the proceedings of a meeting to be annulled?

   3.2 The Community legal acts which may be reviewed by the ECJ include regulations, directives, and decisions, but not recommendations or mere expressions of opinion (EEC 189). This makes good sense, because, as the latter two have no legal effect, they can hardly be quashed by a Court of law. The 'proceedings' in issue lie on the borderline. Clearly, they did not constitute a regulation or directive, but if they counted as a legal *decision*, this would have been an 'act' reviewable under EEC 173, and would presumably have had to be quashed for failure to state its reasons as required by EEC 190. In fact, the Commission argues that the proceedings are a legal act and so reviewable, but does not plead lack of reasons as its main ground for seeking annulment; instead it relies on EEC 228 which, where applicable, says that international agreements will be negotiated by the Commission (and not, as was done with the new ERTA, by individual Member States). It is discussed further at 3.8 below.

3.3 The defendant Council argued that its proceedings bound no one, and conferred no rights, in short were merely a recognition by the Six of their common basis for negotiations on road transport with the non-Member States. Moreover, even if the proceedings could be, and were, 'annulled' it would make no difference, since the Member States had in fact co-ordinated their negotiating positions.

3.4 The Commission seems to try to turn this last point on its head by suggesting that the fact of later co-ordination points to the binding nature of the Council proceedings.

3.5 The ECJ held that the name given to the proceedings was not decisive as to their legal nature. If it had been one of the three acts mentioned in EEC 189 (regulation, directive, decision) presumably it would have to have been quashed for not stating its reasons as required by EEC 190, and so the Court assumes a fourth category of innominate legal acts.

3.6 However, said the Court, the question of whether the proceedings were such an act depended on the answer to a further important point: who—Member States or Community—had power to make the new Agreement. It could not be both, so, if the States still have the power, the Council's proceedings look like a mere recommendation, while if treaty-making power in this field has shifted to the Community, they take on a more juridical character.

3.7 *The treaty-making power.* EEC 210 provides that the Community shall have legal personality, so it has the capacity to make international agreements. But it also needs the power to do so, for this grant of legal power is matched by a diminution of the treaty-making power of each Member State.

3.8 EEC 228 provides that the Commission negotiates and the Council, after consulting the Assembly, concludes international agreements where *this Treaty* so provides. Nothing in the Treaty expressly takes from the States and gives to the Community the power to conclude international agreements on road transport. The question to be settled, therefore, is whether the existence, or at least the later exercise, of Community powers on road transport within the Member States (conferred by EEC 75) also shifts the international powers to the Community.

3.9 In support of such a shift is the obvious fact that the great trucks do not stop at the Community's border. The Advocate-General, however, argues against it with a wincing reference to the practice whereby 'the United States Supreme Court supplements the powers of the federal bodies', and with a discreet warning to the Court against judicial law-making. From this it follows, for him, that the Commission's action is inadmissible because, as legal power remains with the Member States, the Council can have none, and the Court cannot annul something that has no legal value.

3.10 The Court disagrees.

3.11 *The substance.* As far as the particular agreement is concerned, however, the Court was faced with several problems. First, what was going on was merely a renegotiation of an older agreement made when the treaty-making power certainly belonged to the States. Secondly, the Council proceedings occurred at a very late stage in the ERTA renegotiation. Thirdly, by the date of the judgment, the new agreement had already been negotiated and signed by the Member States. Fourthly, the other States would hardly have been pleased if, having dealt for almost a decade with individual sovereign States, they had all vanished to be replaced by the Commission negotiating on behalf of the Community. And fifthly, some of the other signatories were Eastern bloc countries who did not recognize the EEC as an international entity in any field.

3.12 So the ECJ accepts the principle of the transfer of the treaty-making power by the exercise of a Community power in a given field, treats the Council proceedings as a juridical act, but does not annul them.

TEXT

GROUNDS OF JUDGMENT

1. By an application lodged on 19 May 1970 the Commission of the European Communities has requested the annulment of the Council's proceedings of 20 March 1970 regarding the negotiation and conclusion by the Member States of the Community, under the auspices of the United Nations Economic Commission for Europe, of the European Agreement concerning the work of crews of vehicles engaged in international road transport (AETR).

2. As a preliminary objection, the Council has submitted that the application is inadmissible on the ground that the proceedings in question are not an act the legality of which is open to review under the first paragraph of Article 173 of the Treaty.

3. To decide this point, it is first necessary to determine which authority was, at the relevant date, empowered to negotiate and conclude the AETR.

4. The legal effect of the proceedings differs according to whether they are regarded as constituting the exercise of powers conferred on the Community, or as acknowledging a co-ordination by the Member States of the exercise of powers which remained vested in them.

5. To decide on the objection of inadmissibility, therefore, it is necessary to determine first of all whether, at the date of the proceedings in question, power to negotiate and conclude the AETR was vested in the Community or in the Member States.

1 The initial question

6. The Commission takes the view that Article 75 of the Treaty, which conferred on the Community powers defined in wide terms with a view to implementing the common transport policy, must apply to external relations just as much as to domestic measures in the sphere envisaged.

7. It believes that the full effect of this provision would be jeopardized if the powers which it confers, particularly that of laying down 'any appropriate provisions', within the meaning of subparagraph (1) (c) of the Article cited, did not extend to the conclusion of agreements with third countries.

8. Even if, it is argued, this power did not originally embrace the whole sphere of transport, it would tend to become general and exclusive as and where the common policy in this field came to be implemented.

9. The Council, on the other hand, contends that since the Community only has such powers as have been conferred on it, authority to enter into agreements with third countries cannot be assumed in the absence of an express provision in the Treaty.

10. More particularly, Article 75 relates only to measures internal to the Community, and cannot be interpreted as authorizing the conclusion of international agreements.

11. Even if it were otherwise, such authority could not be general and exclusive, but at the most concurrent with that of the Member States.

12. In the absence of specific provisions of the Treaty relating to the negotiation and conclusion of international agreements in the sphere of transport policy—a category into which, essentially, the AETR falls—one must turn to the general system of Community law in the sphere of relations with third countries.

13. Article 210 provides that 'The Community shall have legal personality'.

14. This provision, placed at the head of Part Six of the Treaty, devoted to 'General and Final Provisions', means that in its external relations the Community enjoys the capacity to establish contractual links with third countries over the whole field of objectives defined in Part One of the Treaty, which Part Six supplements.

15. To determine in a particular case the Community's authority to enter into international agreements, regard must be had to the whole scheme of the Treaty no less than to its substantive provisions.

16. Such authority arises not only from an express conferment by the Treaty—as is the case with Articles 113 and 114 for tariff and trade agreements and with Article 238 for association agreements—but may equally flow from other provisions of the Treaty and from measures adopted, within the framework of those provisions, by the Community institutions.

17. In particular, each time the Community, with a view to implementing a common policy envisaged by the Treaty, adopts provisions laying down common rules, whatever form these may take, the Member States no longer have the right, acting individually or even collectively, to undertake obligations with third countries which affect those rules.

18. As and when such common rules come into being, the Community alone is in a position to assume and carry out contractual obligations towards third countries affecting the whole sphere of application of the Community legal system.

19. With regard to the implementation of the provisions of the Treaty the system of internal Community measures may not therefore be separated from that of external relations.

20. Under Article 3 (e), the adoption of a common policy in the sphere of transport is specially mentioned amongst the objectives of the Community.

21. Under Article 5, the Member States are required on the one hand to take all appropriate measures to ensure fulfilment of the obligations arising out of the Treaty or resulting from action taken by the institutions and, on the other hand, to abstain from any measure which might jeopardize the attainment of the objectives of the Treaty.

22. If these two provisions are read in conjunction, it follows that to the extent to which Community rules are promulgated for the attainment of the objectives of the Treaty, the Member States cannot, outside the framework of the Community institutions, assume obligations which might affect those rules or alter their scope.

23. According to Article 74, the objectives of the Treaty in matters of transport are to be pursued within the framework of a common policy.

24. With this in view, Article 75 (1) directs the Council to lay down common rules and, in addition, 'any other appropriate provisions'.

25. By the terms of subparagraph (a) of the same provision, those common rules are applicable 'to international transport to or from the territory of a Member State or passing across the territory of one or more Member States'.

26. This provision is equally concerned with transport from or to third countries, as regards that part of the journey which takes place on Community territory.

27. It thus assumes that the powers of the Community extend to relationships arising from international law, and hence involve the need in the sphere in question for agreements with the third countries concerned.

28. Although it is true that Articles 74 and 75 do not expressly confer on the Community authority to enter into international agreements, nevertheless the bringing into force, on 25 March 1969, of Regulation no. 543/69 of the

Council on the harmonization of certain social legislation relating to road transport necessarily vested in the Community power to enter into any agreements with third countries relating to the subject-matter governed by that regulation.

29. This grant of power is moreover expressly recognized by Article 3 of the said regulation which prescribes that: 'The Community shall enter into any negotiations with third countries which may prove necessary for the purpose of implementing this regulation.'

30. Since the subject-matter of the AETR falls within the scope of Regulation no. 543/69, the Community has been empowered to negotiate and conclude the agreement in question since the entry into force of the said regulation.

31. These Community powers exclude the possibility of concurrent powers on the part of Member States, since any steps taken outside the framework of the Community institutions would be incompatible with the unity of the Common Market and the uniform application of Community law.

32. This is the legal position in the light of which the question of admissibility has to be resolved.

2 Admissibility of the application

33. The admissibility of the application is disputed by the Council on various grounds, based on the nature of the proceedings in question, and to a lesser extent on the Commission's alleged lack of interest in the matter, its previous attitude, and the fact that the application is out of time.

(a) SUBMISSION RELATING TO THE NATURE OF THE PROCEEDINGS OF 20 MARCH 1970

34. The Council considers that the proceedings of 20 March 1970 do not constitute an act, within the meaning of the first sentence of the first paragraph of Article 173, the legality of which is open to review.

35. Neither by their form nor by their subject-matter or content, it is argued, were these proceedings a regulation, a decision or a directive within the meaning of Article 189.

36. They were really nothing more than a co-ordination of policies amongst Member States within the framework of the Council, and as such created no rights, imposed no obligations and did not modify any legal position.

37. This is said to be the case more particularly because in the event of a dispute between the institutions admissibility has to be appraised with particular rigour.

38. Under Article 173, the Court has a duty to review the legality 'of acts of the Council ... other than recommendations or opinions'.

39. Since the only matters excluded from the scope of the action for annulment open to the Member States and the institutions are 'recommendations or opinions'—which by the final paragraph of Article 189 are declared to have no binding force—Article 173 treats as acts open to review by the Court all measures adopted by the institutions which are intended to have legal force.

40. The objective of this review is to ensure, as required by Article 164, observance of the law in the interpretation and application of the Treaty.

41. It would be inconsistent with this objective to interpret the conditions under which the action is admissible so restrictively as to limit the availability of this procedure merely to the categories of measures referred to by Article 189.

42. An action for annulment must therefore be available in the case of all measures adopted by the institutions, whatever their nature or form, which are intended to have legal effects.

43. The nature of the proceedings in question has to be determined in the light of the foregoing.

44. In the course of the meeting on 20 March 1970, the Council, after an exchange of views between its members and the representative of the Commission, reached a number of 'conclusions' on the attitude to be taken by the Governments of the Member States in the decisive negotiations on the AETR.

45. These proceedings were concerned partly with the objective of the negotiations and partly with negotiating procedure.

46. As regards the objective to be pursued, the Council settled on a negotiating position aimed at having the AETR adapted to the provisions of the Community system, apart from the concession of certain derogations from that system which would have to be accepted by the Community.

47. Having regard to the objective thus established, the Council invited the Commission to put forward, at the appropriate time and in accordance with the provisions of Article 75 of the Treaty, the necessary proposals with a view to amending Regulation no. 543/69.

48. As regards negotiating, the Council decided, in accordance with the course of action decided upon at its previous meetings, that the negotiations should be carried on and concluded by the six Member States, which would become contracting parties to the AETR.

49. Throughout the negotiations and at the conclusion of the agreement, the States would act in common and would constantly co-ordinate their positions according to the usual procedure in close association with the Community

institutions, the delegation of the Member State currently occupying the Presidency of the Council acting as spokesman.

50. It does not appear from the minutes that the Commission raised any objections to the definition by the Council of the objective of the negotiations.

51. On the other hand, it did lodge an express reservation regarding the negotiating procedure, declaring that it considered that the position adopted by the Council was not in accordance with the Treaty, and more particularly with Article 228.

52. It follows from the foregoing that the Council's proceedings dealt with a matter falling within the power of the Community, and that the Member States could not therefore act outside the framework of the common institutions.

53. It thus seems that in so far as they concerned the objective of the negotiations as defined by the Council, the proceedings of 20 March 1970 could not have been simply the expression or the recognition of a voluntary co-ordination, but were designed to lay down a course of action binding on both the institutions and the Member States, and destined ultimately to be reflected in the tenor of the regulation.

54. In the part of its conclusions relating to the negotiating procedure, the Council adopted provisions which were capable of derogating in certain circumstances from the procedure laid down by the Treaty regarding negotiations with third countries and the conclusion of agreements.

55. Hence, the proceedings of 20 March 1970 had definite legal effects both on relations between the Community and the Member States and on the relationship between institutions.

(*b*) ALTERNATIVE SUBMISSIONS ON ADMISSIBILITY

56. The Council contends that analysis of the consequences which an annulment of the proceedings on 20 March 1970 might involve confirms that the latter were devoid of all legal effect.

57. Such an annulment would cancel the recognition of the co-ordination between Member States, but would not affect either the reality of that co-ordination or the subsequent action of those States in the negotiation of the AETR.

58. The Council claims that the Commission's action therefore cannot achieve its aim, and is thus devoid of purpose.

59. Under Article 174, 'If the action is well founded the Court of Justice shall declare the act concerned to be void.'

60. If that were done, the Council's proceedings would have to be deemed non-existent in so far as they had been annulled by the Court; the parties to

the dispute would then be restored to their original position, and would have to reconsider the disputed questions so as to resolve them in accordance with Community law.

61. It is thus incontestable that the Commission has an interest in pursuing its action.

62. Next, the Council considers that the Commission is disqualified from pursuing such an action because the Commission itself is responsible for the situation in question through having failed to take, at the proper time, the steps necessary to allow Community powers to be exercised, by submitting suitable proposals to the Council.

63. However, since the questions put before the Court by the Commission are concerned with the institutional structure of the Community, the admissibility of the application cannot depend on prior omissions or errors on the part of the applicant.

64. Moreover, an evaluation of the objections raised by the Council can only be undertaken as part of the examination of the substance of the dispute.

65. Finally, the Council objects that the application is out of time, on the ground that the proceedings of 20 March 1970 did nothing more than restate principles laid down at previous meetings of the Council, of which the last one took place on 17 and 18 March 1969.

66. The proceedings of 20 March 1970, however, cannot be regarded as simply a confirmation of previous discussions, since Regulation no. 543/69 of 25 March 1969 brought about a decisive change in the allocation of powers between the Community and the Member States on the subject-matter of the negotiations.

67. For all these reasons, the application is admissible.

3 Substance

68. Essentially, the Commission disputes the validity of the proceedings of 20 March 1970 on the ground that they involved infringements of provisions of the Treaty, more particularly of Articles 75, 228, and 235 concerning the distribution of powers between the Council and the Commission, and consequently the rights which it was the Commission's duty to exercise in the neogitations on the AETR.

(*a*) SUBMISSION RELATING TO INFRINGEMENT OF ARTICLES 75 AND 228

69. The Commission claims that in view of the powers vested in the Community under Article 75, the AETR should have been negotiated and con-

cluded by the Community in accordance with the Community procedure defined by Article 228 (1).

70. Although the Council may, by virtue of these provisions, decide in each case whether it is expedient to enter into an agreement with third countries, it does not enjoy a discretion to decide whether to proceed through intergovernmental or Community channels.

71. By deciding to proceed through intergovernmental channels it made it impossible for the Commission to perform the task which the Treaty entrusted to it in the sphere of negotiations with third countries.

72. In the absence of specific provisions in the Treaty applicable to the negotiation and implementation of the agreement under discussion, the appropriate rules must be inferred from the general tenor of those articles of the Treaty which relate to the negotiations undertaken on the AETR.

73. The distribution of powers between the Community institutions to negotiate and implement the AETR must be determined with due regard both to the provisions relating to the common transport policy and to those governing the conclusion of agreements by the Community.

74. By the terms of Article 75 (1), it is a matter for the Council, acting on a proposal from the Commission and after consulting the Economic and Social Committee and the Assembly, to lay down the appropriate provisions, whether by regulation or otherwise, for the purpose of implementing the common transport policy.

75. According to Article 228 (1), where agreements have to be concluded with one or more third countries or an international organization, such agreements are to be negotiated by the Commission and concluded by the Council, subject to any more extensive powers which may have been vested in the Commission.

76. As a subsidiary point, since the negotiations took place under the auspices of the United Nations Economic Commission for Europe, the first paragraph of Article 116 has also to be taken into account. By the terms of that paragraph, from the end of the transitional period onwards, Member States shall 'proceed within the framework of international organizations of an economic character only by common action', the implementation of such common action being within the powers of the Council, basing its decisions on proposals submitted by the Commission.

77. If these various provisions are read in conjunction, it is clear that wherever a matter forms the subject of a common policy, the Member States are bound in every case to act jointly in defence of the interests of the Community.

78. This requirement of joint action was in fact respected by the proceedings of 20 March 1970, which cannot give rise to any criticism in this respect.

79. Moreover, it follows from these provisions taken as a whole, and particularly from Article 228(1), that the right to conclude the agreement was vested in the Council.

80. The Commission for its part was required to act in two ways, first by exercising its right to make proposals, which arises from Article 75(1) and the first paragraph of Article 116, and, secondly, in its capacity as negotiator by the terms of the first subparagraph of Article 228(1).

81. However, this distribution of powers between institutions would only have been required where negotiations were undertaken at a time when the vesting of powers in the Community had taken effect, either by virtue of the Treaty itself or by virtue of measures taken by the institutions.

82. In this connection it must be borne in mind that an earlier version of the AETR had been drawn up in 1962, at a period when, because the common transport policy was not yet sufficiently developed, power to conclude this agreement was vested in the Member States.

83. The stage of negotiations of which the proceedings in question formed part was not aimed at working out a new agreement, but simply at introducing into the version drawn up in 1962 such modifications as were necessary to enable all the contracting parties to ratify it.

84. The negotiations on the AETR are thus characterized by the fact that their origin and a considerable part of the work carried out under the auspices of the Economic Commission for Europe took place before powers were conferred on the Community as a result of Regulation no. 543/69.

85. It appears therefore that on 20 March 1970 the Council acted in a situation where it no longer enjoyed complete freedom of action in its relations with the third countries taking part in the same negotiations.

86. At that stage of the negotiations, to have suggested to the third countries concerned that there was now a new distribution of powers within the Community might well have jeopardized the successful outcome of the negotiations, as was indeed recognized by the Commission's representative in the course of the Council's deliberations.

87. In such a situation it was for the two institutions whose powers were directly concerned, namely, the Council and the Commission, to reach agreement, in accordance with Article 15 of the Treaty of April 1965 establishing a Single Council and a Single Commission of the European Communities, on the appropriate methods of co-operation with a view to ensuring most effectively the defence of the interests of the Community.

88. It is clear from the minutes of the meeting of 20 March 1970 that the Commission made no formal use of the rights to submit proposals open to it under Articles 75 and 116.

89. Nor did it demand the simple application of Article 228(1) in regard to its right of negotiation.

90. It may therefore be accepted that, in carrying on the negotiations and concluding the agreement simultaneously in the manner decided on by the Council, the Member States acted, and continue to act, in the interest and on behalf of the Community in accordance with their obligations under Article 5 of the Treaty.

91. Hence, in deciding in these circumstances on joint action by the Member States, the Council has not failed in its obligations arising from Articles 75 and 228.

92. For these reasons, the submission must be rejected.

COMMENTS

1. The word actually used by the Council and translated above as 'proceedings' is the French *délibérations*. This may seem studiously vague, yet it is the word used in the authentic French text of the ECSC Treaty to describe a proceeding of the Assembly or Council which may be the subject of judicial review (ECSC 38). The official English translation renders it by 'act'. ECSC 38 has come to life in recent disputes involving the location of the Parliament: e.g. Cases 230/81 and 108/33 *Luxemburg* v. *Parliament*.

2. It seems as if the ECJ wished to achieve two aims. The first was not to jeopardize the existing ERTA negotiation. With an eye on the future, however, the Court's second aim was to increase, at the expense of the Member States, Community powers in the field of international agreements. The extent of these powers may be investigated in actions brought under EEC 228 to secure a preliminary Opinion of the Court as to whether a proposed agreement is compatible with the Treaty: e.g. Opinion 1/75 *Local Cost Standard*; Opinion 1/76 *Laying-up Fund*. The issue has also arisen in fisheries disputes, e.g. Cases 3, 4, and 6/76 *Kramer*; Case 63/83 *Kent Kirk*. See Hartley, *FCL*, 156–62.

16 Case 13/83 *Parliament v. Council*

1. *The action.* The European Parliament, under EEC 175, brought an action against the Council for breaking the Treaty by failing to introduce and implement a common transport policy and by not reaching a decision on sixteen Commission proposals, to which the Parliament had already given its approval. The Commission intervened in support of the Parliament, and the Netherlands purported to argue on behalf of the Council.

2. *The salient, simplified facts*

2.1 Goods and people are legally free to move about the Community, so the means by which they do so—transport—is clearly of great importance; it is, however, an extremely complex area comprising differing means of transport (road, rail, water, and air) and carriers ranging from the great nationalized services to the one-man van. Both these facts are recognized by the Treaty provisions discussed below.

2.2 While some positive steps had been taken (see extract no. 15 above), for the most part the Council had not, for some twenty years, managed to act decisively on numerous Commission proposals and Parliamentary resolutions.

2.3 In 1982, therefore, the Parliament's President wrote threatening the Council with an action under EEC 175 and calling for action in the framing of a common transport policy, the introduction of freedom to provide services, and the taking of decisions on certain specified Commission proposals.

2.4 The Council's answer was bland as butter. It declined to discuss 'the legal aspects', but reported the actions already taken, and announced its resolve to 'make further solid progress' and 'actively to proceed to examine the pending proposals'.

2.5 Parliament took the view that this answer was neither a yea nor a nay and brought the first suit for inaction to be filed by one institution against another.

3. *The legal issues.* These are important on the practical, the constitutional, and the procedural level. The first relates to the nature of the obligation to introduce a common transport policy and to liberalize services; the second concerns the means by which Parliament may, to some extent, control the Council; the third is intertwined with this, and is treated in terms of the relation between EEC 175 and 173.

3.1 *Transport.* The importance of transport within a free trade area is emphasized by the fact that it is one of the two spheres—the other being agriculture—in which the Treaty requires 'the adoption of a common policy' (EEC 3 (*e*)). EEC Title IV is devoted to transport by rail, road, and inland waterway, and EEC 75 states that the Council, on a proposal from the Commission and after consulting the Economic and Social Committee and the Assembly, *shall*, during the transitional period, lay down common rules for cross-border transport, and the conditions on which carriers may provide services in other Member States. It was common ground in the lawsuit that this had not been done, but, as the Court accepts, the Council is on firm ground in pointing out that its failure does not relate to a clear and specific obligation.

3.2 *Services*. The fact that a similar inactivity had prevailed in the general freedom to provide services did not prevent the ECJ from holding that EEC 59 took effect at the expiry of the transitional period: Case 33/74 *Van Binsbergen* (above, extract no. 11). Freedom to provide transport services, however, is expressly stated to be governed by the transport Title (EEC 61 (1)). The Netherlands Government, nonetheless, argued that EEC 59 became comprehensively effective at the end of the transitional period; it therefore governed transport, and so the Council's inaction was of no consequence. The Commission was more doubtful, although it pointed out that the transitional period had expired fifteen years previously. The ECJ's response is subtle: in the absence of a common policy, EEC 59 is not directly effective within the sphere of transport; nonetheless its principles—especially the removal of discrimination against carriers on the grounds of nationality or residence—are precise enough to have been implemented; consequently the Council has broken the Treaty by failing to act.

3.3 EEC 175. The wording of EEC 175 is as follows (emphasis added):

Should the Council or the Commission, in infringement of this Treaty, fail to *act*, the Member States and the *other institutions* of the Community may bring an action before the Court of Justice to have the infringement established. The action shall be admissible only if the institution concerned has first been *called upon* to act. If, within two months of being so called upon, the institution concerned has not *defined its position*, the action may be brought within a further period of two months.

Any natural or legal person may, under the conditions laid down in the preceding paragraph, complain to the Court of Justice that an institution of the Community has failed to address to that person any act other than a recommendation or opinion.

Constitutional, as well as procedural, issues are bound up in the arguments on this obscure provision; consequently, both Lenz A–G and the Court devote much attention to the question of admissibility.

3.4 By failure to *act*, the Article must mean failure to adopt some measure having legal effect—i.e. one which if it had been taken, could have been challenged under EEC 173. Otherwise there would be no point in the last phrase, excluding complaints concerning the absence of recommendations or opinions (which have no legal effect: EEC 189).

3.5 At first sight, it would seem obvious that the Parliament—which is a

Community institution (EEC 4)—may bring an action under EEC 175, and—unlike a citizen or firm—may do so without showing that it would be directly affected by the act requested. Yet the word can hardly embrace all the institutions listed in EEC 4, since it seems unlikely that the Court itself could bring such an action. Furthermore, it is clear that EEC 175 is using the word imprecisely for, under its first paragraph, the privileged plaintiffs may attack only Council and Commission, while the third appears to permit citizens and firms to use EEC 175 against them plus Parliament and the Court.

3.6 A further argument against the Parliament as plaintiff is the fact that EEC 173 and 175 are meant to be two sides of the same coin. If Council or Commission adopt a legal act, it may be challenged under the former Article; and the latter is available if, in breach of the Treaty, they fail to do so. But the only institutions who may be plaintiffs by the express terms of EEC 173 are Council and Commission. There is thus an argument that Parliament was not meant to be plaintiff under EEC 175 since, if it calls upon the Council to act and the Council promptly answers 'no', that decision seems to be immune from challenge by the Parliament under EEC 173.

3.7 The next set of problems concerns the meaning of 'call upon' and 'define its position' in EEC 175. The kernel is clear: the Council is requested to act. If it says 'yes', it has taken a decision and the act will follow; if it says 'no' it has also taken a decision which may be challenged under EEC 173; if it does not answer then, after two months, suit can be brought under EEC 175. The problem arises when the Council replies promptly but unhelpfully by simply saying that it has the matter under review. Has it 'defined its position' so as to block an action under EEC 175 while simultaneously evading a decision which could be challenged under EEC 173? The Court solves this problem in the way one might expect by indicating that this kind of equivocal response does not 'define a position' so as to avoid an action under EEC 175.

3.8 Underneath all these technical disputes on interpretation lies the real political conflict. The Council contends, first, that the adoption of common rules in so difficult a sphere as transport is a matter of policy, not law; and secondly that the institutional balance of the Treaty requires the denial of legal weapons to a Parliament whose role is defined as 'advisory and supervisory' (EEC 137). The ECJ sees no problem in the coexistence of both political and legal powers.

TEXT

DECISION

On 24 January 1983 the European Parliament brought proceedings pursuant to the first paragraph of Article 175 of the EEC Treaty for a declaration that by failing to introduce a common policy for transport and in particular to lay down the framework for such policy in a binding manner Council had infringed the EEC Treaty and in particular Articles 3 (*e*), 61, 74, 75, and 84 thereof, and that it had infringed the EEC Treaty by failing to reach a decision on sixteen enumerated proposals on transport matters submitted to it by the Commission.

The adoption of a common transport policy is one of the actions which must be undertaken by the community under Article 3 of the Treaty with a view to establishing a common market and progressively approximating the economic policies of Member States.

According to Article 75 (1) the Council must, on a proposal from the Commission and after consulting the Economic and Social Committee and the European Parliament, lay down:

(*a*) Common rules applicable to international transport to or from the territory of a Member State or passing across the territory of one or more Member States;
(*b*) The conditions under which non-resident carriers may operate transport services within a Member State;
(*c*) Any other appropriate provisions.

Admissibility

The Council, the defendant in the case, raised an objection of inadmissibility on two grounds: it argued first that the applicant had no right to bring proceedings on this point and secondly that the conditions laid down in Article 175 regarding the procedure to be followed before the initiation of proceedings had not been complied with.

1. RIGHT TO BRING PROCEEDINGS

The Council explained that this action was a further chapter in the Parliament's efforts to increase its influence in decision-making within the Community. The Parliament had no supervisory authority over the Council such as to provide a basis for an action for failure to act.

It added that the scheme of the Treaty could not be interpreted in such a way as to give the Parliament a right to bring proceedings. In so far as the Treaty did not give the Parliament any authority to supervise the legality of measures taken by the Council and by the Commission, it would be illogical to grant it a right of action where one of those institutions failed to act according to law.

The European Parliament and the Commission challenged that reasoning and referred to the wording of Article 175, which they said, could not be interpreted in such a way as to deny the Parliament the right to bring an action for failure to act.

The Court emphasized that the first paragraph of Article 175 expressly gives 'the other institutions of the Community', *inter alia* the right to bring an action against the Council or the Commission for their failure to act. That provision thus gives all the Community institutions the same right to initiate proceedings.

The first ground of inadmissibility was therefore rejected.

2. THE CONDITIONS REGARDING THE PROCEDURE TO BE FOLLOWED BEFORE INITIATING PROCEEDINGS

The council took the view that the conditions laid down in Article 175 regarding the procedure to be followed before initiating proceedings had not been fulfilled. The letter of the President of the European Parliament of 21 September 1982 did not constitute a request to act as provided for in Article 175; furthermore, the Council had 'defined its position' on that letter, within the meaning of Article 175, by providing the Parliament with a complete analysis of the Council's activities in the field of the common transport policy, referred to by the letter of 21 September 1982.

The Council argued that it could be inferred from its reply to that letter that it had viewed the correspondence between the two institutions as a contribution to political dialogue and not as the first step in a legal dispute.

The Parliament and the Commission took the view that the letter of the Parliament of 21 September 1982 set out sufficiently clearly the measures requested by the Parliament under the second paragraph of Article 175, and that the reply of the President of the Council, dated 22 November 1982, was significant precisely because it failed to define a position with regard to any of those measures, so that the Parliament was left without a reply to its complaint that the Council had failed to act.

The Court held that the conditions required by the second paragraph of Article 175 were fulfilled. After expressly referring to that provision, the Parliament had clearly stated in the letter from its President that it was requesting the Council to act, as referred to in Article 175, and had added a list of the measures which in its view the Council was obliged to take in order to compensate for its failure to act.

The Council's reply, however, simply summarized the action already taken by the Council in the transport sector but did not deal with 'the judicial aspects' of the correspondence initiated by the Parliament.

The second ground of inadmissibility was also rejected.

Subject matter of the action

In its defence the Council submitted that the Parliament had failed to address the key issue in the dispute, that is, whether the word 'act' as used in Article 175 can be interpreted as including the establishment of a common transport policy.

The Council took the view that the procedure provided for in Article 175 was intended for cases where the institution in question was legally obliged to adopt a specific legal measure and that it was not well suited to the resolution of cases involving the establishment of a system of measures in a complex legislative process. According to Article 176 the institution which has failed to act is required 'to take the necessary measures' to comply with the judgment of the Court. The applicant had not however indicated the specific measures which the Council had failed to adopt.

The Parliament accepted that a common transport policy would probably not be adopted at a single stroke but would have to be brought into existence by means of several successive measures. It considered it clear, however, that it was necessary to 'act' in one manner or another in order to establish, in accordance with a programme, the necessary set of measures.

The Court recalled that the Parliament had made two separate claims: one concerning the failure to establish a common transport policy and to establish its framework, and another regarding the failure of the Council to reach a decision on sixteen proposals on transport matters submitted to it by the Commission. Only the first claim raised the issue of whether the wording of Article 175 and its place in the system of legal remedies provided for by the Treaty made it possible for the Court to declare that the Council had failed to act, in breach of its obligations under the Treaty.

The substance of the Council's objection was therefore the question whether in this case the European Parliament had in its first claim indicated with sufficient precision the measures which it asserted the Council had failed to adopt, so that if the Court upheld the Parliament's claim it would render a judgment which could be complied with by the Council, under Article 176.

It followed that even if the Parliament's first claim was well founded it could only be upheld to the extent to which the Council's alleged failure to adopt a common transport policy amounted to a failure to adopt measures sufficiently specific in nature to enable them to be individually identified and implemented in accordance with Article 176. It was therefore necessary to examine the arguments of the parties regarding the alleged lack of a common transport policy.

The first claim: failure to establish a common transport policy

1. THE COMMON TRANSPORT POLICY IN GENERAL

The European Parliament accepted that the Treaty allowed the Council a wide discretion with regard to the content of the common transport policy. That discretion was however limited in two respects: first, it did not permit the Council to ignore the time-limits laid down by the Treaty and in particular that established in Article 75 (2); secondly, the Council was required to lay down a common framework consisting of a coherent set of principles, taking general account of the complex economic factors at work in the transport sector.

In those circumstances, it said, the basic principles which the Council should have adopted should at least observe certain objectives and cover certain areas.

The Commission stated that there were still large gaps in all areas of transport policy, in spite of the numerous proposals submitted by it to the Council over a period of more than twenty years. It referred to the inadequacy of the measures taken regarding the transport of goods by road, the obstacles presented by the large number of border controls, the unsatisfactory situation of railway accounts, the large structural overcapacity in the area of water-borne transport, and the almost total absence of Community action with regard to sea and air transport.

The Council did not dispute the existence of the gaps referred to. However, it raised a series of arguments intended to show that those gaps could not be considered tantamount to a failure to act as referred to in Article 175 of the Treaty.

The Council went on to give details of the action it had already taken in the field, a summary of which had been provided to the Parliament.

The Court concluded from those arguments that the parties were in agreement that there was not yet a consistent set of regulations which could be regarded as a common transport policy within the meaning of Articles 74 and 75 of the Treaty.

It was therefore necessary to decide whether, in the absence of a set of measures which could be regarded as a common transport policy, the Council's failure to act was one for which it could be held to account under Article 175 of the Treaty.

The Council's argument based on its discretion was, in principle, correct. According to the scheme of the Treaty it was for the Council, in accordance with the procedural rules laid down in the Treaty, to establish the objectives of the common transport policy and decide upon the means of achieving them.

Similarly, it was for the Council to set priorities in the harmonization of legislation and administrative practice in this sector and to decide what the content of such harmonization should be.

The failure to adopt a common policy provided for by the Treaty, therefore, is not necessarily a failure to act sufficiently specific in nature to fall within the purview of Article 175. That remark is applicable in this case, even if it is true that work under Article 75 must be carried on continuously in order to make the progressive establishment of a common transport policy possible, and although it is also true that according to Article 75 (2) a substantial portion of that work should have been completed before the end of the transitional period.

2. FREEDOM TO PROVIDE SERVICES IN THE TRANSPORT SECTOR

The Parliament and the Commission argued that the provisions of Article 75 (1) (a) and (b) regarding the common rules applicable to international transport and the conditions under which non-resident carriers may operate transport services within a Member State were not only subject to a time-limit but also imposed obligations on the Council of a sufficiently specific nature that they could provide the basis for a declaration of failure to act under Article 175 of the Treaty. Both institutions emphasized the close link between those provisions and the freedom to provide services, the implementation of which is one of the principle tasks of the Community.

The Council disputed that contention, arguing that even in the context of Article 75 (1) (a) and (b) the content and objectives of the rules to be adopted were not sufficiently precise.

The Commission and the Netherlands Government emphasized the importance of the freedom to provide services.

The Court was therefore led to give detailed attention to the arguments of the parties regarding the freedom to provide services in the transport sector and its relationship to the establishment of a common policy in that sector.

The Commission took the view that Articles 59 and 60 are not directly applicable in the transport sector. Under Article 61 the freedom to provide services in the transport sector was to be implemented under the rules provided for by Article 75 (1) (a) and (b). That provision was intended to give the Council an appropriate period, which might if necessary extend beyond the end of the transitional period, to establish freedom to provide services in the transport sector within the framework of a common policy. That appropriate period could not however be extended indefinitely; more than fifteen years after the end of the transition period it should be approaching expiry.

In those circumstances, the Commission argued, in its judgment the Court should, by way of admonition, indicate when the reasonable period provided for by Article 61 came to an end.

The Court pointed out that Article 61 (1) provided that freedom to provide services in the field of transport was to be governed by the provisions of the Title relating to transport. According to the Treaty the application of the principles of the freedom to provide services (Articles 59 and 60) was therefore to be ensured by the implementation of the common transport policy and more particularly by the establishment of common rules on international transport and the conditions under which non-resident carriers may operate transport services within a Member State, the rules and conditions referred to in Article 75 (1) (a) and (b), which of necessity concern freedom to provide services.

The Parliament, the Commission, and the Netherlands Government were therefore correct to argue that the Council's obligations under Article 75 (1) (a) and (b) included the obligation to establish freedom to provide services in the transport sector, and that the scope of that obligation was clearly defined by the Treaty.

It followed that the Council does not have the discretion in that regard which it has in other areas of the common transport policy. In those circumstances the obligations laid down by Article 75 (1) (a) and (b), in so far as they are intended to establish freedom to provide services, are sufficiently precise to serve as the basis for a declaration of failure to act under Article 175. Under Article 75 (1) the Council was required to extend the freedom to provide services to the transport sector before the end of the transition period. Since the Council had failed to adopt the measures which should have been adopted before the end of the transition period measures whose object and nature could be identified with sufficient precision, the Court held that the Council had failed to act.

The Court added that it was for the Council to introduce the measures which it considered necessary to accompany the required measures of liberalization, and to decide in what order such measures should be adopted.

The second claim: failure to arrive at a decision on sixteen proposals submitted by the Commission

The European Parliament's second claim concerns the Council's failure to make a decision regarding sixteen proposals, listed in the application, submitted to it by the Commission.

The Court held that in so far as the proposals based on Article 75 (1) (a) and (b) were intended to contribute to the establishment of freedom to provide services in the transport sector, they were already covered by the Court's declaration that the Council had failed to act in that respect. In so far as they did not fall within that description, they belonged to the category of measures which might accompany the required liberalization measures, the adoption of which was a matter for the Council's discretion.

The Court held:
1. The Council has infringed the Treaty by failing to ensure freedom to provide services in the sphere of international transport and to lay down the conditions under which non-resident carriers may operate transport services in a Member State.
2. The remainder of the application is dismissed.

COMMENTS

1. The case should bear fruit in the practical sphere of transport; for competition in the air, see Joined Cases 209–213/84 *Ministère Public* v. *Lucas*

Asjes. Its implications at the constitutional level are even more important, for the Parliament now has another weapon against Council inaction.

2. The Court met the argument that Parliament's role was purely political by saying that this 'is not capable of affecting the interpretation of the provisions of the Treaty on the rights of action of the institutions'. Whether the statement (it can hardly be called a reason) is entirely candid must be decided in the light of the next extract. The case above vindicated the Parliament's right to sue for things not done; the next deals with its liability to be sued for what it did.

17 Case 294/83 *Les Verts* v. *Parliament*

1. *The action.* The European Ecology Party—the Greens (in French, Les Verts)—brought an action under EEC 173 against the Parliament, asking the ECJ to annul a decision to spend money on what was described by the Parliament as an information campaign leading up to its 1984 elections.

2. *The facts.* These are somewhat confused by the existence of several separate, and confederated, Ecology Parties, but the details can be disregarded. The applicant party has legal personality.

   2.1 The first direct elections took place in 1979; the Parliament's life is five years.

   2.2 The applicant party was in existence in 1982 but was not represented in the Parliament until 1984.

   2.3 EEC 142 enables the Parliament to adopt its own rules of procedure, which must include the power to spend money on its internal organization (see Financial Regulation of 21 December 1977, art. 18; OJ 1977 L 356/8).

   2.4 In the 1982 and subsequent budgets some 43m. ECU (approximately £25m.) was appropriated (as Item 3708) towards the 1984 elections.

   2.5 In a set of earlier cases, the Greens had challenged the Budget, but, by brief orders, the Court held their action inadmissible: Case 216/83 *Greens* v. *Parliament*.

   2.6 By a 1982 decision, Parliament settled how the budget sum allocated would be distributed: the lion's share went to parties who had gained seats in 1979; the lesser amount was available both to them and to new political groupings which put up candidates for the 1984 election.

   2.7 The Greens thought this unfair, but also challenged the decision on narrower legal grounds: that it was *ultra vires*, and that it was a misuse of powers in order to ensure the re-election of existing Members of Parliament. The Court decided on only the first ground.

3. *The legal issues.* The political issues in the previous extract were channelled into technical argument about the interpretation of EEC 175; the same happens here with EEC 173, and concerns the question of whether Parliament can be sued and whether the Greens can sue.

   3.1 *Defendant.* EEC 173 seems clear on the first point: the Court 'shall review the legality of acts of the Council and the Commission', and the next sentence confers jurisdiction 'for this purpose'. Only under ECSC 38 may the Parliament's acts be reviewed, and then only at the suit of the Commission or a Member State. Yet the ECJ reviews the growth of Parliament's powers since 1958 and concludes that to hold it unaccountable would betray the Court's mission to ensure that 'in the *interpretation* of this Treaty the law is observed' (EEC 164). Thus the ECJ finds in the Treaty itself a mandate to write words into EEC 173, thereby inevitably extending its own jurisdiction.

3.2 *Plaintiff.* Having held that the Parliament can be sued, the problem still remains that the Greens are not a privileged plaintiff. The expenditure decision was not specifically addressed to them (indeed it was addressed to its own author) and so they can sue under the second paragraph of EEC 173 only if it is 'of direct and individual concern' to them. One of the Greens' problems is that—on the Community level—they did not exist when the decision was taken. Nonetheless, the ECJ, finds the criteria of direct and individual concern to be satisfied.

3.3 *Vires.* Although EEC 138(3) forecasts a uniform electoral procedure, this has not been achieved. The principle of direct elections is governed by a 1976 Council Decision and Act, Article 7(2) of which provides that, until the attainment of uniformity, elections in each Member State are governed by the law of that State (see Rudden and Wyatt, *BCL*, 133). This must include the funding of campaign costs. The Parliament argued that its expenditure was simply an information campaign to explain its workings to the populace, but—as the money had to be spent during the election period—the Court was not convinced.

TEXT

DECISION

The Court's jurisdiction to hear an action under Article 173 against an act of the European parliament

The applicant association considers that, having regard to Article 164 of the Treaty, the power to review the legality of measures adopted by the institutions, which is granted to the Court by Article 173 of the Treaty, may not be limited to acts of the Council and the Commission without giving rise to a denial of justice.

The European Parliament also considers that the list of potential defendants to be found in Article 173 of the Treaty (the Council and the Commission) is not exhaustive.

It must be emphasized that the European Economic Community is a community based on law inasmuch as both the Member States and the institutions are subject to judicial review of the conformity of measures adopted by them with the basic constitutional charter represented by the Treaty.

An interpretation of Article 173 of the Treaty which would exclude measures adopted by the European Parliament from those which could be attacked would lead to a result which is contrary both to the spirit of the Treaty as expressed in Article 164 thereof and to its overall structure. The measures adopted by the European Parliament in the sphere governed by the EEC Treaty could encroach on the power of Member States or of the other institutions, or exceed the limits of the Parliament's powers without it being possible to submit those measures to review by the Court.

It must therefore be considered that an action for annulment will lie against measures adopted by the European Parliament which are intended to have legal effects *vis-à-vis* third parties.

The decision of 1982 and the rules of 1983 as measures intended to produce legal effects vis-à-vis third parties

The applicant association emphasizes that it has legal personality and that the contested decisions, since they entail the granting of aid to rival political groupings are certainly of direct and individual concern to them.

The European Parliament considers that in the present state of the Court's case-law concerning that condition, the applicant association's action is inadmissible.

It should first be noted that the contested measures are of direct concern to the applicant association. They constitute a complete set of rules which are sufficient in themselves and require no implementing provision, since the share of the appropriations to be allocated to each of the political groupings concerned is automatic and leaves no room for discretion.

It remains to be verified whether the applicant association is individually concerned by the contested measures.

In that connection it is necessary to consider principally the 1982 Decision. That decision approved the principles of allocating the appropriations entered in Item 3708 to the political groupings. It then fixed the share of those appropriations which was to be granted to the political groupings constituted in the Assembly elected in 1979 and to the non-attached members of that Assembly (69 per cent), and the share of the appropriations to be divided among all the political groupings, whether or not represented in the Assembly elected in 1979, which took part in the 1984 elections (31 per cent). Finally, it divided the 69 per cent between the political groupings and the non-attached members. The 1983 Rules must be regarded as an integral part of the above.

The 1982 Decision concerns all political groupings, even though the treatment accorded to them varies according to whether or not they were represented in the Assembly elected in 1979.

It must therefore be considered that the applicant association, which was already in existence at the time the 1982 Decision was adopted and which was likely to put up candidates in the 1984 elections, is individually concerned by the contested measures.

It must therefore be concluded that its application is admissible.

Substance of the case

In its first three submissions, the applicant association describes the scheme set up by the European Parliament as a scheme for the reimbursement of election campaign expenses.

In the first submission, the applicant association contends that the Treaty provides no legal basis for the adoption of such a scheme.

The second submission asks the Court to declare that, at all events, the question is covered by the concept of 'uniform electoral procedure' referred to in Article 138 (3) of the Treaty and, for that reason, in accordance with Article 7 (2) of the action concerning the election of the representatives of the Assembly by direct universal suffrage, is within the competence of the national legislature.

Finally, the applicant association's third submission complains of the lack of equal opportunity as between the political groupings inasmuch as those already represented at the Parliament elected in 1979 shared twice in the allocation of the appropriations entered in Item 3708. They shared first in the 69 per cent reserved for the political groups and non-attached members of the Assembly elected in 1979 and shared once again in the allocation of the 31 per cent reserve fund.

The European Parliament replies to the first two submissions together. It points out a contradiction between the two submissions: either the question is or is not within the powers of the Community, but the applicant association cannot put forward both of those arguments at the same time.

The European Parliament emphasizes that the scheme in question is not a scheme for the reimbursement of election campaign expenses but a contribution to an information campaign intended to make the Parliament more widely known among the electorate on the occasion of the elections, as is clear both from the remarks on Items 3708 and from the implementing rules. Since there is no question of reimbursement of election campaign expenses, the first and second submissions are without foundation.

Furthermore, the European Parliament contends that the Court should reject the third submission because the equality of opportunity of the various political groupings has not been affected. The purpose of the rules is to permit the effective dissemination of information regarding the Parliament.

In order to consider whether or not the first three submissions are well founded, the real nature of the financing scheme established by the contested measures must first be established.

It should first be noted that the contested measures are at the very least ambiguous. The 1982 Decision merely indicates that it deals with the allocation of the appropriations entered in Item 3708, whereas the informal memorandum intended to provide a synthesis of those rules speaks quite openly of financing the election campaign. With regard to the 1983 Rules, they do not state whether the expenditure which may be reimbursed thereunder must have served to provide information concerning the European Parliament itself or information concerning the positions which the political groupings have adopted or intend to adopt in the future.

It should be noted that the funds could be spent only during the election campaign. That is clear in regard to the 31 per cent reserve fund, which was shared among the groupings which took part in the 1984 elections. The expenditure which could be reimbursed was that incurred in connection with the 1984 European elections during the period from 1 January 1983 until forty days after the elections.

The same is true in regard to the 69 per cent of the appropriations shared among the political groups. Under those circumstances, it must be considered that the financing scheme set up cannot be distinguished from a scheme providing for the flat-rate reimbursement of election campaign expenses.

Secondly, it must be considered whether the contested measures were adopted in breach of Article 7(2) of the Act concerning the election of the representatives of the Assembly by direct universal suffrage of 20 September 1976.

According to that provision, 'pending the entry into force of a uniform electoral procedure and subject to the other provisions of this Act, the electoral procedure shall be governed in each Member State by its national provisions.'

The question of the reimbursement of election campaign expenses is not one of the points regulated by the Act of 1976. Consequently, in the present state of Community law, the establishment of a scheme for the reimbursement of election campaign expenses and the laying down of detailed arrangements for that purpose remain within the competence of the Member States.

There is therefore no need to rule on the other submissions.

The Court decided as follows:

1. The Decision of the Bureau of the European Parliament of 12 October 1982 allocating the appropriations entered in Item 3708 of the General Budget of the European Parliament, and the Rules adopted by the enlarged Bureau on 29 October 1983 governing the use of the appropriations for reimbursement of the expenditure incurred by the political groupings having taken part in the 1984 elections are void.
2. Each party is to bear its own costs.

COMMENTS

1. The Parliament did not raise the question of admissibility; it did not, that is, plead that it was missing from the possible defendants named in EEC 173.

The ECJ, however, raises the issue since it must justify its own jurisdiction under EEC 173.

2. The budget appropriation decision looks like a juridical act concerning several categories of entitled persons, defined in the abstract—in other words, its legal effect seems very similar to that of a Regulation. In numerous actions by individuals against such general acts, the Court has repeatedly held them inadmissible. Yet it contrived to give the Greens *locus standi* by holding them affected directly and *individually*. It must be admitted that this is difficult to reconcile with numerous earlier cases (for an example, see extract no. 19 below), but perhaps the Court is, if not overtly, reasoning from consequences: the Greens can stand for election, but if, once elected, they cannot sue then, every five years, only the old and established parties will be favoured.

3. Parliament's failure to plead that it was not a named defendant under EEC 173 was, no doubt, motivated by acceptance of legal responsibility for its own legal acts. Since Parliament can sue under EEC 175 (above, extract no. 15) and be sued under EEC 173, the ECJ will one day have to decide whether—although not named as plaintiff—it can sue under EEC 173; and, if so, whether it can mount a general attack like the Member States, Council, and Commission or whether, like individuals, it can challenge only those acts which touch it directly.

4. The Court annuls the decision, yet the money has been spent. EEC 176 requires the institution whose act has been declared void 'to take the necessary measures to comply with the judgment'. Perhaps the Parliament ought to require candidates (both winners and losers) who had received funds to repay them.

18 Case 34/86 *Council* v. *Parliament*[1]

1. *The action.* The Council brought an action against the Parliament under EEC 173, seeking either partial annulment of the 1986 Budget or annulment of the whole in the form in which the Parliament had purported to adopt it. The applicant was supported by the Federal Republic of Germany, France, and the UK.

2. *The salient, simplified facts*

2.1 The action concerns the procedure for the adoption of the Community budget, one of the few areas in which, under EEC 203, the Parliament has real legal power.

2.2 Community spending is divided into that which the Community is legally obliged to disburse (largely under the CAP) and the rest, a much smaller proportion known as 'non-compulsory expenditure' or NCE.

2.3 The rate of increase in NCE over that spent in the previous year is set by the Commission. However, under EEC 203 (9), para. 5, this rate can be increased by the Parliament and the Council *if they both agree* the new figure.

2.4 In the adoption of the 1986 Budget the Parliament increased NCE far beyond the Council limits, and the latter made clear its disagreement: the difference amounted to almost £50m. Nonetheless, the President of the Parliament purported to 'declare that the budget has been finally adopted' under EEC 203 (7).

2.5 The UK obtained an interim order limiting the Commission to acting on the non-contentious parts of the 1986 draft budget, and the Council brought this action.

3. *The legal issues*

3.1 After the success of the Greens in Case 294/83 (above extract no. 17), the problem of whether the Parliament can be sued under EEC 173 is easily resolved.

3.2 Similarly, although the precise facts are somewhat complex, the need for agreement between Council and Parliament is clearly spelled out in EEC 203 (9), para. 5, and so the latter's unilateral 'adoption' of the budget is obviously invalid.

3.3 The major problem facing the ECJ is that of what precise order to make. Its judgment on the 1986 budget is not handed down until half-way through that year, so that a simple quashing of both the budget and any action already taken under it would result in chaos. The Council wanted the ECJ to reinstate as a budget the draft which had emerged at an earlier stage, but the Court is understandably reluctant to make a budget for the

[1] Judgment was delivered just as this work was going to press; consequently the decision cannot here be given the close scrutiny it merits.

Community. It therefore 'annuls' the declaration adopting the entire budget but makes an imaginative extension of EEC 174, which in terms confers power to save something from the wreckage of only a *regulation* which the Court has held void.

TEXT
DECISION
Admissibility

The Parliament denied in the first place that the Council might rely on Article 173 of the EEC Treaty for the purposes of seeking the annulment of the budget as an act of the European Parliament.

It had to be pointed out that the Court had already held in its judgment in Case 294/83 *Parti Ecologiste, Les Verts* v *European Parliament* that by virtue of Article 173 an action for annulment might be brought against the acts of the European Parliament which were intended to have legal effects *vis-à-vis* third parties.

The general budget of the Communities was the instrument which set out forecasts of, and authorized in advance, the revenue and expenditure for each year. It followed that once the President of the Parliament made the declaration referred to in Article 203 (7), the budget ranked among the acts which were capable of producing legal effects *vis-à-vis* third parties.

Substance

It was possible to make three findings of fact in regard to the way in which the provisions of the maximum rate of increase had been applied:

1. The Commission, the Council, and the Parliament had all concurred in the view that the maximum rate of increase as fixed by the Commission was not adequate to enable the Community to function properly during the financial year 1986.

2. The Council and the Parliament had been unable to agree on a new maximum rate of increase although the positions which those two institutions finally adopted were quite close to each other.

3. The appropriations adopted by the Parliament at the second reading and ratified by the budget as adopted on 18 December 1985 by the President of the Parliament had accepted by implication the figures on the maximum rate established by the Council.

The finding under 2 was disputed by the Council which argued that, in exceeding the increases proposed at the second reading by the Council, the

Parliament had accepted by implication the figures on the maximum rate established by the Council.

It had to be stated in that respect that, although the Treaty provided that the maximum rate was to be fixed by the Commission on the basis of objective factors, no criterion had been laid down for the modification of that rate.

According to the fifth subparagraph of Article 203 (9), it was sufficient that the Council and the Parliament came to an agreement.

In view of the importance of such an agreement, which conferred on the two institutions, acting in concert, the freedom to increase the appropriation in respect of the NCE in excess of the rate declared by the Commission, that agreement might not be inferred on the basis of the presumed intention of one or other of those institutions.

The finding under 3 above was disputed by the Parliament which maintained that NCE for the financial year 1986 relating to the enlargement and the absorption of the 'cost of the past' had no equivalent in the financial year 1985. That expenditure could not therefore be covered by the procedure laid down by Article 203 (9).

That argument could not be accepted. The expression 'expenditure of the same type' in Article 203 (9) could only refer to the expenditure mentioned later in the same sentence, namely NCE. It followed, therefore, that the Treaty did not recognize the existence of NCE whose increase fell outside the scope of the maximum rate of increase.

In its defence, the Parliament further charged the Council with having acted illegally in submitting an incomplete draft budget, particularly inasmuch as it did not include the appropriations necessary in order to cover the enlargement and the absorption of the 'cost of the past'.

Whatever the impact of that argument might be on the exceeding of the maximum rate of increase by the amendments adopted by the Parliament, it was sufficient to state on that point that the determination of the exigencies posed, for the budget of the Communties, by special situations such as the accession of new Member States or the absorption of the 'cost of the past' was not a matter for the Court, but for the Council and the Parliament acting in concert.

It had therefore to be held that the act of the President of Parliament of 18 December 1985 whereby he declared the budget for 1986 finally adopted occurred at a time when the budgetary procedure had not yet been completed for want of an agreement between the institutions concerned on the figures to be adopted for the new maximum rate of increase. That act was therefore vitiated by illegality.

Consequences to be drawn

Although it was incumbent on the Court to ensure that the institutions which made up the budgetary authority kept within the limits of their powers, it might not intervene in the process of negotiation between the Council and the Parliament which was to result, with due regards for those limits, in the establishment of the general budget of the Communities.

It was therefore necessary to reject the Council's principal claim for a partial annulment of the budget, the effect of which would be to bring into force the version of that document resulting from the proposal made by the Council to the Parliament on 29 November 1985.

It had next to be remarked that the irregularity attaching to the act of the President of the Parliament of 18 December 1985 was to be traced to the fact that the two institutions had not reached agreement on the figures concerning the new maximum rate of increase.

Looking back on the situation as it presented itself at the time of the second reading of the budget by the Parliament, the Court was left with the impression that the respective positions adopted by the two institutions could hardly have constituted a serious obstacle to the possibility of arriving at an agreement.

It had to confine itself to holding that, since that essential agreement was lacking, the President of the Parliament could not lawfully declare that the budget had been finally adopted. That declaration had to be annulled, thus depriving the 1986 budget of its validity.

It was for the Council and the Parliament to take the necessary measures to comply with this judgment and to resume the budgetary procedure at the point at which the Parliament, at its second reading, had increased its appropriations in respect of NCE beyond the maximum rate of increase fixed by the Commission and without having come to an agreement with the Council on the figure for a new rate.

The declaration that the 1986 budget was illegal came at a time when a substantial part of the financial year 1986 had already elapsed.

In those circumstances, the need to guarantee the continuity of the European public service and also important reasons of legal certainty, which were to be compared with those which applied in the case of the annulment of certain regulations, justified the Court in exercising the power expressly conferred upon it by the second paragraph of Article 174 of the EEC Treaty.

In the particular circumstances of this case it had to be held that the annulment of the act of the President of the Parliament might not call in question the validity of the payment made and the commitments entered into in implementation of the 1986 budget up to the date of this judgment.

On those grounds, the European Court:

1. declared void the act of the President of the European Parliament of 18 December 1985, whereby he declared that the budget for 1986 had been finally adopted;
2. declared that the annulment of the aforesaid act of the President of the

European Parliament might not call in question the validity of the payment made and the commitments entered into in implementation of the budget for 1986 as published in the Official Journal, before the date of delivery of this judgment.

Judgment given 3 July 1986.

COMMENTS

1. Since the judgment left the Community without a budget, EEC 204 limits spending month by month to one-twelfth of the sums appropriated in the previous year's budget. The 1985 appropriations, of course, covered a smaller Community, since Portugal and Spain were then not members.

2. The institutional structure of the Community is marked more by separation, than by concentration, of powers. The Council, the Commission, and the Parliament are chosen in different ways and none of these institutions can control the other two. Members of the Council are, at least in theory, responsible to national Parliaments; Commissioners, although appointed by Governments, must be 'completely independent' (Merger Treaty 10 (2)); and the European Parliament is directly elected by the peoples of twelve countries. The general result is a separation of institutions, persons, powers, and political accountability. What the four preceding extracts demonstrate is the growth of interdependent *legal* accountability before the ECJ. The Council, Commission, and Parliament collaborate to make *laws*, but are becoming more and more answerable to the guardian of the *law*.

3. Just as the Court, in the absence of political will expressed in regulations and directives, made the internal market work (see the preceding sections), so it seems as if institutional problems which prove intractable to negotiated political solution are being passed to the Court. A simple example is to be found in the problem of the Parliament's seat. This ought to be determined 'by common accord of the Governments of the Member States' (EEC 216) but, in the conspicuous absence of any such agreement, is the subject of lawsuits by Luxemburg to keep part of the Parliament's activities there (cases 230/81, 108/83), and by France to keep part in Strasbourg (Case 51/86).

4. In Case 34/86, the Court resists the temptation offered by the Council to endow with legal validity an earlier version of the draft budget. It emphasizes that the task of making the budget, both politically and legally, is for the other institutions. Nonetheless, the Court observes sadly that the difference between the Council and the Parliament 'could hardly have constituted a serious obstacle'.

5. Comparisons must be treated cautiously, but it is interesting to note that within a week of this decision, the US Supreme Court declared unconstitutional a key provision of the Gramm–Rudman–Hollings Act. This

attempted to control federal budget deficits by establishing a mechanism to align spending and revenue, in the form of automatic cuts to be imposed by an officer of Congress, the Comptroller General. Thus the elective body of the US constitution was seeking to extend its powers at the expense of the executive, just as the European Parliament was attempting to override the Council.

III
Community Blunders

The first two parts contained cases selected to show the creation and development of Community common law. Many of them were preliminary rulings on interpretation given under EEC 177; and the extracts illustrate both the Court's community vision and the practical role it has played in fostering the legal framework of a thriving internal market. The last three were based on EEC 173-5 and concerned the interplay between Community institutions.

But the relation between institutions and Community citizens and firms is also of crucial importance, a fact recognized by the treaty in its provisions for judicial review of Community acts. In Case 294/83 *Les Verts* v. *Parliament* (above, extract no. 17), the Court said that the treaty established a complete system of legal remedies; but it must be admitted that the actual provisions are far from perfect. They combine norms of different juridical categories, ranging from that which confers jurisdiction on the Court, through those which attempt to list the substantive criteria to be applied in reviewing legality, and those specifying, dispensing with, or ignoring, the period within which an action must be begun, to those spelling out (or failing to spell out) the consequences of a successful attack.

The Articles in question comprise EEC 173-6, 184, 177 (*b*), and 178, together with 215; their interrelationship is delicate. EEC 173 is intended to be the main provision. It begins by saying that the Court *shall* review the legality of acts of the Council and the Commission other than recommendations or opinions; the last phrase demonstrates, if it were necessary, that things which have no legal effect (EEC 189) cannot be illegal. The next sentence *gives the Court jurisdiction* in actions by Member States, Council, or Commission on grounds of *ultra vires*, failure to comply with an essential procedural requirement, misuse of powers, and breach of either the Treaty or of 'any rule of law' affecting its application. The named plaintiffs need show no particular interest to have *locus standi*, but it looks as if the ECJ simply has no jurisdiction to hear a complaint which does not allege one of the listed grounds.

Nothing else in EEC 173 expressly confers on the Court any other jurisdiction in judicial review. An extension must, however, be implicit in the second paragraph which allows individuals to attack, on the same grounds, decisions and only decisions. This will often suffice—if the Commission takes a decision addressed to a firm, the firm can seek judicial review (as in Cases 56 and 58/64 *Consten and Grundig*, above, extract no. 8). If, however, an individual tries to attack something called a regulation, the Court has no jurisdiction save to allow him to attempt to persuade them that, despite its name, the measure in question is really a decision against him personally. Consequently, all EEC 173 suits by individuals against regulations begin (and most of them end) with an examination of admissibility.

EEC 175 is meant to be the other side of the coin; whereas EEC 173 allows acts to be challenged, EEC 175 does the same for inaction in breach of the Treaty, and draws a similar distinction between classes of plaintiff. Both remedies are subject to the same short time period of two months.

Together they set out, deliberately, to prevent individuals from challenging, or calling for, general measures. All is not lost, however, for the individual has two other ways of questioning a Community regulation: one is the ECJ, the other in a national court. The first will occur when, as often happens, a general regulation has to be applied by the Commission to concrete cases. The application will be by way of decision affecting the individual or firm involved, and the decision may be challenged in the ECJ under EEC 173. It is perfectly possible, however, that the decision is simply a straightforward exercise of the power conferred on the Commission by a regulation, and that what the applicant really objects to is the latter. In that situation, EEC 184 comes to the rescue by allowing, regardless of any time-limit, an attack to be mounted against the regulation. The grounds of attack are those listed in EEC 173 (thus it is an indirect review of the regulation's legality) and the result of a successful attack is a finding of the regulation's 'inapplicability' (whatever that may mean: see Hartley, *FCL*, 427). Examples will be found in: Case 20/71 *Sabbatini*; Case 92/78 *Simmenthal* v. *Commission*.

On the other hand many regulations—above all in the field of agriculture— are applied and administered by national agencies. Complaints about them will be litigated in the national courts, and it is here that EEC 177 (*b*) comes into its own. That provision enables the domestic court to seek a ruling, not merely on the meaning, but on the *validity* of a Community act. Nothing in the Treaty explicitly deals with the criteria for validity, nor with the effect of a ruling of invalidity. Yet—perhaps many years after its adoption—a regulation may thus be called in question by a national court.

The final weapon of the aggrieved individual is to sue the Community for damages under EEC 178, which confers jurisdiction on the ECJ, and EEC 215 which sets out studiously vague criteria for liability. This action must be brought within five years (Court Statute, art. 43).

Most complaints about Community action arise in connection with the common agricultural policy, and provoke strings of cases on very complex facts, figures, and documents. The extracts given below attempt to illustrate the foregoing brief account of remedies against the Community by concentrating on just one area. This should ensure a certain economy of effort by limiting the facts which need to be mastered, and may also provide the student with some insight into the common agricultural policy, and into the way in which the Community responded to the challenge of the discovery of something new to eat.

The Isoglucose Story: Prologue

In the simple Europe before the 1970s, cereals were cereals and sugar, sugar. Each is a quite different sector of agriculture, and each is subject to its own regime under the Common Agricultural Policy. The Americans, however, discovered a way to turn cereals into sugar—although that is, of course, a gross over-simplification of a more complex process. As corn grows, the plant makes simple sugars from which, in its seed, it makes starch. Enzymes (or our digestive process) can break this down again into its simple sugar components. The discovery was of an enzyme which breaks down the starch, not into a glucose, but to an equally simple sugar which tastes much sweeter. It is called variously isoglucose, isomerose, or 'glucose with a high fructose content'. This is not crystalline like the stuff we put in our tea, but liquid; nonetheless, it is a perfectly acceptable substitute for (and thus competitor with) sugar in the manufacture of soft drinks, jam, ice-cream, and confectionery.

Its introduction to the US agricultural scene caused relatively few problems, since that country produces too much grain and not enough sugar. In the EEC, however, there is too much of both. A small number of Community firms, within four groups of companies, went into the isoglucose business, thus straddling the two sectors of grain and sugar.

Their prospects must have looked promising. Under the then CAP, not only would their output in the sweeteners market be only slightly restrained, but, in the grain sector, they would benefit from the lower prices for their raw material resulting (quite deliberately) from a system of production refunds granted to the producers of certain cereals used to make starch. Almost immediately on their entry into the market, however, they lost the benefit of these refunds and were soon subjected to levies and quotas on their product. To date the lawsuits cover some 500 pages of the European Court Reports.

The firms' setbacks were all imposed by regulations issued under the Treaty's title on agriculture. EEC 43 (2) empowers the Council to act thus, on a proposal from the Commission and after consulting the Assembly; however, in terms of substance, this must be done within the objectives of the CAP spelled out in EEC 39, to which EEC 40 (3) adds that, in any case, there must be no discrimination between producers or consumers within the Community. What this means, essentially, is that there must, of course, be no discrimination between producers of the same product; hence, there must be no discrimination between producers of comparable products; and 'comparable' means 'competing'. As we have seen, isoglucose competes with sugar for a large sector of the sweet, food, and soft-drinks market.

Act I: Production Refunds

The basic CAP regime in the cereals sector is laid down in Regulation 2727/75 (see Rudden and Wyatt, BCL, 210). Some firms will buy some cereals for their starch content, if the price is low enough. If not, they will use chemical substitutes. The prices provoked by the basic regime were too high for these buyers. Consequently, 1975 Regulations, recognizing the need for cereals to remain competitive, gave production refunds in respect of certain cereals used to make starch and glucose. The aim of the scheme was to enable the grower to sell at a price low enough to compete with substitutes and to make up his income by claiming a refund from his national agricultural intervention authority (Regulation 2742/75 OJ 1975 L281/57). A year later, however, an amending Regulation increased the refunds except for materials used to make *isoglucose*; and they were to lose all refund in a year's time. The new scheme provided that the grower would get his higher refund in all cases; but, if the buyer used the product to make isoglucose, the national intervention agency was to claw from him the difference between the higher refund and the lower. Details were worked out by the Commission. (Council Regulation 1862/76 OJ 1976 L206/3; Commission Regulation 2158/76 OJ 1976 L241/21).

Regulations, says EEC 190, must state the reasons on which they are based. Those given in the preamble of the Council measure just described were:

Whereas ... it is necessary to increase production refunds; whereas, however, given the objectives of the production refund system, such an increase should not be retained in the case of products used in the manufacture of glucose having a high fructose content [i.e. isoglucose]; whereas the best method of implementing a measure of this type is to provide for recovery from the manufacturers concerned of the amount of the increase ...

According to the isoglucose manufacturers, the real reason for discriminating against them was the threat they posed to sugar producers. This was not mentioned by the Council, and no reason was given for the future entire withdrawal of refunds; the firms consequently thought the measure invalid.

The isoglucose producers had bought their raw material at a low price reflecting the increased refund paid to their seller, and were now expected to pay to the Community, via their national agricultural agency, the difference between the old and the new refund. Their problem was how to get a ruling on the validity of the Regulation. EEC 173 allows them to challenge only decisions; if the act in question is called a 'regulation' it is open to attack by a firm only if it can be shown to be, in effect, a disguised decision which is of direct and individual concern to the firm. On the other hand, EEC 177 (*b*) allows any national court simply to ask the ECJ to rule on the validity of any Community act (save, of course, the Treaties themselves), so regulations can easily be challenged provided their validity is relevant to the solution of some dispute before a national court.

The extracts from the two cases which follow illustrate the interplay between the two Treaty Articles. The first is a challenge under EEC 173, which both Council and Commission resist as being inadmissible. The plaintiff can show that the contested Regulation in fact affects only a small number of firms (four groups), but, because it is framed as being applicable to any isoglucose manufacturer, the ECJ follows the Advocate-General and nonsuits the plaintiff for lack of *locus standi*.

The second case in effect raises exactly the same questions about the same Regulation. The firm whose action under EEC 173 had been declared inadmissible challenged its national intervention agency's claim for the refunds paid to the supplier. The Dutch court, seised of the dispute, used EEC 177 to ask a number of questions as to the validity of the Regulation: were the reasons adequate? did it not discriminate against isoglucose producers? was its haste not a breach of the principle of legal certainty? and was it not a misuse of powers? It should be particularly noted that these are the kind of complaints often made in a direct action under EEC 173 for judicial review.

The ECJ was, of course, bound to hear the case and thus found itself deciding the very questions it had refused even to consider in the earlier action.

19 Case 101/76 *KSH* v. *Council and Commission*

TEXT

DECISION

1. The application seeks the annulment of Article 2 of Council Regulation (EEC) No. 1862/76 and Commission Regulation (EEC) no. 2158/76 laying down rules for the application of the Council Regulation.

2. The Council takes the view that the application is inadmissible in so far as it is directed against Regulation no. 1862/76, because it is brought against a measure of general application which does not concern the applicant directly and individually, and raises this objection before any discussion of the substance of the case.

3. The Commission considers that the question of the admissibility of the application arises in identical terms with regard to Regulation no. 1862/76 and Regulation no. 2158/76 since these two regulations are both in the nature of a legislative provision of the type referred to in the second paragraph of Article 173 of the EEC Treaty.

4. For the purposes of its defence it expressly adopts the submissions put forward in the Council's defence.

5. Article 173 of the EEC Treaty empowers a natural or legal person to contest a decision addressed to that person or a decision which, although in the form of a regulation or a decision addressed to another person, is of direct and individual concern to the former.

6. The objective of this provision is in particular to prevent the Community institutions from being in a position, merely by choosing the form of a regulation, to exclude an application by an individual against a decision which concerns him directly and individually.

7. The choice of form cannot change the nature of the measure.

8. In order to make a decision as to the admissibility of the application it is therefore necessary to examine whether the contested measures are regulations or decisions within the meaning of Article 173 of the Treaty.

9. By virtue of the second paragraph of Article 189 of the Treaty the criterion for distinguishing between a regulation and a decision is whether the measure at issue is of general application or not.

10. The nature of the contested measures must therefore be studied and in particular the legal effects which it is intended to or does actually produce.

11. It is necessary in this connection to consider the provisions in question in the context of the rules on production refunds for starches. ...

[The Court then describes the scheme, and continues:]

20. A regulation which provides for the reduction of a production refund for a whole marketing year with regard to a certain product processed from cereals and rice and for its complete abolition from the following marketing year is by its nature a measure of general application within the meaning of Article 189 of the Treaty.

21. It in fact applies to objectively determined situations and produces legal effects with regard to categories of persons regarded generally and in the abstract.

22. It only affects the applicant by virtue of its capacity as a producer of glucose having a high fructose content without any other specification.

23. Moreover, the nature of a measure as a regulation is not called in question by the possibility of determining more or less precisely the number or even the identity of the persons to whom it applies at a given moment as long as it is established that it is applied by virtue of an objective legal or factual situation defined by the measure in relation to the objective of the latter.

24. Moreover, the fact that a legal provision may have different actual effects for the various persons to whom it applies is not inconsistent with its nature as a regulation when that situation is objectively defined.

25. To refuse to acknowledge that rules on production refunds amounted to a regulation only because they concerned a specific product and to take the view that such rules affected the manufacturers of that product by virtue of circumstances which differentiated them from all other persons would enlarge the concept of a decision to such an extent as to jeopardize the system of the Treaty which only permits an application for annulment to be brought by any person against an individual decision which affects him as the person to whom it is addressed or against a measure which affects him as in the case of such a person.

26. For the same reasons it is necessary to sustain the objection raised by the Commission.

27. It follows that the application must be dismissed as inadmissible.

On those grounds, the Court hereby:
1. dismisses the application as inadmissible;
2. orders the applicant to bear the costs.

20 Case 125/77 *KSH* v. *Netherlands Intervention Agency*

TEXT

DECISION

The College van Beroep voor het Bedrijfsleven, pursuant to Article 177 of the Treaty, referred to the Court of Justice various questions concerning the validity of Council Regulation (EEC) no. 1862/76 and also the validity and interpretation of Commission Regulation (EEC) no. 2158/76 of 31 August 1976 laying down rules for the application of Regulation.

The reference by the national court shows that the plaintiff companies in the main action appealed against a decision of the Netherlands intervention agency, by which that agency claimed, in pursuance of the provisions of Council Regulation (EEC) no. 1862/76 and of Commission Regulation (EEC) no. 2158/76 payment of a levy applicable to the processing, carried out during the period from 1 August to 31 October 1976 inclusive, of maize starch into glucose having a high fructose content.

The file shows that the plaintiffs before the national court are starch producers who manufacture isoglucose, a glucose syrup having a high fructose content, the sale of which on the Community market in appreciable quantities goes back only to 1976 and which is manufactured from starch obtained from various cereals but most frequently from maize, a substantial part of which is imported from non-member countries.

Although isoglucose has in many respects the same characteristics as cane or beet sugar it differs in certain respects from the two latter products especially inasmuch as, in the present state of technical knowledge, it cannot be crystallized and at present can only compete with sugar in industries using sugar in a liquid form.

[The Court describes the production refunds system, and continues:]

Therefore, in the case of products used subsequently for the manufacture of glucose having a high fructose content, Article 2 of Regulation no. 1862/76 by using the expedient of 'recovery' in fact refused the increase in the production refund for the 1976/77 marketing year and abolished it as from the following marketing year.

The reasons on which Article 2 of Regulation no. 1862/76 is based, in so far as they emerge from the preamble to that regulation, are limited to the mere statement that, 'given the objectives of the production refund system, such an increase should not be retained in the case of products used in the manufacture of glucose having a high fructose content'.

However, the statement of reasons, laconic as it is, even omitting to mention the abolition of refunds for the manufacture of that product, must nevertheless be examined and assessed in the context of the whole of the rules of which Regulation no. 1862/76 forms an integral part.

The statements quoted above from the preambles to the Regulations show that the primary objectives of production refunds, as regards the market in starches, is to abolish the disadvantage to which the starch industry is subjected by reason of the application of common prices for the raw materials used by the industry and to enable it to maintain competitive prices in comparison with the prices of substitute chemical products.

When considered in the context of the system in which they took effect, the refusal to increase the refund and its subsequent elimination for starch intended for the manufacture of isoglucose, a product which is not or is hardly in competition with substitute chemical products, may be explained by the nature of the above-mentioned objectives of the system of production refunds to which reference is made in the preamble to Regulation no. 1862/76.

That reference to the purposes of the refund system, which moreover are well known to the circles concerned, satisfies the requirement under Article 190 of the Treaty for a statement of reasons and thus the validity of Regulation no. 1862/76 cannot be challenged on those grounds.

The national court in its second question asks whether Article 2 of Regulation no. 1862/76 is incompatible with the principle of non-discrimination which is fundamental to the Treaty and which is set out in particular in Article 40 of the treaty and whether Article 2 of the regulation is for that reason invalid.

Koninklijke Scholten-Honig NV, the only one of the plaintiffs which has submitted observations, lays particular stress on the fact that when Regulation no. 1862/76 puts manufacturers of starch for the production of isoglucose into an exceptional situation, it discriminates between the latter and the manufacturers of starch for other purposes.

The second subparagraph of Article 40 (3) of the Treaty provides that the common organization of agricultural markets 'shall exclude any discrimination between producers or consumers within the Community'.

The prohibition of discrimination laid down in the above-mentioned provision is merely a specific enunciation of the general principle of equality which is one of the fundamental principles of Community law.

This principle requires that similar situations shall not be treated differently unless the differentiation is objectively justified.

It must therefore be ascertained whether isoglucose is in a situation comparable to that of other products of the starch industry, in particular in the sense that they can be substituted for isoglucose in the specific use to which the latter product is normally put.

It is clear that there is no competition between starch and isoglucose or between isoglucose and the other products derived from starch except possibly glucose.

It emerges from the file that the considerable differences in the sweetening powers of isoglucose on the one hand and glucose on the other mean that the two products have different applications so that they cannot be in a comparable competitive situation with regard one to the other. Furthermore as isoglucose is a product which is at least partially interchangeable with sugar, the maintenance of the production refund in favour of manufacturers of isoglucose might at a subsequent stage have constituted discrimination against manufacturers of sugar who, for their part, do not enjoy an equivalent advantage.

Hence Article 2 of Regulation no. 1862/76 does not infringe the rule of non-discrimination between Community producers set out in the second subparagraph of Article 40 (3) of the Treaty.

The national court asks in the third question whether the alteration effected by Regulation no. 1862/76 in the system of granting refunds to the starch industry is incompatible with the principle of legal certainty, and, if so, whether the said regulation is in whole or in part invalid, in so far as it makes provision for the said alteration.

The plaintiff company referred to above lays particular stress on the fact that the sudden change of policy effected by Regulation no. 1862/76 conflicts with the principle of legal certainty.

It is necessary to call attention in the first place to the fact that isoglucose, a product which moreover was not in existence at the time of the adoption of Regulation no. 120/67, which brought into force a compulsory system of production refunds, does not fall within the category of products which this system is designed to help.

Moreover, as far as concerns the complaint that the change in the system of production refunds was introduced suddenly, it is advisable to bear in mind that pursuant to the provisions of Article 2 of Regulation no. 1862/72 the amount of the refund for starch processed into isoglucose was retained but not increased for the 1976/77 marketing year before being abolished as from the following marketing year.

The arguments with regard to legitimate expectation therefore have no foundation.

The national court asks in the fourth question whether the Council and the Commission, by adopting Regulations nos. 1862/76 and 2158/76 respectively, have misused their powers by altering the system of production refunds with a view to helping the sugar industry—which was not one of the objectives of the common organization of the market in cereals.

In formulating the Common Agricultural Policy the institutions are entitled to take account of the interplay of different markets.

Therefore the Council and the Commission could lawfully take into consideration the risk that production refunds in respect of starch for the manufacture of isoglucose might disturb the sugar market, although the said refunds did not appear to be necessary for attainment of the objectives of the organization of the market in cereals.

There can therefore be no question of a misuse of powers on the part of the Council or the Commission.

On those grounds, the Court in answer to the questions referred to it by the College van Beroep voor het Bedrijfsleven by a decision of 12 October 1977, hereby rules:

1. consideration of the questions raised has disclosed no factor of such a kind as to affect the validity of Council Regulation (EEC) no. 1862/76 and Commission Regulation (EEC) no. 2158/76.

COMMENTS

1. Not that when an action is brought under EEC 177 to test the *validity* of a Community act, the Court is forced to look closely at the facts.

2. In order to decide whether there has been unlawful discrimination in the treatment afforded to producers, the ECJ, in this case, compares the situation of isoglucose with that of other starch products. The Court concludes that they are not substitutes and so not competitors; hence a Regulation which treats them differently is not unfair. In the next case, the comparison is between isoglucose and sugar.

Act II: Production Levies

The next stage in the story is the adoption, in 1977, of a specific scheme for isoglucose, outside the common sugar organization (Regulations 1110/77 and 1111/77 OJ 1977 L134/1 and 4). The main Regulation (1111/77) recited that isoglucose is a direct substitute for liquid sugar; that there was a surplus of sugar, much of which had to be exported [at a loss]; and that isoglucose manufacturers should contribute to export costs by paying a levy. Essentially, the scheme adopted worked as follows. Sugar producers paid nothing on sales within their basic quota; for sales in the Community above that basic quota, they paid a levy; and indeed there was a maximum quota beyond which they could not sell in the Community at all. By contrast, the isoglucose scheme imposed a levy (though at a smaller basic rate) on *all* that was produced.

The firms were in competition with sugar producers and thought this scheme discriminatory, since it imposed a heavier burden on one set of producers within the same sector of the market. But the scheme was set out in a Regulation, so that they had no *locus standi* to challenge it directly under EEC 173. The English law of procedure came to their aid, and the English subsidiary of the Dutch firm simply brought an action in the Queen's Bench for a declaration that the Regulation was void. Such a question could clearly not be decided by a national court, and it took Donaldson J (as he then was) just five minutes to make a reference under EEC 177 (*b*). His question was simplicity itself: is the Regulation valid?

Other—equally straightforward—questions on other regulations were added, and the reference was joined with one from a Dutch court. In the proceedings, the Council and Commission defended the measures and the Advocate-General submitted that they were all valid. For ease of comprehension, many of the procedural and factual complexities are deleted from the extract which follows. Its purpose is to show the reasoning which led the ECJ to quash the scheme.

21 Joined Cases 103 and 145/77 *Royal Scholten-Honig* v. *Agricultural Intervention Board*

TEXT

DECISION

The national court has asked whether Regulations nos. 1111/77 and 1110/77 are invalid on one or more of the grounds pleaded before it by the plaintiffs.

It appears from the file that the most important grounds pleaded against the validity of the rules in question may be summarized as follows:

(*a*) They offend against the principle of proportionality by imposing on isoglucose manufacturers an altogether unfair charge to the advantage of sugar manufacturers.

(*b*) They contain no provision, and were followed by no rules of application, for the protection of the legitimate expectation of the plaintiffs.

(*c*) They infringe the Treaty because their provisions do not seek to attain or are in contradiction with the objectives of the common agricultural policy set out in Article 39 of the Treaty both jointly and severally.

(*d*) They infringe the Treaty because they embody a manifest discrimination contrary to the second subparagraph of Article 40 (3) of the Treaty.

(*e*) The levy is excessive and disproportionate as is shown by the fact that its effect is to make the manufacture of isoglucose unprofitable as compared with sugar on a market on which such products might otherwise be competitive so that it is thus eliminating a competitor from the market.

(*f*) The Commission and the Council have misused their powers inasmuch as they have sought by means of the levy to compensate for the real or supposed advantage of isoglucose from the point of view of competition.

(*g*) The regulations are based on an altogether inappropriate and/or false estimate of the costs of production of isoglucose and/or on an altogether erroneous appreciation of the role of isoglucose and of its potential market.

The first question to be examined is whether Regulation no. 1111/77, in establishing the production levy for isoglucose, infringed the prohibition on discrimination laid down in the second subparagraph of article 40 (3) of the Treaty.

In this respect inquiry must be made whether isoglucose and sugar are in comparable situations.

The second recital in the preamble to Regulation no. 1111/77 states that 'isglucose is a direct substitute for liquid sugar obtained from sugar-beet or cane' and the seventh recital states that isoglucose is 'a substitute product in direct competition with liquid sugar'.

As the Council has subsequently recognized as the markets in sugar and isoglucose are closely linked and there are structural surpluses in the Community sugar sector, any Community decision on one of those products necessarily affects the other.

Nevertheless it must be pointed out that isoglucose manufacturers and sugar manufacturers are treated differently as regards the imposition of the production levy.

In fact, in contrast to the production levy which only affects Quota B sugar, the levy applied by Article 9 of Regulation no. 1111/77 is applied to the whole of isoglucose production. Within the limits of Quotas A and B, sugar manufacturers enjoy a guarantee of marketing at the intervention price and are entitled to the benefit of the export refund system whereas isoglucose manufacturers do not enjoy any similar advantages. Even when account is taken of the fact that of the amount of the production levy on isoglucose was limited, the difference in treatment still exists as the isoglucose manufacturers do not enjoy the marketing guarantees provided for manufacturers of normal sugar.

It is also important to note that it emerges from the Commission's calculations that each increase in the total production of sugar outside the basic quota has the effect of increasing the average charge to be borne by the manufacturer so that the latter is in a position to reduce the amount of the said charge by limiting his production whereas for the isoglucose manufacturer a limitation on production remains without any effect as regards the amount per unit of weight of the production levy brought into force by Regulation no. 1111/77.

Moreover the Council and the Commission emphasize the practical difficulties which certain alternative solutions would have presented, in particular the establishment of a quota system for isoglucose, regard being had to the fact that the latter is a product newly arrived on the Community market and that its production is in the process of increasing rapidly.

However, inconveniences of the type alleged cannot justify the imposition of a charge which is manifestly unequal. Accordingly the provisions of Regulation no. 1111/77 establishing the production levy system for isoglucose offend against the general principle of equality of which the prohibition on discrimination set out in Article 40 (3) of the Treaty is a specific expression.

The answer must therefore be that Regulation no. 1111/77 is invalid to the extent to which Articles 8 and 9 thereof impose a production levy on isoglucose of 5 units of account per 100 kg of dry matter for the period corresponding to the sugar marketing year 1977/78.

There is therefore no need to examine the other grounds put forward by the plaintiffs or to give a ruling on the validity of Regulation no. 1110/77.

However, the above answer will leave the Council free to take any necessary measures compatible with Community law for ensuring the proper functioning of the market in sweeteners.

On those grounds, the Court in answer to the question referred to it hereby rules:

Council Regulation no. 1111/77 of 17 May 1977 is invalid to the extent to which Articles 8 and 9 thereof impose a production levy on isoglucose of 5 units of account per 100 kg of dry matter for the period corresponding to the sugar marketing year 1977/78.

COMMENTS

1. The ECJ sees in the non-discrimination clause of EEC 40 (3) merely a specific enunciation of a fundamental principle of Community law—equality of treatment in like situations. Having accepted that the Regulation under attack appears to treat two products differently, the Court investigates whether they are alike. In this context, that means whether they are substitutes on the relevant market. If they are, the difference may be upheld only if justified by some other reason. This justification must be made by the Community institutions which seek to impose the difference in treatment.

2. If a legal act is successfully attacked under EEC 173, then the ECJ must declare it void (EEC 174), and its author must do what is necessary to comply with the annulment (EEC 176). In principle, the Court's judgment has effect *ex tunc* and *erga omnes*; which is a shorthand way of saying that the annulment has retrospective effect and anyone may treat the measure as never having existed. Uncertainty is lessened by the fact that an attack under EEC 173 must be mounted within two months; and, under EEC 174, the ECJ can annul a regulation but allow some of its effects to survive: See Case 264/82 *Timex*.

3. But a reference under EEC 177 is simply a question by one court faced with a particular domestic dispute. The effect on other courts (and other people) of a ruling on *interpretation* was discussed in connection with Case 28/62 *Da Costa en Schaake*, above extract no. 2. The Article also allows national courts to query the *validity* of Community legal acts, but says nothing whatever about the effect on others or on the institutions concerned of a preliminary ruling that the measure in question is invalid. It can hardly amount to an annulment, that is to say, the Court's judgment cannot itself, as it were, 'repeal' the measure: see Case 16/65 *Schwarze*.

Of course, the court which made the reference cannot apply the measure. In pure theory, it seems to remain valid for other courts, and certainly some other court could make a reference, in effect asking the ECJ to reverse itself and hold the measure valid. This has never happened, however, and seems unlikely. But to go to the other extreme and hold that a ruling of invalidity under EEC 177 is the same as annulment under EEC 173 would cause serious problems, for there is no time-limit whatever on the making of a reference by a national court. The problem was discussed at some length by several Advocates-General: Case 31/70 *Getreide und Futtermittel Handelsgesellschaft* v. *Hauptzollamt Hamburg Altona*; Case 16/65 *Schwarze*; Case 185/73 *Hautpzollamt Bielefeld* v. *König*; Case 112/76 *Manzoni* v. *Fonds National de Retraite des Ouvriers Mineurs*. Finally, in Case 66/80 *ICC*, the ECJ held directly that other national courts could either ignore, or refer, a regulation held invalid in an earlier preliminary ruling.

4. This does not solve the problem of a national court confronted with a regulation which is technically distinct from, but in substance the same as, one already held invalid. Recently, the English Divisional Court, while emphasizing that it was not passing on the validity of the second regulation, has—with the consent of the parties—adopted the same solution as that which flowed from the declaration of invalidity of the first: Case 181/84 *Man Sugar*.

5. Practical difficulties are eased by the way in which the ECJ, by analogy with EEC 176, when it rules that a measure is invalid, calls on the institution concerned to correct the situation. Thus, in this case, the Court says that its answer 'will leave the Council free to take any necessary measures compatible with Community law for ensuring the proper functioning of the market in sweeteners'. This decision was handed down in October 1978, and in June of the following year the Council adoted (or tried to adopt) a Regulation which formally repealed the offending parts of Regulation 1111/77 and set up a new scheme analogous to that applied to sugar. The grave difficulties which beset this attempt are revealed in Act IV.

Act III: Actions for Compensation

While the proceedings in the preceding extracts had been under way, the producers had lost money. They had suspended production because, if they had failed to persuade the ECJ that the levy was unlawful, manufacture of isoglucose would have been uneconomic. The Dutch firm KSH had invested in the building of a huge plant at Tilbury, which it had had to sell off. It ended up in liquidation, while two other firms had each made large losses. So there were a few victims, each having sustained quantifiable and foreseeable damage by the adoption of the challenged (and invalid) regulation.

The preceding extract shows how the Regulation imposing production levies was successfully attacked in references under EEC 177. That article is followed by EEC 178 which gives the ECJ jurisdiction in claims for compensation. The relevant law for determining liability is contained in EEC 215, whose second paragraph says: 'In the case of non-contractual liability, the Community shall, in accordance with the general principles common to the laws of the Member States, make good any damage caused by its institutions or by its servants in the performance of their duties.' Clearly the invalid measure was issued by the Community institutions; it appears to have caused grave losses. In its judgment on validity, the ECJ had rebutted the institutions' arguments by saying 'inconveniences of the type alleged cannot justify the imposition of a charge which is manifestly unequal'. The plaintiffs must have thought they had a good case. Three actions were brought, two of which were joined. The arguments, Advocate-General's submissions, and much of the judgment are either the same or very similar in all three. Only the fundamentals are extracted.

22 Joined Cases 116 & 124/77 *Amylum and Tunnel* v. *Council and Commission*

TEXT

DECISION

The applicants are not claiming from the national authorities reimbursement of the production levies overpaid but are seeking to obtain compensation from the Community for losses resulting in particular from the reduction in sales of isoglucose and from operating deficits and other losses which they claim to have suffered as a result of the introduction of the levy laid down by Regulation no. 1111/77 and declared invalid by the Court in its judgment of 25 October 1978. According to Amylum the damage caused to it by the entry into force of Regulation no. 1111/77 consists, for the most part, on the one hand in the reduction in its profit margin resulting from the replacement of sales of isoglucose by alternative sales of starch and glucose and, on the other hand, in the loss of its profit margin resulting from the reduction in grinding during the early months following the establishment of the levy, a step made necessary by the absence during that period of outlets for the alternative products. Amylum is also claiming the cost of the bank guarantee referred to above and the expenditure in which it claims to have been involved in the defence of its interests before the Belgian authorities.

According to Tunnel the damage for which it is claiming compensation and which is attributable to the isoglocuse production levy established by Regulation no. 1111/77 consists in the loss of production of its factory, the loss of profits resulting from the production of dry starch instead of isoglucose, additional costs for storage and handling of starch as well as losses incurred by reason, on the one hand, of higher unit costs in its undertaking due to reduced isoglucose production and, on the other hand, of supplementary investments effected to increase production of substitute products.

Since the Court has already established in its judgment of 25 October 1978 that the imposition of an isoglucose production levy was incompatible with the principle of equality, the first question which arises in these cases is whether the illegality is such as to involve the Community in liability under the second paragraph of Article 215 of the Treaty. A finding that a legal situation resulting from legislative measures by the Community is illegal is insufficient by itself to involve it in liability. In this connection the Court referred to its consistent case-law in accordance with which the Community does not incur liability on account of a legislative measure which involves choices of economic policy unless a sufficiently serious breach of a superior rule of law for the protection of the individual has occurred. Having regard to the principles in the legal systems of the Member States, governing the liability of public authorities for damage caused to individuals by legislative measures, the Court has stated that in the context of Community legislation in which one of the chief features is the exercise of a wide discretion essential for the implementation of the common agricultural policy, the liability of the Community can arise only exceptionally in cases in which the institution concerned has manifestly and gravely disregarded the limits on the exercise of its powers.

This is confirmed in particular by the fact that, even though an action for damages under Articles 178 and 215 of the Treaty constitutes an independent action, it must nevertheless be assessed having regard to the whole of the system of legal protection of individuals set up by the Treaty. If an individual takes the view that he is injured by a Community legislative measure which he regards as illegal he has the opportunity, when the implementation of the measure is entrusted to national authorities, to contest the validity of the measure, at the time of its implementation, before a national court in an action against the national authority. Such a court may, or even must, in pursuance of Article 177, refer to the Court of Justice a question on the validity of the Community measure in question. The existence of such an action is by itself of such a nature as to ensure the efficient protection of the individuals concerned.

These considerations are of importance where, as in these cases, the Court, within the framework of a reference for a preliminary ruling, has declared a production levy to be illegal and where the competent institution, following that finding, has abolished the levy concerned with retroactive effect.

It is appropriate to inquire in the light of these considerations whether, in the circumstances of these cases, there has been, on the part of the Council and the Commission, a grave and manifest disregard of the limits which they are required to observe in exercising their discretion within the framework of the common agricultural policy.

In this respect it must be recalled that the Court did not declare invalid any isoglucose production levy but only the method of calculation adopted and the fact that the levy applied to the whole of the isoglucose production. Having regard to the fact that the production of isoglucose was playing a part in increasing sugar surpluses it was permissible for the Council to impose restrictive measures on such production.

Although, in its judgment of 25 October 1978, giving a preliminary ruling within the framework of a consideration of the validity of Regulation no. 1111/77, the Court found that the charges borne in pursuance of that regulation by isoglucose producers by way of production levy were manifestly unequal as compared with those imposed on sugar producers, it does not follow that, for the purposes of an assessment of the illegality of the measure in connection with Article 215 of the Treaty, the Council has manifestly and gravely disregarded the limits on the exercise of its discretion.

In fact, even though the fixing of the isoglucose production levy at five units of account per 100 kg of dry matter was vitiated by errors, it must nevertheless be pointed out that, having regard to the fact that an appropriate levy was fully justified, these were not errors of such gravity that it may be said that the conduct of the defendant institutions in this respect was verging on the arbitrary and was thus of such a kind as to involve the Community in non-contractual liability.

It must also be recalled that Regulation no. 1111/77 was adopted in particular to deal with an emergency situation characterized by growing surpluses of sugar and in circumstances which, in accordance with the principles set out in Article 39 of the Treaty permitted a certain preference in favour of sugar beet, Community production of which was in surplus, whilst Community production of maize was to a considerable extent deficient.

It follows from these considerations that the Council and the Commission did not disregard the limits which they were required to observe in the exercise of their discretion in the context of the common agricultural policy in such a serious manner as to incur the non-contractual liability of the Community.

The applications must be dismissed as unfounded.

On those grounds, the Court hereby:

1. dismisses the applications;
2. orders the applicants to pay the costs.

COMMENTS

1. The notion that a law-maker may be liable to pay compensation for adopting a law which is then held invalid is unfamiliar to the English. It could not, of course, arise in respect of their statutes, for these cannot be invalidated; in principle, only their maker may repeal them. It might, however, arise where subordinate legislation is quashed.

2. The plaintiffs Amylum and Tunnel were not seeking to recover sums paid to the national authorities, so this is not some sort of restitution action. It is a pure claim for compensation.

3. EEC 215 instructs the ECJ to seek inspiration from the general principles of law common to the Member States. Some of these do have a 'public law' of liability for bungled, or discriminatory, legislation.

4. The ECJ refers to this body of law in repeating its general rule on liability for unlawful legislation. It is not enough that the regulation be unlawful and so quashed; it is not enough that, while in existence, it caused loss; its adoption still gives rise to no liability 'unless a sufficiently serious breach of a superior rule of law for the protection of the individual has occurred'. Thus the Court

grades rules of law according to some notion of their intrinsic value: some are superior to others. Among these superior rules, some have the function of protecting individuals, and in the preceding case the ECJ described the non-discrimination rule as being a specific application of a fundamental principle of equality. Even so, compensation is not payable unless this principle is infringed in a sufficiently serious way.

5. Breach of '*any* rule of law' is one of the grounds mentioned in EEC 173 as enabling a Community act to be declared void in direct proceedings for judicial review. But it does not follow that, because a legislative measure has been quashed under EEC 173 or declared invalid under EEC 177 (*b*), therefore its author must pay damages. In this case, the ECJ holds that the mere existence of ways of getting the measure annulled 'is by itself of such a nature as to ensure the efficient protection of the individuals concerned'. This may well be true in long-term economic theory: firms would adjust, withdrawing some production facilities, switching product, or laying off employees. But, first, any particular manufacturer may not be able to hold out until the long run—the Dutch firm went under. And, secondly, the short-term injury goes uncompensated; if it is passed on in higher prices, the buyers lose.

6. The ECJ finds for the defendants in a series of steps which merit reflection. First, it recalls that the judgment on validity did not decide that no levy should be charged, merely that it should be calculated so as to impose an equal burden on the two comparable products. But the firms were not objecting to a levy; only to one which, being 'manifestly unequal' presumably placed them at a market disadvantage in the competition for customers. Secondly, the Court says that the Community's errors were not so grave as to verge on the arbitrary, which suggests that attention is being paid to the mental element involved. The Advocate-General submits that liability for an invalid regulation depends on the presence of (his emphasis) *serious* fault. Thirdly the ECJ points out that the Regulation was provoked by an emergency, namely the sugar surplus. But the plaintiffs did not build this mountain: it was the result of the generous prices set by the Council and Commission in the regulations for the common market in sugar; and in the preceding case, the ECJ had held that there should be no discrimination. Finally, it is understandable that the Court should be reluctant to expose the Community to liability to an indefinite range of plaintiffs and in an incalculable amount. But in the present case, the possible plaintiffs were few in number, the nature of the damage that would be caused by hindering their competition with sugar was foreseeable, and their particular losses were both calculable and grave.

7. There have been many other actions for compensation for unlawful Community acts (see Hartley, *FCL*, 487). At first, the ECJ held that they could not succeed unless the act itself had been set aside in proceedings under EEC

173 or 177 (Case 25/62 *Plaumann* v. *Commission*). This ruling was severely criticized, and later the Court changed its mind and held that the action for compensation was independent (Case 4/69 *Lütticke* v. *Commission*; Case 5/71 *Zuckerfabrik Shöppenstedt* v. *Commission*). From this point on, the action for compensation becomes a complement to that for judicial review. The firm which has no *locus standi* to attack a regulation under EEC 173, has been the addressee of no decision applying the regulation so as to be able to use EEC 173 against the former and EEC 184 against the latter, and cannot persuade a national court to query the regulation's validity under EEC 177 (*b*), may bring an action for compensation under EEC 215. Indeed a plaintiff could claim compensation for a *valid* measure if, for instance, it did not contain an adequate transitional period to enable the firm to adjust (Case 74/74 *CNTA* v. *Commission*). All this, however, is true more in theory than in reality.

8. In practice, few such actions have succeeded, even where the measure whose adoption caused the loss has been quashed. The case under discussion is a striking example. Others, which in various ways test the criterion of a 'sufficiently serious breach of a superior rule of law' are: Cases 5, 7, and 13–24/66 *Kampffmeyer* v. *Commission*; Cases 83 and 94/76, 4, 15, and 40/77 *Dried milk 2*; and the string of cases known as *Gritz and Quellmehl*: 64/76 *et al.*; 238/78; 241/78 *et al.*; 261 and 262/78.

9. Even where, as a result of the Commission's errors, an individual has been jailed, we find the defendant invoking the need for him to prove 'a sufficiently serious breach of a superior rule of law'. The case is given later (extract no. 26).

Act IV: The Parliament Slighted

The next stage concerns matters of such fundamental importance that much of the Court's judgment is given in full. All that need be done is to set the scene.

The basic thrust of the isoglucose Regulation 1111/77 was declared invalid in a judgment of October 1978 (above, extract no. 21). The isoglucose production levy was not being collected at all, so that, having been treated worse, the product was now in a better market position than sugar. A new regulation was therefore needed, which would treat both products equally. The empowering provision of the Treaty (EEC 43 (2)) requires that agricultural measures of this nature be drafted by the Commission and that the Assembly be consulted before their adoption by the Council.

In March 1979—five months after the judgment—the Commission draft was ready. Like the sugar regime, the scheme was to come into force at the beginning of July. Its general provisions announced a basic quota for every isoglucose producer in the Community (equal to twice its production for the half year ending in April 1979) which could be sold freely; the method of calculating a maximum quota was then given, and sales above the basic but below the maximum were subject to a levy; production exceeding the maximum could not be sold in the Community. The draft Regulation thus resembles the sugar scheme and, so far, is 'abstract' in nature, capable of covering any Community isoglucose firm. However, its Annex went on to apply its own methods of calculation to six separate manufacturers, spelling out the precise number of tonnes comprising the basic quota of each.

A fortnight after receiving this draft, the Council (as it was bound to do under EEC 43 (2)), sent it to the Parliament, pointing out that it was to come into force the following July and asking for it to be considered at Parliament's April session.

The draft came before the Parliament in April and May, but no final decision was taken. It was being reconsidered by the Agriculture Committee when the Parliament died. In June 1979 were held the first direct elections for the European Parliament, and the powers of the old members came to an end on 17 July when the new Parliament held its first session: Council Decision on Direct Elections, 1976, art. 10 (4) (see Rudden and Wyatt, *BCL*, 133).

Meanwhile, a regulation was urgently needed. Consequently, in June, the Council adopted the draft, which appeared as Regulation 1293/79 (OJ 1979 L162/10). Up to this moment, every regulation adopted under EEC 43 (2) had begun by saying 'having regard to the opinion of the European Parliament [or, in the earlier years, Assembly]'. This one said 'having regard to the fact that the European Parliament has been consulted' and went on to explain that 'the European Parliament has been consulted [but] did not deliver its opinion' and that 'the judgment of the Court of Justice must be implemented before too long [and] it is extremely important for the public that the isoglucose arrangements be adopted before the beginning of the sugar year on 1 July 1979.'

The Council action infuriated both the firms and the new Parliament. At the time it was thought that the latter had no individual cause of action before the ECJ, because it is missing from the list of permitted plaintiffs under EEC 173 (but consider now the implications of Case 294/83 *Les Verts* v. *Parliament*, above, extract no. 17).

At first glance, moreover, it would seem that the firms could not use EEC 173, because no individual may challenge a regulation. This particular measure, however, did two things: it laid down a general regime—the normal province of a regulation; then, in its Annex, it applied its own scheme to particular firms—which is what a decision does. If, as commonly happens, the Regulation had merely laid down abstract rules and then told the Commission to apply them to particular cases, the latter's act in relation to any given firm would have been a decision addressed to that firm. This, the firm could have challenged under EEC 173; and, when the Commission explained that it was empowered to take the decision by the regulation, the firm could have used EEC 184 to attack the whole regulation, pleading any of the grounds set out in EEC 173. This circuity should not be necessary when the regulation applies its own criteria to individual firms.

Consequently, two of the firms named filed actions under EEC 173 against that provision of the Annex fixing their respective quotas; they thus brought into question the whole Regulation. The Parliament decided to intervene, basing its step on the Court Statute, art. 37: 'Member States and other institutions of the Community may intervene in cases before the Court' (see Rudden and Wyatt, *BCL*, 119).

The litigation, then, involved three issues.

1. *Admissibility*. The Council challenged the firms' right to bring proceedings under EEC 173 against a regulation. However, the curious form of this Regulation has been discussed above. It is interesting to note that the Commission did not bother to argue the admissibility point, confining itself to the rather weary observation that if, on the grounds of inadmissibility, the ECJ did not decide the validity of the Regulation in this case, it would soon be faced with a reference on the very same question under EEC 177 (*b*).

2. *Intervention*. As laid down in the Treaties, the Parliament's standing before the Court is rather strange. At that time it could not, apparently, be

Act IV: The Parliament Slighted

plaintiff or defendant under EEC 173 but could bring a suit for inaction under EEC 175. Under the Court Statute, it probably cannot file briefs in actions under EEC 177 (art. 20) but, says Article 37, may apparently intervene 'in cases before the Court'. The intervener must support one of the parties.

3. *Annulment.* Two sorts of reason for annulment were pleaded. The firms argued the merits: having, in the earlier case protested that they were treated differently from sugar, they now maintained that it was unfair to treat in the same way an industry which had existed for 150 years, and the fledgling isoglucose enterprises; and that their quotas should not be calculated by reference to a half-year during which, because of the legal uncertainties, output was low. They, and of course the Parliament, also argued one of the clear grounds of illegality spelled out in EEC 173: breach of an essential procedural requirement.

This raised the question of what is meant on the numerous occasions when the Treaty empowers the Council to make laws only 'after consulting the Assembly'. Did sending the draft count as consultation, or was consultation complete only when the Council received a reply? It should be pointed out that the Council was never bound by this reply; if, having read it with respect, the Council ignored Parliament's views and adopted its original draft, there would be no breach of the Treaty whatever: EEC 137 confers upon the Assembly only 'advisory and supervisory powers'.

The Commission supported the Council, observing that the Parliament had had plenty of time to deliver its opinion on the draft.

The Parliament naturally contended that the Council had at least to receive and consider its opinion. Furthermore, the Council's preamble to the Regulation pleaded the urgency of the matter and its importance to the public: to this, the Parliament rejoined that it was for the Parliament, and not the Council, to determine the public interest; and, as EEC 139 empowers either the Council or the Commission to convoke a special session, this could have been done if the draft was so important.

If the ECJ were persuaded that the consultation procedure required by the Treaty had not been followed, it would have to declare the Regulation void. Its decision, however, would not be given until the autumn of 1980, so that simple annulment would retrospectively undermine a scheme of eighteen months' standing. Consequently, both Commission and Advocate-General submitted that the ECJ should make use of its power under EEC 174 which ends with an enigmatic sentence to the effect that the Court shall, if necessary, 'state which of the effects of the regulation which it has declared void shall be considered as definitive'. This invitation to salve something from the wreckage was not accepted by the Court.

The two cases were not joined, but the arguments and decision are similar, and the Advocate-General gave only one submission. The extract which follows omits some of the discussion of the detailed merits of the new scheme.

23 Case 138/79 *Roquette Frères* v. *Council*

TEXT

DECISION

1. It is apparent from consideration of the application that it is an application for a declaration that Regulation no. 1293/79 is void in so far as it fixes a production quota for isoglucose in respect of the applicant.

2. In support of its application, the applicant, apart from various substantive submissions, makes a formal submission that its production quota fixed by the said regulation be declared void on the ground that the Council adopted that regulation without having received the opinion of the European Parliament as required by Article 43 (2) of the EEC Treaty which action constitutes an infringement of an essential procedural requirement within the meaning of Article 173 of the said Treaty.

3. By order of 16 January 1980 the Court allowed the Parliament to intervene in support of the applicant's claims of infringement of essential procedural requirements. By order of 13 February 1980 it also allowed the Commission to intervene in support of the Council.

4. The Council contended that both the application and the intervention in favour of the applicant were inadmissible. Alternatively it contended that the application should be rejected as unfounded.

5. Before considering the questions of admissibility raised by the Council and the claims made by the applicant it is well to recall briefly the history of the adoption of the contested regulation and the provisions thereof.

6. In Joined Cases 103 and 145/77 the Court held that Council Regulation no. 1111/77 laying down common provisions for isoglucose was invalid. The Court found that the system offended against the general principle of equality (in those cases between sugar and isoglucose manufacturers) of which the prohibition on discrimination as set out in Article 40 (3) of the Treaty was a specific expression. The Court however added that its judgment left the Council free to take any necessary measures compatible with Community law for ensuring the proper functioning of the market in sweeteners.

7. On 7 March 1979 following that judgment the Commission submitted a proposal for an amendment of Regulation no. 111/77 to the Council. By letter of 19 March 1979 received by the Parliament on 22 March the Council asked the Parliament for its opinion pursuant to the third subparagraph of Article 43 (2) of the Treaty. In its letter seeking an opinion it wrote that:

This proposal takes account of the position after the judgment of the Court of 25 October 1978 in anticipation of new arrangements for sweeteners which should enter into force on 1 July 1980. ... Since the regulation is intended to apply as from 1 July 1979, the Council would welcome it if the European Parliament could give an opinion on the proposal at its April session.

8. The urgency of the consultation requested in the Council's letter related to the fact that in order to avoid inequality of treatment between sugar manufacturers and isoglucose manufacturers the proposed regulation was basically intended to subject isoglucose production to rules similar to those applying to sugar manufacture until 30 June 1980 pursuant to the common organization of the market in sugar. In particular it was a question of making transitional arrangements for production quotas for isoglucose which were to apply from 1 July 1979 which was the beginning of the new sugar marketing year.

9. The President of the Parliament immediately referred the matter to the Committee on Agriculture for further consideration and to the Committee on Budgets for its opinion. The Committee on Budgets forwarded its opinion to the Committee on Agriculture on 10 April 1979. On 9 May 1979 the Committee on Agriculture adopted the motion for a resolution of its Rapporteur. The report and draft resolution adopted by the Committee on Agriculture were debated by the Parliament at its session on 10 May 1979. At its session on 11 May the Parliament rejected the motion for a resolution and referred it back to the Committee on Agriculture for reconsideration.

10. The parliamentary session from 7 to 11 May 1979 was to be the last before the sitting of the Parliament elected by direct universal suffrage as provided for by the Act concerning the election of the representatives of the Assembly by direct universal suffrage and fixed for 17 July 1979. At its meeting on 1 March 1979 the Bureau of the Parliament had decided not to provide for an additional session between those of May and July. It had however stated:

The Enlarged Bureau ...

—is nevertheless of the view that in so far as the Council or Commission consider it necessary to provide for an additional session they may, pursuant to Article 1 (4) of the Rules of Procedure, call for an extraordinary session of the Parliament; any such session would be for the purpose only of considering reports which had been adopted following urgent consultation.

At its meeting on 10 May 1979 the Bureau was to confirm its position in the following words:

—confirms the position adopted at the above-mentioned meeting when it was decided not to provide for an additional session between the last session of the present

Parliament and the session of the Parliament elected by direct universal suffrage, provided always that where the majority of the effective members of the Parliament, the Council, or the Commission desire the hoding of an additional session they may, pursuant to the provisions of Article 1 (4) of the Rules of Procedure, ask for the Parliament to be summoned;

—decides further having regard to the provisions of Article 139 of the EEC Treaty that where the President has such an application before him the Enlarged Bureau will meet to consider how it should be dealt with.

11. On 25 June 1979 the Council without obtaining the opinion requested adopted the regulation proposed by the Commission which thus became Regulation no. 1293/79 amending Regulation no. 1111/77. The third reference in the preamble to Regulation no. 1293/79 refers to consultation of the Parliament. The Council nevertheless took account of the absence of an opinion from the Parliament by observing in the third recital in the preamble to the regulation that 'the European Parliament which was consulted on 19 March 1979 on the Commission proposal did not deliver its opinion at its May part-session; whereas it had referred the matter to the Assembly for its opinion'.

12. The Court is asked to declare Regulation no. 1293/79 void in so far as it amends Regulation no. 1111/77.

Admissibility of the application

13. In the Council's view the application is inadmissible for it is directed against a regulation and the conditions provided for in the second paragraph of Article 173 of the Treaty are not satisfied. The contested measure is claimed not to constitute a decision in the form of a regulation and not to be of direct and individual concern to the applicant. The applicant maintains on the other hand that the contested regulation is a set of individual decisions one of which is taken in respect of the applicant and is of direct and individual concern to it.

[The Court considered the Regulation and its Annex and continued:]

16. It follows that Article 9 (4) of Regulation no. 1111/77 (as amended by Article 3 of Regulation no. 1293/79) in conjunction with Annex II, itself applies the criteria laid down to each of the undertakings in question who are the addressees and thus directly and individually concerned. Regulation no. 1293/79 therefore is a measure against which the undertakings concerned manufacturing isoglucose may bring proceedings for a declaration that it is void pursuant to the second paragraph of Article 173 of the Treaty.

Admissibility of the Parliament's intervention

17. The Council queries the possibility of the Parliament's intervening voluntarily in the proceedings pending before the Court. In the Council's view a power to intervene of this kind is to be equated with a right of action which the Parliament does not have under the Treaty. In that respect it observes that Article 173 of the Treaty does not mention the Parliament among the institutions entitled to seek a declaration that a measure is void and that Article 20 of the Statute of the Court does not mention it among the institutions invited to lodge observations pursuant to the procedure under Article 177 for a preliminary ruling.

18. Article 37 of the Statute of the Court provides:

Member States and institutions of the Community may intervene in cases before the Court.

The same right shall be open to any other person establishing an interest in the result of any case submitted to the Court, save in cases between Member States, between institutions of the Community, or between Member States and institutions of the Community.

Submissions made in an application to intervene shall be limited to supporting the submissions of one of the parties.

19. The first paragraph of that article provides that all the institutions of the Community have the right to intervene. It is not possible to restrict the exercise of that right by one of them without adversely affecting its institutional position as intended by the Treaty and in particular Article 4 (1).

20. Alternatively the Council alleges that even if the Parliament's right to intervene has to be accepted such right would depend upon the existence of a legal interest. Such an interest may no doubt be presumed but it does not prevent the Court from checking, if necessary, that it exists. In the present case, in the Council's view, if the Court were to consider the matter it would lead to find that the Parliament had no interest in the outcome of the proceedings.

21. That submission must be rejected as incompatible with Article 37 of the Statute of the Court. Although the second paragraph of Article 37 of the Statute of the Court provides that persons other than States and the institutions may intervene in cases before the Court only if they establish an interest in the result, the right to intervene which institutions, and thus the Parliament, have under the first paragraph of Article 37 is not subject to that condition. [The Court then held that the Regulation infringed neither the principle of equality of treatment nor that of proportionality.]

Infringement of essential procedural requirements

32. The applicant and the Parliament in its intervention maintain that since Regulation no. 1111/77 as amended was adopted by the Council without regard to the consultation procedure provided for in the second paragraph of Article 43 of the Treaty it must be treated as void for infringement of essential procedural requirements.

33. The consultation provided for in the third subparagraph of Article 43 (2), as in other similar provisions of the Treaty, is the means which allows the Parliament to play an actual part in the legislative process of the Community. Such power represents an essential factor in the institutional balance intended by the Treaty. Although limited, it reflects at Community level the fundamental democratic principle that the peoples should take part in the exercise of power through the intermediary of a representative assembly. Due consultation of the Parliament in the cases provided for by the Treaty therefore constitutes an essential formality disregard of which means that the measure concerned is void.

34. In that respect it is pertinent to point out that observance of that requirement implies that the Parliament has expressed its opinion. It is impossible to take the view that the requirement is satisfied by the Council's simply asking for the opinion. The Council is, therefore, wrong to include in the references in the preamble to Regulation no. 1293/79 a statement to the effect that the Parliament has been consulted.

35. The Council has not denied that consultation of the Parliament was in the nature of an essential procedural requirement. It maintains however that in the circumstances of the present case the Parliament, by its own conduct, made observance of that requirement impossible and that it is therefore not proper to rely on the infringement thereof.

36. Without prejudice to the questions of principle raised by that argument of the Council it suffices to observe that in the present case on 25 June 1979 when the Council adopted Regulation no. 1293/79 amending Regulation no. 1111/77 without the opinion of the Assembly the Council had not exhausted all the possibilities of obtaining the preliminary opinion of the Parliament. In the first place the Council did not request the application of the emergency procedure provided for by the internal regulation of the Parliament although in other sectors and as regards other draft regulations it availed itself of that power at the same time. Further the Council could have made use of the possibility it had under Article 139 of the Treaty to ask for an extraordinary session of the Assembly especially as the Bureau of the Parliament on 1 March and 10 May 1979 drew its attention to that possibility.

37. It follows that in the absence of the opinion of the Parliament required by Article 43 of the Treaty Regulation no. 1293/79 amending Council Regu-

lation no. 1111/77 must be declared void without prejudice to the Council's power following the present judgment to take all appropriate measures pursuant to the first paragraph of Article 176 of the Treaty.

On those grounds, the Court hereby:

1. declares Regulation no. 1293/79 to be void.

COMMENTS

1. The case provides a good example of a decision which, although in the form of a regulation, is of direct and individual concern (EEC 173).

2. The ECJ annulled the whole Regulation, one of whose provisions repealed the parts of the earlier Regulation which the court had declared invalid in Cases 103 and 145/77. Does the annulment of the repeal revive the invalid norms?

3. Its main importance, however, lies in its effects on the balance of power of the institutions. This is recognized by the Court which sees in the consultation procedure a (pale) reflection, at Community level, of 'the fundamental democratic principle that the peoples should take part in the exercise of power through the intermediary of a representative assembly'. The 1986 Single European Act amends the treaty in this direction, by stipulating in a number of areas (though not agriculture) that the Council shall not merely consult but shall act 'in co-operation with' the European Parliament. This is given some teeth by amendments to EEC 149, which requires Council unanimity to adopt a measure rejected by the Parliament or to amend a measure approved by both Parliament and Commission (see Rudden and Wyatt, BCL, 79).

4. An unsolved, largely political, problem would arise in the many areas where consultation or co-operation is required, if the Parliament simply refused to reply to the Council. The Court's decision in the particular actions is discreetly stated to be 'without prejudice to the questions of principle' raised by this sort of scenario.

Act V: Retroactive Regulations

In June 1980—a year after adopting the 1979 Regulation—the Council was still in difficulties over the sweeteners market. The actions against the 1979 Regulation (see extract no. 23) were pending; but in any event, the Regulation, even if upheld, expired at the end of June. So the Council, having prudently this time waited for the opinion of the Parliament, issued a Regulation imposing quotas for the following twelve months, based on those 'applicable during the period 1 July 1979 to 30 June 1980' (Regulation 1592/80, art. 2, OJ 1980 L160/12).

This was a mistake: if the cases on the 1979 Regulation (as they did) went against the Council, and the measure was annulled, then there were no quotas for the year 1979–80. Two firms began actions but they need not detain us.

After the decision in Cases 138 and 139/79 annulling the 1979 Regulation (extract no. 23), the Council tried again. Having read the judgment, the institutions realized that the Court had found nothing wrong with the scheme itself, but had declared it void solely because the Parliament had not been consulted. Here was a chance to reinstate the whole regime.

Consequently, and after scrupulous consultation of the Parliament, a new Regulation was adopted in February 1981. Its legislative technique is rather complex, since in form it merely amends Regulation 1111/77. In essence, however, it simply enacted the 1979 quota scheme with retroactive effect back to 1 July 1979. Once again, an Annex applied its methods, and laid down figures for the basic quota of each of the six producers. A separate Regulation corrected the mistake of Regulation 1592/80 described above 'in order to avoid any doubts as to its legality' (Regulations 387 and 388/81, OJ 1981 L44/1 and 4).

So, after all this travail, the producers found that their output for the past eighteen months was retrospectively subject to the old regime of quotas comparable to those for sugar. Furthermore, those firms who had paid levies under the scheme declared invalid in Cases 103 and 145/77 (above, extract no. 21), or its successor declared void in Case 138/79 (above, extract no. 23), would not be able to recover them.

Unfortunately for the firms, in Case 138/79 the ECJ had seen nothing wrong with the scheme; it had been annulled for purely procedural (though important) reasons. The producers, therefore, had to find other grounds for their new actions under EEC 173, and there is an understandable note of desperation in their pleadings. Their main complaint was that the adoption of

Act V: Retroactive Regulations

retroactive measures was a breach of a general principle against retroactivity found in the legal systems of all the Member States. In addition, they alleged that the reintroduction of a scheme on which the Parliament had not originally been consulted, and which the ECJ had annulled, was a barefaced insult to both institutions. They pleaded also, failure to give adequate reasons in breach of EEC 190; and finally put forward an argument (rejected, and not dealt with in extract no. 24 below) based on the financing of the Community. Three separate cases were brought, but the arguments and much of the judgments are similar, and the Advocate-General made only one submission.

24 Case 108/81 *Amylum* v. *Council*

TEXT

DECISION

I First submission: breach of the principle that Community measures may not have retroactive effect

4. As the Court has already held although in general the principle of legal certainty, as the applicant states, precludes a Community measure from taking effect from a point in time before its publication, it may exceptionally be otherwise where the purpose to be achieved so demands and where the legitimate expectations of those concerned are duly respected.

5. As regards the first of those two conditions it is well to call to mind certain matters of fact or law which are moreover well known to the parties. During the period of application of the contested regulation sugar producers were, in particular, subject to quotas and production levies. Isoglucose is a product which may be substituted for sugar and is in direct competition with it. Any Community decision concerning one of those products necessarily has repercussions on the other. Having regard to that situation, although the Court declared Regulation no. 1293/79 void for infringement of an essential procedural requirement, namely the absence of the Parliament's opinion, the Court nevertheless considered that it was a matter for the Council, in view of the fact that isoglucose production was contributing to an increase in sugar surpluses and that it was open to it to impose restrictive measures on that production, to take such measures in the context of the agricultural policy as it judged to be useful, regard being had to the similarity and interdependence of the two markets and the specific nature of the isoglucose market.

6. If, following the declaration of the nullity of Regulation no. 1293/79, the Council had adopted no measure restrictive of isoglucose production—in the present case the reinstatement with effect from 1 July 1979 of the quotas allocated and the levies imposed on the producers—the objective which it was pursuing, namely the stabilization, in the general interest, of the sugar market, could not have been achieved or could only have been achieved to the detriment of sugar producers, who alone would have had to finance the costs of Community surpluses, or even to the detriment of the Community

as a whole, whilst isoglucose producers whose production competed with that of sugar undertakings would have escaped all restraints.

7. The Court is unable to uphold the argument put forward by the applicant that the application of Regulation no. 1293/79, until it was declared void by the Court, had held isoglucose producers to observe the quotas which it laid down and thus rendered superfluous their reinstatement by the contested regulation. In fact, in addition to the legal basis which the contested regulation gave to the system of quotas during the period in question from 1 July 1979 to 30 June 1980, the maintenance of levies during that period, which was necessary to attain the objectives of public interest pursued by the Council, made it necessary to fix the quotas upon which the amount of those levies depended.

8. Thus the Council was lawfully entitled to consider that the objective to be achieved in the general interest, namely the stabilization of the Community market in sweeteners without arbitrary discrimination between traders, required the contested provisions to be retroactive in nature and thus the first of the conditions which the Court lays down for the applicability *ratione temporis* of a Community measure to a date prior to the date of its publication may be regarded as satisfied.

9. To ascertain whether the second of the conditions set out above is satisfied it is necessary to inquire whether the action of the Council in Regulation no. 387/81 has frustrated a legitimate expectation on the part of the applicants to the effect that the production of isoglucose would not be regulated during the period from 1 July 1979 to 30 June 1980, the period to which that regulation makes applicable Article 9 relating to quotas and production levies on isoglucose which it inserted in Regulation no. 1111/77.

10. It should first be pointed out that the contested provisions of Regulation no. 387/81 do not include any new measures and merely reproduce the provisions of Council Regulation no. 1293/79 declared void by the Court.

11. In view of the fact that Council Regulation no. 1293/79 of 25 June 1979 retained its full effect within the Community legal order until it was declared void, so that the national authorities responsible for its implementation were required to subject the production of isoglucose to the restrictive system which it laid down, such a legitimate expectation could only be founded on the unforeseeability of the reinstatement with retroactive effect of the measures contained in Regulation no. 1293/79 declared void by the Court.

12. In the present case the applicant cannot claim any legitimate expectation worthy of protection.

13. In the first place the traders concerned by the rules in question are limited in number and are reasonably well aware of the interdependence of the markets in liquid sugar and isoglucose, of the situation of the Community

market in sweeteners, and therefore of the consequences which, following the declaration that Regulation no. 1293/79 was void, the imposition on the production of sugar in respect of the period from 1 July 1979 to 30 June 1980 of stabilization measures from which the production of isoglucose would have been entirely exempt might have had.

14. Secondly by adopting successive Regulations the Council had clearly manifested its intention of regulating the production of all sweeteners in the Community and to that end of subjecting the production of isoglucose to a restrictive system based on a system of quotas and production levies.

15. Thirdly it could not have escaped the notice of the applicant that in both judgments of the Court which declared void Regulation no. 1293/79 (which also fixed its own production quota), the Court rejected the grounds on which the applicant companies Roquette and Maizena were contesting the substantive validity of that regulation and was at pains, at the same time as pronouncing it void for failure to obtain the Parliament's opinion, to state that such nullity was without prejudice to 'the Council's power following the present judgment to take all appropriate measures pursuant to the first paragraph of Article 176 of the Treaty'.

16. Finally, from the publication of the Commission's proposal in the Official Journal of 20 December 1980 the applicant knew that the Commission had, as early as 3 December 1980, submitted to the Council a proposal to reinstate, for the period from 1 July 1979 to 30 June 1980, the system of quotas and levies in the form in which that system had been laid down by Regulation no. 1293/79 and in which it was to be reinstated by the contested provisions of Regulation no. 387/81.

17. In challenging the retroactivity of those provisions the applicant further claims that they disturb the institutional equilibrium of the Communities. That claim cannot be upheld. On the one hand, there is no provision of the Treaty which precluded the Parliament from being called upon to express its views on a retroactive reinstatement of Regulation no. 1293/79 although it had not given its opinion on that regulation. On the other hand, the fact that the Court, in declaring that regulation void, did not think fit to make use of the power given to it by the second paragraph of Article 174 to state which of the effects of the regulation which it had declared void should be considered definitive, gives no ground for regarding the retroactive effect given to the contested provisions of Regulation no. 387/81, adopted by the Council in the context of the first paragraph of Article 176 of the Treaty, as a trespass on the prerogatives of the Court.

II Second submission: breach of the duty to state the reasons upon which a measure is based

18. The applicant claims that the Council has given inadequate reasons for the retroactive effect given to Regulation no. 387/81 and therefore has infringed the provisions of Article 190 of the Treaty.

19. According to the case-law of the Court the statement of the reasons on which a measure is based, which is required by Article 190 of the Treaty, must be adapted to the nature of the measure in question. It must enable the reasoning of the Community institution responsible for the measure to emerge clearly and unequivocally so as to enable those concerned to recognize the reasons for the measure adopted and the Court to exercise its power of review.

20. The statement of the reasons on which Council Regulation no. 387/81 is based states first that 'Council Regulations provided for the application of a system of production quotas for the period from 1 July 1979 to 30 June 1980' and, secondly, that 'in Cases 138/79 and 139/79 the Court of Justice of the European Communities, on 29 October 1980, annulled regulation (EEC) no. 1293/79, which amended Regulation (EEC) no. 1111/77, on the grounds of an infringement of an essential procedural requirement; ... in rejecting all the alleged complaints of breach of the principles of the law of competition, of proportionality, and of non-discrimination made against the system of production quotas introduced by Regulation (EEC) no. 1293/79, the Court affirmed that the latter regulation was substantively in conformity with Community law; ... it is therefore appropriate to reinstate *inter alia* the system of quotas concerned retroactively.

21. Laconic as these reasons may be, they satisfy the requirement laid down by Article 190 of the Treaty. In fact, by referring to the system of production quotas, which moreover was well known to those concerned, the provisions of the preamble to the contested regulation set forth in essence the objective pursued by the institution responsible for the contested measure, namely to ensure continuity in time of the system restricting isoglucose production—a system in respect of which the Court, in its judgments in Cases 138/79 and 139/79 of 29 October 1980, rejected the substantive criticisms made against it by the applicant undertakings—in order to ensure an equal division of burdens on the production of isoglucose and that of liquid sugar which are in direct competition on the market in sweeteners.

22. The submission as to breach of the requirement to state the reasons on which the measure was based must therefore be rejected as unfounded.

On those grounds, the Court (Second Chamber) hereby:
1. dismisses as unfounded the application for a declaration that Council Regulation no. 387/81 is void.

IV
Judicial Technique

Neither of the final two cases to be discussed deals with a problem which is exclusive to the Community: the first concerns the confidentiality of communications between lawyer and client, the second a tort action; they are thus the kind of dispute that might come before any court in any country. In both of them, the submissions of the Advocates-General are both meticulous and lengthy. Here, however, only extracts from the judgments are given, in the hope that this will enable the reader to stand back from the detailed legal issues involved and to focus on the Court's methods of reasoning.

25 Case 155/79 *AM & S Europe Limited* v. *Commission*

1. *The action.* A company incorporated in England brought an action under EEC 173 against a decision of the Commission which said 'AM & S Europe Ltd. is hereby required to produce for examination all documents for which legal privilege is claimed as listed in [the company's] letter of 26 March 1979 to the Commission'. Under the Court Statute, art. 37, the French and UK Governments intervened, as did the Consultative Committee of the Bars and Law Societies of the European Community ('CCBE').

2. *The salient, simplified facts*

2.1 The lawsuit arose in the context of Community competition law, whose regulations empower the Commission to investigate suspected breaches of EEC 85 and 86 and, for this purpose, to inspect and copy documents (see Rudden and Wyatt, *BCL*, 291).

2.2 While scrutinizing a number of undertakings which produce and distribute zinc (one being AM & S), the Commission requested that certain documents be produced. The company refused, on the grounds of legal confidentiality (also described as 'professional privilege'), whereupon the Commission took the decision quoted above.

2.3 The company began this (obviously admissible) action under EEC 173, the written and oral stages were held, and, in January 1981, Warner A-G presented lengthy submissions which concluded in favour of the company and recommended that the decision be quashed (in fact, since the composition of the Court had changed since the action began, the oral stage and Advocate-General's submission were heard twice).

2.4 A month later, the Court made an Order reopening the oral procedure and instructing the company to send the disputed documents, in a sealed envelope, to the Court. They were scrutinized by the Reporting Judge and the Advocate-General whose report (likewise sealed) was sent to the company, the Commission, the CCBE, and the intervening Governments. The Court also set a date for the next oral hearing and asked the parties and interveners to give a comparative survey of the relevant law of the Member States; later it refused an application for extension of time.

2.5 In January 1982 the new Advocate-General Sir Gordon Slynn presented lengthy submissions which largely agreed with those of his predecessor. He too concluded that, as regards most of the documents, the decision should be quashed.

3. *The legal issues*

3.1 No text of Community law, whether in Treaty or regulation, deals with the question of confidentiality between lawyer and client. (When the draft basic Regulation (17/62) was being considered by the Parliament, some protection was written in, but this was deleted by the Council and does not appear in the version adopted.) Thus the ECJ must find the normative source of its decision in EEC 164 which enjoins the Court to ensure that 'the law is observed' and in EEC 173 which includes among its grounds of illegality, breach of 'any rule of law'.

3.2 During the investigation, however, the Commission was quite prepared to concede that certain documents were protected by lawyer/client confidentiality. The problem was the familiar one of *who decides* which documents fall into the protected category. The company's strongest argument was that it should decide, while the defence contended that the Commission was entitled to look at all the documents in order to determine whether the company's claim was valid in respect of any, and if so which. The company retorted that this would destroy confidentiality entirely, and render any protection illusory.

3.3 As a fall-back position, AM & S argued that the ECJ itself should decide disputed documents. The theoretical difficulty here, however, is that the Court has no general jurisdiction at all (EEC 4 (1)) and no article of the Treaty allows it to undertake this task. Even if a decision were challenged under EEC 173, this gives the Court jurisdiction only to decide legality, not matters of fact—for instance whether the addressee of a particular letter is or is not a practising lawyer.

3.4 The Commission pointed out—quite correctly—that there was no harmony in the range of protection afforded by the domestic laws of the Member States. Indeed, much of the submissions of the two Advocate-Generals is devoted to a comparative survey which illustrates this; and the diversity is demonstrated in a report by Professor David Edward, President of the CCBE. A striking example is the fact that in England the privilege is a private right of the client, so that he can waive it if he chooses; while in some other systems it is treated as a matter of public policy which may still bind the lawyer.

3.5 The UK Government supported the company and suggested that, by agreement, the Commission and the firm in question could submit any dispute, and send the document, to an independent person or body. The CCBE also took the side of the company, contending that lawyer/client confidentiality was a fundamental human right and so part of 'the law' in terms of EEC 164. The French Government, on the other hand, supported the Commission, arguing that the legal privilege claimed was not a principle common to the laws of all the Member States.

3.6 In the welter of these conflicting views, it is not easy to focus on the precise problems. The first relates to a possible distinction between advice given by a lawyer and information furnished to him by his client; in fact the Court encompasses both in the term 'correspondence'. The second concerns the distinction between general legal advice (on, say, the impact of accession to the Community, or on the laws of a particular country where the client is thinking of trading) and that necessitated by a threatened lawsuit. The Court asked for comment only on the second of these categories, although its decision deals with documents in the first.

3.7 A further set of issues concerns the question of *what lawyer*. The following categories are relevant: (1) those not licensed to practise in the Community (e.g. Swiss or US attorneys); (2) those licensed in the Community but working, not as independent professionals, but as employees of an enterprise; which, in turn, could be the client ('in-house lawyers'), a related company, or a third party; (3) independent lawyers licensed in a Member State of the Community.

TEXT

DECISION

1. By application lodged at the Court Registry on 4 October 1979 Australian Mining & Smelting Europe Limited (hereinafter referred to as 'AM & S Europe'), which is based in the United Kingdom, instituted proceedings pursuant to the second paragraph of Article 173 of the EEC Treaty to have Article 1 (*b*) of an individual decision notified to it declared void. That provision required the applicant to produce for examination by officers of the Commission charged with carrying out an investigation all the documents for which legal privilege was claimed, as listed in the appendix to AM & S Europe's letter of 26 March 1979 to the Commission.

2. The application is based on the submission that in all the Member States written communications between lawyer and client are protected by virtue of a principle common to all those States, although the scope of that protection and the means of securing it vary from one country to another. According to the applicant, it follows from that principle which, in its view, also applies 'within possible limits' in Community law, that the Commission may not when undertaking an investigation pursuant to Regulation no. 17 of 1962, claim production, at least in their entirety, of written communications between lawyer and client if the undertaking claims protection and takes 'reasonable steps to satisfy the Commission that the protection is properly claimed' on the ground that the documents in question are in fact covered by legal privilege.

3. On the basis of that premise the applicant contends that it is a denial of the principle of confidentiality to permit an authority seeking information or undertaking an investigation, such as the Commission in this instance, against which the principle of protection is relied upon, to inspect protected documents in breach of their confidential nature. However, it concedes that 'the Commission has a prima facie right to see the documents ... in the possession

of an undertaking' by virtue of Article 14 of Regulation no. 17, and that by virtue of that right 'it is still the Commission that takes the decision whether the documents are protected or not, but on the basis of a description of the documents' and not on the basis of an examination of the whole of each document by its inspectors.

4. In that respect the applicant accepts that initially the undertaking claiming protection must provide the Commission with sufficient material on which to base an assessment: for example, the undertaking may provide a description of the documents and show the Commission's inspectors 'parts of the documents', without disclosing the contents for which protection is claimed, in order to satisfy the Commission that the documents are in fact protected. Should the Commission remain unsatisfied as to the confidential nature of the documents in question the undertaking would be obliged to permit 'inspection by an independent third party who will verify the description of the contents of the documents'.

5. The contested decision, based on the principle that it is for the Commission to determine whether a given document should be used or not, requires AM & S Europe to allow the Commission's authorized inspectors to examine the documents in question in their entirety. Claiming that those documents satisfy the conditions for legal protection as described above, the applicant has requested the Court to declare Article 1 (*b*) of the above-mentioned decision void, or alternatively, to declare it void in so far as it requires the disclosure to the Commission's inspector of the whole of each of the documents for which the applicant claims protection on the grounds of legal confidence.

6. The United Kingdom, intervening, essentially supports the argument put forward by the applicant, and maintains that the principle of legal protection of written communications between lawyer and client is recognized as such in the various countries of the Community, even though there is no single, harmonized concept the boundaries of which do not vary. It accepts that the concept may be the subject of differing approaches in the various Member States.

7. As to the most suitable procedure for resolving disputes which might arise between the undertaking and the Commission as to whether certain documents are of a confidential nature or not, the United Kingdom proposes that if the Commission's inspector is not satisfied by the evidence supplied by the undertaking, an independent expert should be consulted, and, should the dispute not be resolved, the matter should be brought before the Court of Justice by the party concerned following the adoption by the Commission of a decision under Regulation no. 17.

8. The view taken by the Consultative Committee of the Bars and Law Societies of the European Community (hereinafter referred to as 'the Con-

sultative Committee'), which has also intervened in support of the applicant's conclusions, is that a right of confidential communication between lawyer and client (in both directions) is recognized as a fundamental, constitutional, or human right, accessory or complementary to other such rights which are expressly recognized, and that as such that right should be recognized and applied as part of Community law. After pointing out that the concept is not a static one, but is continually evolving, the Consultative Committee concludes that if the undertaking and the Commission cannot agree as to whether a document is of a confidential nature or not, the most appropriate procedure would be to have recourse to an expert's report, or to arbitration. Assuming, moreover, that the Court is the sole tribunal with jurisdiction to settle such a dispute it ought in that case to be necessary for it only to determine whether or not the contested documents are of a confidential nature on the basis of an expert's report obtained pursuant to an order under Article 49 of the Rules of Procedure.

9. To all those arguments the Commission replies that even if there exists in Community law a general principle protecting confidential communications between lawyer and client, the extent of such protection is not to be defined in general and abstract terms, but must be established in the light of the special features of the relevant Community rules, having regard to their wording and structure, and to the needs which they are designed to serve.

10. The Commission concludes that, on a correct construction of Article 14 of Regulation no. 17, the principle on which the applicant relies cannot apply to documents the production of which is required in the course of an investigation which has been ordered under that article, including written communications between the undertaking concerned and its lawyers.

11. The applicant's argument is, the Commission maintains, all the more unacceptable inasmuch as in practical terms it offers no effective means whereby the inspectors may be assured of the true content and nature of the contested documents. On the contrary, the solutions which the applicant proposes would have the effect, particularly in view of the protracted nature of any arbitration procedure (even assuming that such a procedure were permissible in law) of delaying considerably, or even of nullifying, the Commission's efforts to bring to light infringements of Articles 85 and 86 of the Treaty, thereby frustrating the essential aims of Regulation no. 17.

12. The Government of the French Republic, intervening in support of the conclusions of the Commission, observes that as yet Community law does not contain any provision for the protection of documents exchanged between a legal adviser and his client. Therefore, it concludes, the Commission must be allowed to exercise its powers under Article 14 of Regulation no. 17 without having to encounter the objection that the documents whose disclosure it considers necessary in order to carry out the duties assigned to it by that

regulation are confidential. To permit the legal adviser and the undertaking subject to a proceeding in a matter concerning competition to be the arbiters of the question whether or not a document is protected would, in the opinion of the French Government, not be compatible with Community law and would inevitably create grave inconsistencies in the application of the rules governing competition.

13. It is apparent from the application, as well as from the legal basis of the contested decision, that the dispute in this case is essentially concerned with the interpretation of Article 14 of Regulation no. 17 of the Council of 6 February 1962 for the purpose of determining what limits, if any, are imposed upon the Commission's exercise of its powers of investigation under that provision by virtue of the protection afforded by the law to the confidentiality of written communications between lawyer and client.

14. Once the existence of such protection under Community law has been confirmed, and the conditions governing its application have been defined, it must be determined which of the documents referred to in Article 1 (*b*) of the contested decision may possibly be considered as confidential and therefore beyond the Commission's powers of investigation. Since some of those documents have in the meantime been produced to the Commission by the applicant of its own volition, the documents to be considered now are those which were lodged in a sealed envelope at the Court Registry on 9 March 1981, pursuant to the Court's order of 4 February 1981 reopening the oral procedure in this case.

(a) The interpretation of Article 14 of Regulation no. 17

15. The purpose of Regulation no. 17 of the Council which was adopted pursuant to the first subparagraph of Article 87 (1) of the Treaty, is 'to ensure compliance with the prohibitions laid down in Article 85 (1) and in Article 86' of the Treaty and 'to lay down detailed rules for the application of Article 85 (3)'. The regulation is thus intended to ensure that the aim stated in Article 3 (*f*) of the Treaty is achieved. To that end it confers on the Commission wide powers of investigation and of obtaining information by providing in the preamble that the Commission must be empowered, throughout the Common Market, to require such information to be supplied and to undertake such investigations 'as are necessary' to bring to light infringements of Articles 85 and 86 of the Treaty.

16. In Articles 11 and 14 of the Regulation, therefore, it is provided that the Commission may obtain 'information' and undertake the 'necessary' investigations, for the purpose of proceedings in respect of infringements of the rules governing competition. Article 14 (1) in particular empowers the Commission to require production of business records, that is to say, docu-

ments concerning the market activities of the undertaking, in particular as regards compliance with those rules. Written communications between lawyer and client fall, in so far as they have a bearing on such activities, within the category of documents referred to in Articles 11 and 14.

17. Furthermore, since the documents which the Commission may demand are, as Article 14 (1) confirms, those whose disclosure it considers 'necessary' in order that it may bring to light an infringement of the Treaty rules on competition, it is in principle for the Commission itself, and not the undertaking concerned or a third party, whether an expert or an arbitrator, to decide whether or not a document must be produced to it.

(b) Applicability of the protection of confidentiality in Community law

18. However, the above rules do not exclude the possibility of recognizing, subject to certain conditions, that certain business records are of a confidential nature. Community law, which derives from not only the economic but also the legal interpretation of the Member States, must take into account the principles and concepts common to the laws of those States concerning the observance of confidentiality, in particular, as regards certain communications between lawyer and client. That confidentiality serves the requirements, the importance of which is recognized in all of the Member States, that any person must be able, without constraint, to consult a lawyer whose profession entails the giving of independent legal advice to all those in need of it.

19. As far as the protection of written communications between lawyer and client is concerned, it is apparent from the legal systems of the Member States that, although the principle of such protection is generally recognized, its scope and the criteria for applying it vary, as has, indeed, been conceded both by the applicant and by the parties who have intervened in support of its conclusions.

20. Whilst in some of the Member States the protection against disclosure afforded to written communications between lawyer and client is based principally on a recognition of the very nature of the legal profession, inasmuch as it contributes towards the maintenance of the rule of law, in other Member States the same protection is justified by the more specific requirement (which, moreover, is also recognized in the first-mentioned States) that the rights of the defence must be respected.

21. Apart from these differences, however, there are to be found in the national laws of the Member States common criteria inasmuch as those laws protect, in similar circumstances, the confidentiality of written communications between lawyer and client provided that, on the one hand, such communications are made for the purposes and in the interests of the client's

rights of defence and, on the other hand, they emanate from independent lawyers, that is to say, lawyers who are not bound to the client by a relationship of employment.

22. Viewed in that context Regulation no. 17 must be interpreted as protecting, in its turn, the confidentiality of written communications between lawyer and client subject to those two conditions, and thus incorporating such elements of that protection as are common to the laws of the Member States.

23. As far as the first of those two conditions is concerned, in Regulation no. 17 itself, in particular in the eleventh recital in its preamble and in the provisions contained in Article 19, care is taken to ensure that the rights of the defence may be exercised to the full, and the protection of the confidentiality of written communications between lawyer and client is an essential corollary to those rights. In those circumstances, such protection must, if it is to be effective, be recognized as covering all written communications exchanged after the initiation of the administrative procedure under Regulation no. 17 which may lead to a decision on the application of Articles 85 and 86 of the Treaty or to a decision imposing a pecuniary sanction on the undertaking. It must also be possible to extend it to earlier written communications which have a relationship to the subject-matter of that procedure.

24. As regards the second condition, it should be stated that the requirement as to the position and status as an independent lawyer, which must be fulfilled by the legal adviser from whom the written communications which may be protected emanate, is based on a conception of the lawyer's role as collaborating in the administration of justice by the courts and as being required to provide, in full independence, and in the overriding interests of that cause, such legal assistance as the client needs. The counterpart of that protection lies in the rules of professional ethics and discipline which are laid down and enforced in the general interest by institutions endowed with the requisite powers for that purpose. Such a conception reflects the legal traditions common to the Member States and is also to be found in the legal order of the Community, as is demonstrated by Article 17 of the Protocols on the Statutes of the Court of Justice of the EEC and the EAEC, and also by Article 20 of the Protocol on the Statute of the Court of Justice of the ECSC.

25. Having regard to the principles of the Treaty concerning freedom of establishment and the freedom to provide services the protection thus afforded by Community law, in particular in the context of Regulation no. 17, to written communications between lawyer and client must apply without distinction to any lawyer entitled to practice his profession in one of the Member States, regardless of the Member State in which the client lives.

26. Such protection may not be extended beyond those limits, which are

determined by the scope of the common rules on the exercise of the legal profession as laid down in Council Directive 77/249 EEC, which is based in its turn on the mutual recognition by all the Member States of the national legal concepts of each of them on this subject.

27. In view of all these factors it must therefore be concluded that although Regulation no. 17, and in particular Article 14 thereof, interpreted in the light of its wording, structure, and aims, and having regard to the laws of the Member States, empowers the Commission to require, in the course of an investigation within the meaning of that Article, production of the business documents the disclosure of which it considers necessary, including written communications between lawyer and client, for proceedings in respect of any infringements of Articles 85 and 86 of the Treaty, that power is, however, subject to a restriction imposed by the need to protect confidentiality, on the conditions defined above, and provided that the communications in question are exchanged between an independent lawyer, that is to say one who is not bound to his client by a relationship of employment, and his client.

28. Finally, it should be remarked that the principle of confidentiality does not prevent a lawyer's client from disclosing the written communications between them if he considers that it is in his interests to do so.

(c) The procedures relating to the application of the principle of confidentiality

29. If an undertaking which is the subject of an investigation under Article 14 of Regulation no. 17 refuses, on the ground that it is entitled to protection of the confidentiality of information, to produce, among the business records demanded by the Commission, written communications between itself and its lawyer, it must nevertheless provide the Commission's authorized agents with relevant material of such a nature as to demonstrate that the communications fulfil the conditions for being granted legal protection as defined above, although it is not bound to reveal the contents of the communications in question.

30. Where the Commission is not satisfied that such evidence has been supplied, the appraisal of those conditions is not a matter which may be left to an arbitrator or to a national authority. Since this is a matter involving an appraisal and a decision which affect the conditions under which the Commission may act in a field as vital to the functioning of the common market as that of compliance with the rules on competition, the solution of disputes as to the application of the protection of the confidentiality of written communications between lawyer and client may be sought only at Community level.

31. In that case it is for the Commission to order, pursuant to Article 14 (3) of Regulation no. 17, production of the communications in question and, if necessary, to impose on the undertaking fines or periodic penalty payments

under that regulation as a penalty for the undertaking's refusal either to supply such additional evidence as the Commission considers necessary or to produce the communications in question whose confidentialit . in the Commission's view, is not protected in law.

32. The fact that by virtue of Article 185 of the EEC Treaty any action brought by the undertaking concerned against such decisions does not have suspensory effect provides an answer to the Commission's concern as to the effect of the time taken by the procedure before the Court on the efficacy of the supervision which the Commission is called upon to exercise in regard to compliance with the Treaty rules on competition, whilst on the other hand the interests of the undertaking concerned are safeguarded by the possibility which exists under Articles 185 and 186 of the Treaty, as well as under Article 83 of the Rules of Procedure of the Court, of obtaining an order suspending the application of the decision which has been taken, or any other interim measure.

(d) The confidential nature of the documents at issue

33. It is apparent from the documents which the applicant lodged at the Court that almost all the communications which they include were made or are connected with legal opinions which were given towards the end of 1972 and during the first half of 1973.

34. It appears that the communications in question were drawn up during the period preceding, and immediately following, the accession of the United Kingdom to the Community, and that they are principally concerned with how far it might be possible to avoid conflict between the applicant and the Community authorities on the applicant's position, in particular with regard to the Community provisions on competition. In spite of the time which elapsed between the said communications and the initiation of a procedure, those circumstances are sufficient to justify considering the communications as falling within the context of the rights of the defence and the lawyer's specific duties in that connection. They must therefore be protected from disclosure.

35. In view of that relationship and in the light of the foregoing considerations the written communications at issue must accordingly be considered, in so far as they emanate from an independent lawyer entitled to practise his profession in a Member State, as confidential and on that ground beyond the Commission's power of investigation under Article 14 of Regulation no. 17.

36. Having regard to the particular nature of those communications Article 1 (*b*) of the contested decision must be declared void in so far as it requires the applicant to produce the documents mentioned in the appendix to its letter to the Commission of 26 March 1979 and listed in the schedule of

documents lodged at the Court on 9 March 1981 under numbers 1 (*a*) and (*b*), 4 (*a*) to (*f*), 5, and 7.

37. Nevertheless, the application must be dismissed inasmuch as it is directed against the provisions in the above-mentioned Article 1 (*b*) relating to documents other than those referred to above, which are likewise listed in the above-mentioned appendix and schedule and which have not yet been produced to the Commission.

On those grounds, the Court hereby:

1. declares Article 1 (*b*) of Commission Decision no. 79/760 of 6 July 1979 void inasmuch as it requires the applicant to produce the documents which are mentioned in the appendix to the letter from the applicant to the Commission of 26 March 1979 and listed in the schedule of documents lodged at the Court on 9 March 1981 under numbers 1 (*a*) and (*b*), 4 (*a*) to (*f*), 5, and 7.

COMMENTS

1. After noting the differences between national laws on the question of lawyer/client confidentiality, the ECJ finds that they have one thing in common: they protect communications between an independent lawyer and a client threatened with legal proceedings. This protection is then read into Community law on competition investigations.

2. As to the second of the factors, however, the Court does not confine protection to communications dealing only with pending proceedings, but extends it to advice given years before and concerning the general effect of the UK's accession to the Treaty.

3. It is the first limitation which has provoked most reaction. In the first place, protection is denied to communications from 'in-house' lawyers, apparently because in some Member States they are not subject to the professional discipline of their Bar. In the second place, advice from independent but non-Community lawyers, such as US or Swiss firms, must, apparently, be produced to the Commission. The reason for this cannot be their lack of professional discipline.

4. The ECJ does not explain its reasoning in simple terms; it asserts only that 'such protection may not be extended beyond those limits' and refers to Directive 77/249 and to the EEC Court Statute, art. 17 (see Rudden and Wyatt, *BCL*, 116, 261). The latter limits the right of audience before the ECJ to Community lawyers; its second sentence, however, forbids the ordinary citizen to conduct his own case; he *must* be represented. While this may reflect the legal tradition of the six original Member States, it is profoundly inimical to those of Denmark, Ireland, and the UK.

26 Case 145/83 *Adams* v. *Commission* (no. 1)

1. *The action.* Under EEC 215, Mr Adams brought an action against the Commission for damages in respect of his period of imprisonment in Switzerland, his subsequent sentencing, and his wife's suicide.

2. *The facts.* These appear in the judgment.

3. *The legal issues*

   3.1 *Liability.* The first problem is to find some act of, or default by, the Commission giving rise to liability. As to positive acts, the Commission handed to the Swiss copies of certain documents which the plaintiff had furnished; as to omissions, they did not warn Mr Adams that the Swiss proposed to prosecute him.

   3.2 *Limitation.* The Court Statute, art. 43 provides that: 'Proceedings against the Community in matters of non-contractual liability shall be barred after a period of five years from the occurrence of the event giving rise thereto.' The acts and omissions of the Commission occurred in 1974. In 1975 the plaintiff was imprisoned in Switzerland and his wife killed herself. He was later given a suspended sentence, and his appeal was dismissed on 3 May 1978. He started this action on 18 July 1983.

   3.3 It is not clear whether the limitation provision must be applied by the Court of its motion, even if not raised by the defence. In the event, however, the Commission pleaded it, as a subsidiary point.

TEXT

DECISION

1. By an application lodged at the Court Registry on 18 July 1983 Stanley George Adams brought an action under Article 178 and Article 215 (2) of the EEC Treaty against the Commission of the European Communities for compensation for the damage which he claims to have suffered as a result of wrongful acts or omissions on the part of the Commission, or of its servants in the performance of their duties, which led *inter alia* to his arrest, detention, and conviction in Switzerland.

2. The acts and omissions which, according to the applicant, gave rise to the damage which he claims to have suffered are more particularly the following:

The disclosure on various occasions, in breach of confidence, of information and documents which made it possible to identify the applicant as the source of information which led the Commission to impose a fine on the applicant's former employer, the Swiss company Hoffman-La Roche, for certain anti-competitive practices;

The failure to advise the applicant that he had the right to petition the European Commission of Human Rights in respect of the criminal proceedings instituted against him by the Swiss authorities as a result of his activities as the Commission's informant.

In his reply the applicant complains in addition that the Commission failed to warn him of the risk that he would run if he returned to Switzerland.

3. With the agreement of the parties the Court decided that the scope of the proceedings should for the time being be limited to the questions whether there is a basis for liability and whether the applicant's action is time-barred.

The events which gave rise to the dispute

4. The applicant, who was at the time employed by the Swiss company Hoffman-La Roche & Co. AG (hereinafter referred to as 'Roche'), Basle, sent a letter on 25 February 1973 to the Commissioner for Competition in which he described a number of anti-competitive practices engaged in by Roche. In that letter, which was headed 'personal and confidential', the applicant stated that he was still working for Roche but that he planned to leave around July 1973 and to start his own meat business in Italy, near Rome. He concluded his letter as follows:

I request you not to let my name be connected with this matter. However, I remain at your entire disposal for further information, as well as documentary evidence about every point which I have raised in this letter. Furthermore, I am prepared to discuss any point with your assistants or yourself at any time, and if necessary I am prepared to fly to Belgium or Rome for this purpose. Additionally, after I leave Roche around July 1973 I would be prepared even to appear before any court to give sworn evidence on my statements. I trust to hear from you soon to know in what direction I can be of further help.

5. Following a reply from the Director-General of the Commission's Directorate-General for Competition (DGIV), the applicant had an interview in Brussels on 9 April 1973 with two Commission officials. In the course of that interview, he supplied the Commission with certain additional information concerning Roche's activities. Moreover, in April and July 1973 the applicant sent the Commission photocopies of a considerable number of internal documents issued by Roche, including fourteen 'Management Information' memoranda and a letter to the directors of Roche from the company's President.

6. In a letter dated 21 July 1973 the applicant informed the Commission that he would be staying with Roche until the end of October 1973. He did in fact leave Roche on 31 October 1973 and on 1 April 1974 he took up residence with his wife and children in Italy.

7. Subsequently the Commission commenced an investigation into Roche's activities in the areas which the applicant had described to it. As part of that investigation Commission officials, visited the offices of Roche's subsidiaries in Paris and in Brussels on 22 and 29 October 1974 and attempted to obtain copies of the documents supplied to the Commission by the applicant. As the Roche representatives denied any knowledge of those documents, the Commission officials finally handed over edited copies of the 'Management Information' memoranda in question and the letter to the Roche directors from the President. Before doing so they covered up certain details and handwritten notes which they thought might indicate the specific source of the documents copied. In return the Commission officials received confirmation that the documents were authentic.

8. On 9 June 1976 the Commission adopted Decision 76/642/EEC relating to a proceeding under Article 86 of the Treaty establishing the European Economic Community, in which the Commission found that Roche had abused its dominant position in the market for bulk vitamins and imposed a fine of 300,000 units of account on that company. That decision was confirmed in all essential respects by the Court's judgment of 13 February 1979 (Case 85/76, *Hoffmann-La Roche v. EC Commission*).

9. In the meantime, on 8 November 1974, Dr Alder, a Swiss lawyer acting on behalf of Roche, visited the Commission in order to discover how it had come into possession of the documents in question. On that occasion Dr Alder intimated that if the Commission provided information as to the informant's identity, Roche would be willing to provide the necessary data for the Commission's investigation and, in addition, would not institute criminal proceedings against the informant, a step which it was otherwise proposing to take on the basis of section 273 of the Swiss Penal Code which concerns economic espionage in the form of the disclosure of business information. According to the Commission, the officials who took part in the meeting finally 'agreed that they would consider informing Dr Alder whether the person who had passed the documents to the Commission was a Roche employee'. However, when Mr Schlieder was informed of Dr Alder's proposal he gave instructions that in no circumstances would the Commission depart from its general practice of not divulging the identity of its informants. Accordingly, on 6 December 1974, Dr Alder was informed that the Commission had no intention of discussing the origin of the documents in its possession.

10. By a letter dated 18 December 1974, addressed to the Public Prosecutor's Office, Berne, Dr Alder, on behalf of Roche, laid a complaint against a person or persons unknown for economic espionage within the meaning of the above-mentioned section 273 of the Swiss Penal Code. On the basis in particular of the copies of the documents handed over by the Commission

officials to the Roche employees in October 1974, Dr Alder drew the conclusion that the applicant was the main suspect.

11. On 31 December 1974, the applicant was arrested by the Swiss authorities as he crossed the border from Italy with his family. According to the police record of the interrogations whch took place on 31 December 1974 and 1 January 1975, the applicant acknowledged that he was the Commission's informant and that it was 'certainly within the bounds of possibility' that he had given the Commission the documents in question. On 1 January the applicant was charged with economic espionage contrary to section 273 of the Swiss Penal Code. In the course of subsequent interrogations he claimed that he had given the Commission information only verbally and that the record of 31 December 1974 and 1 January 1975 did not properly reflect what he had said.

12. While he was in prison, the applicant was held in solitary confinement and he was not allowed to communicate with his family. His wife was also interrogated by the Swiss police and on 10 January 1975 she committed suicide. On 25 January an official of the Commission received an unsigned letter informing him of the applicant's arrest and asking the Commission to intervene in his favour.

13. At the beginning of February 1975 Dr Alder had a telephone conversation with Mr Schlieder, in the course of which the latter confirmed that the applicant was the Commission's informant. There is however some dispute as to whether Mr Schlieder confirmed that the applicant was the person who had supplied the documents. In any event, on 14 February 1975 a police officer informed Dr Portmann, a colleague of Dr Bollag, the Swiss lawyer retained by the applicant, that a high-ranking official of the Commission had named the applicant as the person who had supplied the documents and as the Commission's informant. Dr Portmann immediately informed the applicant of this.

14. On 21 March 1975 the applicant was released on bail of 25,000 S.fr. The Commission subsequently reimbursed that sum and in addition paid the fees of the applicant's lawyers in connection with the criminal proceedings.

15. On 1 July 1976 the Criminal Court, Basle found the applicant guilty, *inter alia*, of an offence against section 273 of the Swiss Penal Code and sentenced him *in absentia* to one year's imprisonment (suspended). It is clear from the text of the judgment, which was drafted in German, that in the course of the visits of the Commission officials to the Roche subsidiaries in October 1974, the officials had handed over to the Roche employees photocopies of documents supplied by the applicant to the Commission. In addition, it is pointed out in the judgment that the applicant admitted having informed the Commission officials orally of the activities of Roche which, in

his view, constituted anti-competitive schemes. Finally, the judgment indicated that the applicant's identity as the Commission's informant also emerged from the telephone call from Mr Schlieder to Dr Alder.

16. On 27 September 1977 the Court of Appeal for the Canton of Basel-Stadt dismissed the applicant's appeal. That judgment stated, *inter alia*, that in the course of their visit to Roche's French subsidiary, the Commission officials had shown the documents in question to the director of the subsidiary, who had taken copies of them. On 6 January 1978 the Commission sent a letter to the applicant enclosing an English translation of that judgment.

17. The appeals brought by the applicant before the Bundesgericht (Swiss Federal Supreme Court) and an application to reopen the proceedings were subsequently dismissed.

18. In February 1979 the applicant discharged his lawyer, Dr Bollag, and retained Dr Diefenbacher, of Berne. By a letter of 18 August 1980 Dr Diefenbacher informed the Commission that he had come into possession 'of evidence proving in a singular way the direct responsibility of the EEC Commission for Mr Adams's most lamentable fate'.

19. Finally, on 28 May 1982 the applicant lodged a petition, in which he laid a complaint against Switzerland, with the European Commission of Human Rights. In that petition he alleged that the criminal proceedings instituted against him by the Swiss authorities had been conducted in breach of Articles 6 and 10 of the European Convention for the Protection of Human Rights and Fundamental Freedoms of 4 November 1950. By a decision of 9 May 1983 the European Court of Human Rights rejected the petition as inadmissible on the ground that it was out of time.

The hearing before the Court

20. In the course of the proceedings the Court (Second Chamber) heard the applicant and took evidence from Dr Portmann, his former lawyer, and various former and present Commission officials.

21. At that hearing the applicant explained *inter alia* that by his letter of 23 February 1973 he had sought to impose on the Commission an obligation of confidentiality which was continuous and without any date of expiry. Although he had stated in that letter that after he had left Roche he would be prepared to appear before any court, he did not think that it would be necessary for him to do so and, even if it were, he considered that his identity could be kept secret. In addition, [the officials] promised that the applicant's name would not be mentioned in the course of the investigation. The applicant believes that he did not expressly state that the documents sent to the Commission were not to be shown to third parties, or that, taken together, they might reveal to Roche the division from which they came, because he

did not for a moment imagine that the Commission would use them outside the institution. Nor did he ask to be kept informed about the progress of the investigation of Roche. It would, however, have been possible for the Commission to keep him so informed, because, as a result of the letter of 25 February 1973, it was already aware of his plan to set up home in Italy and, in the course of the meeting with [the officials] in April 1973, the applicant had stated that he was going to live in the small town of Latina.

22. Mr Schlieder stated *inter alia* that it had been clear to the Commission that the investigation of Roche would have to wait in any event until the applicant had left the company. The need to protect him after his departure was not discussed because no one seriously thought that there was a possibility that criminal proceedings might be instituted against him. Mr Schlieder did not give instructions for the use of the documents passed by the applicant to the Commission. Even after Dr Alder's visit of 8 November 1974, no one at the Commission believed in the possibility that criminal proceedings might be instituted against the applicant. Dr Alder's threats were therefore merely regarded as a trick for the purpose of obtaining the informant's name. That was why the Commission did not consider it necessary to inform the applicant of those threats. Furthermore it was clear from a letter from the applicant that he had left Roche, and therefore Switzerland, to set up home in Italy. Finally, Mr Schlieder did not remember having had a telephone conversation with Dr Alder at the beginning of February 1975. He stated, however, that after the Commission had received the anonymous letter informing it of the applicant's arrest, it was clear that it had to give the applicant its formal support and help him.

23. Mr Rihoux stated *inter alia* that he had understood the applicant's letter of 25 February 1973 to mean that after the applicant's departure from Roche the Commission was free to do as it thought fit. Moreover, he received no instructions from his superiors as to the manner in which the information obtained from the applicant should be treated. At the meeting of 9 April 1973 with the applicant the question of the confidentiality of the applicant's information was not raised and the applicant gave no information regarding his future address. In October 1974, Mr Rihoux and two of his colleagues, including Mr Pappalardo, visited the Roche subsidiary in Paris, where they made every attempt, without success, to obtain copies of the documents supplied by the applicant. To that end, they read to the Roche employees extracts from those documents, without however showing the said documents to them. The question then arose as to whether the investigation would have to be closed despite the overwhelming proof that the Commission had in its possession. It was therefore necessary to weigh up carefully the interests at stake, namely, the public interest, which required that the provisions of the Treaty should be enforced, and the individual interest, which was contrary

to the Commission's disclosing the informant's identity. In particular, the method by which the documents had been passed to the Commission and the indications on the face thereof militated against their use. It was therefore decided to use, and to pass on to Roche, edited photocopies of the documents which were both anonymous in character and sufficiently convincing for the prosecution of the inquiry. Mr Rihoux stated that no one at the Commission had thought of informing the applicant of the threats made by Dr Alder during his visit to the Commission on 8 November 1974. The applicant had in fact disappeared without informing the Commission of his address and there was no reason to believe that he was going to return to Swtizerland. Finally the Commission took the view that Dr Alder's threats were merely 'bluff'.

24. Mr Pappalardo, who has been assigned to DGIV since September 1983, supplemented Mr Rihoux's evidence by stating that during his visit to the Commission on 8 November 1974 Dr Alder had explained the contents of section 273 of the Swiss Penal Code.

25. Dr Portmann explained that the applicant's defence had been undertaken at his request at the beginning of 1975. Initially, the applicant's lawyers had received instructions only from the applicant himself. Later the lawyers received information from the Commission but no specific instructions.

The objection that the action is time-barred

26. The Commission raises the objection that the applicant's action is time-barred by virtue of Article 43 of the Protocol on the Statute of the Court of Justice of the EEC.

27. In view of the fact that the action is founded on several events which occurred at different times and which became known to the applicant at different times, the pertinence of the objection that the action is time-barred cannot be considered before the question whether any of those events, and if so which, are capable of giving rise to the non-contractual liability of the Commission has been examined. Only after that question has been resolved will it be possible to determine whether the action is barred by virtue of the five-year limitation period laid down in Article 43 of the Protocol on the Statute of the Court of Justice of the EEC. It is therefore necessary, in the first place, to consider the submission regarding the existence of a basis for liability.

The existence of a basis for liability

(*a*) BREACHES OF THE DUTY OF CONFIDENTIALITY AND THE DUTY TO WARN THE APPLICANT

28. The applicant claims that the relationship between the Commission and

himself was in fact confidential in nature, as is clear both from his first letter to the Commission, dated 25 February 1973, and the discussion which he had with the Commission officials at the meeting of 9 April 1973. The existence of a duty of confidentiality follows, moreover, from the general principles common to the laws of the Member States and from the obligations imposed on the Commission by Article 214 of the EEC Treaty and by Article 20 of Council Regulation no. 17 of 6 February 1962.

29. In particular the applicant points out that the fact that he indicated in his letter of 25 February 1973 that he would be prepared to give evidence on oath before the Court as to the accuracy of his statements showed that his identity was to be disclosed by himself alone after the Commission investigation had been completed and the proceedings before the Court initiated. The applicant maintains that he never gave the Commission to understand that after he had left Roche he would no longer insist on that duty of confidentiality in regard to him. Finally, in the applicant's view, the Commission's conduct proved that it considered itself bound by such a duty. Thus on several occasions, both before and after the applicant had left Roche, the Commission deliberately refused to name its informant—until the beginning of 1975 when Mr Schlieder disclosed his name.

30. Although the Commission was therefore bound by a duty of confidentiality towards the applicant, in his view it acted in breach of that obligation on three occasions in particular. In the first place, the disclosure of the copies of the documents to the Roche employees in October 1974 enabled Roche to infer therefrom that the applicant was the most likely informant. Secondly, the Commission failed to warn the applicant of the risk that he would inevitably run if he returned to Switzerland. In the applicant's view, it was the Commission's duty to warn him of that risk, either after the documents had been handed over to the Roche employees or, in any event, after Dr Alder's first visit to the Commission in November 1974, when the Commission was made fully aware of the gravity of that risk. In that respect, the applicant points out that Dr Alder had told the Commission officials that Roche was considering the possibility of criminal proceedings against the informant and that the lawyer had even explained the contents of the relevant provision of the Swiss Penal Code. Thirdly, and finally, in February 1975 Mr Schlieder named the applicant as the Commission's informant.

31. The Commission denies that it was bound by a duty of confidentiality towards the applicant after he had left his employment with Roche. It bases its contention in particular on the applicant's express statement in his letter of 25 February 1973 that, after he had left Roche, he would be willing to appear before any court, in other words not only before the Court of Justice, to confirm on oath the statements he had made. Moreover, the applicant's conduct after he had left Roche gave the Commission good reason to believe

that it was a matter of indifference to him whether he was identified as the informant, since he had not even informed the Commission of his new address. According to the Commission the fact that it repeatedly declined to identify its informant in no way establishes that it considered itself bound by a duty of confidentiality. Its conduct was dictated entirely by its general practice of not divulging the identity of its informants.

32. In any event the Commission contends that even if it were under a duty of confidentiality regarding the applicant's identity, it did not act in breach of that duty. The fact that it handed over photocopies to the Roche employees did not amount to such a breach, since it could not possibly have been foreseen that Roche would be able to identify the source of the documents by examining the copies. The applicant never requested the Commission not to discose those documents to Roche. On the other hand, he agreed that the Commission could use the documents in connection with an investigation of that firm. The Commission had considered that it was necesssary to disclose them to Roche but it nevertheless took care to remove anything which looked as though it might indicate their specific source. Moreover, the documents in question had no evident connection with the applicant, who could have been identified only by someone with a highly detailed knowledge of the organization and the operation of Roche. The applicant had never warned the Commission of such a risk.

33. As regards the possible existence of a duty on the part of the Commission to warn the applicant, the Commission contends that such a duty cannot be inferred from any duty of confidentiality which may have existed. In so far as the applicant is putting forward a separate submission in this respect, the Commission adds that it is impossible to establish in law that, following Dr Alder's visit, it was under a duty to warn the applicant of the risks that he would run if he returned to Switzerland. In addition, the Commission had no reason to believe that Roche would be able to identify the applicant as the informant. Finally, during his telephone conversation with Dr Alder at the beginning of February 1975, Mr Schlieder revealed nothing that Roche and the Swiss authorities did not already know, since by then the applicant had already admitted that he was the Commission's informant.

34. As regards the existence of a duty of confidentiality it must be pointed out that Article 214 of the EEC Treaty lays down an obligation, in particular for the members and the servants of the institutions of the Community 'not to disclose information of the kind covered by the obligation of professional secrecy, in particular information about undertakings, their business relations, or their cost components'. Although that provision primarily refers to information gathered from undertakings, the expression 'in particular' shows that the principle in question is a general one which applies also to information supplied by natural persons, if that information is 'of the kind'

that is confidential. That is particularly so in the case of information supplied on a purely voluntary basis but accompanied by a request for confidentiality in order to protect the informant's anonymity. An institution which accepts such information is bound to comply with such a condition.

35. As regards the case before the Court, it is quite clear from the applicant's letter of 25 February 1973 that he requested the Commission not to reveal his identity. It cannot therefore be denied that the Commission was bound by a duty of confidentiality towards the applicant in that respect. In fact the parties disagree not so much as to the existence of such a duty but as to whether the Commission was bound by a duty of confidentiality after the applicant had left his employment with Roche.

36. In that respect it must be pointed out that the applicant did not qualify his request by indicating a period upon the expiry of which the Commission would be released from its duty of confidentiality regarding the identity of its informant. No such indication can be inferred from the fact that the applicant was prepared to appear before any court after he had left Roche. The giving of evidence before a court implies that the witness has been duly summoned, that he is under a duty to answer the questions put to him, and is, in return, entitled to all the guarantees provided by a judicial procedure. The applicant's offer to confirm the accuracy of his information under such conditions cannot therefore be interpreted as a general statement releasing the Commission from its duty of confidentiality. Nor can any such intention be inferred from the applicant's subsequent conduct.

37. It must therefore be stated that the Commission was under a duty to keep the applicant's identity secret even after he had left his employer.

38. Of the events mentioned by the applicant, the only occasion on which the Commission directly revealed the identity of its informant was the telephone conversation between Mr Schlieder and Dr Alder at the beginning of February 1975. However, that conversation took place after the applicant had caused an anonymous letter to be sent to the Commission informing it of his detention and seeking its help. It is difficult to see how the Commission could have acted on that request without confirming, at least by implication, that the applicant was indeed its informant. Moreover, it transpired subsequently that at that time the applicant had already admitted to the Swiss police that he had given information, at least orally, to the Commission and it is clear from the decisions of the Swiss courts that the confirmation of that fact by Mr Schlieder did not have a decisive bearing on the applicant's conviction. The disclosure of the applicant's identity at that time and in those circumstances cannot be regarded as constituting a breach of the duty of confidentiality which could give rise to the Commission's liability *vis-à-vis* the applicant.

39. On the other hand, it is clear that the handing over of the edited photocopies to members of the staff of the Roche subsidiaries enabled Roche to identify the applicant as the main suspect in the complaint which it lodged with the Swiss Public Prosecutor's Office. It was therefore that handing over of the documents which led to the applicant's arrest and which in addition supplied the police and the Swiss courts with substantial evidence against him.

40. It appears from the documents before the Court that the Commission was fully aware of the risk that the handing over to Roche of the photocopies supplied by the applicant might reveal the informant's identity to the company. For that reason the Commission officials first attempted to obtain other copies of the documents in question from the Roche subsidiaries in Paris and Brussels. When that attempt failed, the Commission prepared new copies of the documents which it considered were the least likely to lead to the discovery of the applicant's identity and it took care to remove from those copies any indication which it considered might reveal the source of the documents. However, since it was not familiar with Roche's practices regarding the distribution of the documents in question within the company, the Commission could not be sure that those precautions were sufficient to eliminate all risk of the applicant's being identified by means of the copies handed over to Roche. The Commission was therefore, in any event, imprudent in handing over those copies to Roche.

41. It is not however necessary to decide whether, in view of the situation at the time and in particular of the information in the Commission's possession, the handing over of the documents is sufficient to give rise to the Commission's liability regarding the consequences of the applicant's being identified as the informant. Although the Commission was not necessarily aware, when those documents were handed over, of the gravity of the risk to which it was exposing the applicant, Dr Alder's visit on 8 November 1974, on the other hand, provided it with all the necessary information in that respect. Following that visit the Commission knew that Roche was determined to discover how the Commission had come into possession of the documents in question and that it was preparing to lay a complaint against the informant under section 273 of the Swiss Penal Code, the contents of which Dr Alder even took care to explain. The Commission also knew that there was a possibility of obtaining from Roche, in return for the disclosure of the informant's identity, an undertaking not to take action against him. It could not however pursue that possibility without the applicant's consent.

42. In those circumstances it was not at all sufficient for the Commission merely to take the view that it was unlikely that the applicant would be identified, that he was probably never going to return to Switzerland, and that, in any event, the Swiss authorities did not intend to institute criminal

proceedings against him. On the contrary, the Commission was under a duty to take every possible step to warn the applicant, thereby enabling him to make his own arrangements in the light of the information given by Dr Alder, and to consult him as to the approach to be adopted in relation to Dr Alder's proposals.

43. Although the applicant had not left any precise address making it possible for the Commission to contact him easily, in his letter of 25 February 1973 he had already indicated his intention of setting up his own meat business in Italy, near Rome. Even in the absence of other indications, that information would have enabled the Commission to make enquiries with a view to discovering where the applicant was staying. It is common ground that the Commission did not even attempt to find the applicant although it allowed almost one month to elapse before communicating to Dr Alder its final refusal to discuss the origin of the documents in its possession, a refusal which was followed by the lodging of Roche's complaint at the Swiss Public Prosecutor's Office.

44. It must therefore be concluded that, by failing to make all reasonable efforts to pass on to the applicant the information which was available to it following Dr Alder's visit of 8 November 1974, even though the communication of that information might have prevented, or at least limited, the damage which was likely to result from the discovery of the applicant's identity by means of the documents which it had handed over to Roche, the Commission has incurred liability towards the applicant in respect of that damage.

(*b*) THE DUTY TO ADVISE THE APPLICANT WITH REGARD TO THE CONVENTION FOR THE PROTECTION OF HUMAN RIGHTS

45. The applicant's final claim is that inasmuch as it undertook in April 1975 to advise Dr Bollag on the preparation of the applicant's defence, the Commission owed a duty of care to the applicant, which consisted in giving him proper professional advice. By failing to advise the applicant in good time of his right to petition the European Commission of Human Rights, the Commission failed to fulfil that duty.

46. The Commission contends that it never undertook to advise the applicant or his lawyer regarding the possibility of petitioning the European Commission of Human Rights. It merely paid the legal costs of the applicant's defence and left it to his lawyers to advise him.

47. The applicant's submission is clearly ill-founded. It is clear from the information before the Court, and in particular from the evidence of Dr Portmann, that the applicant himself retained his lawyers for his defence and that they received instructions only from him. The Commission merely provided the information requested, in particular in relation to the Free

Trade Agreement concluded between the Community and the Swiss Confederation and, in addition, paid the legal costs. The Court considers that the Commission was under no additional duty and that it was not therefore negligent in failing to give specific instructions to the applicant's lawyers in regard to his defence and in not directly advising him in that respect.

The question whether the applicant's action is time-barred

48. According to the Commission, the applicant's action is, in any event, time-barred under Article 43 of the Protocol on the Statute of the Court of Justice of the EEC. All the events on which the applicant has founded his action occurred more than five years before it was brought. In its view, Article 43 does not require that the applicant should have had knowledge of those events in good time. In any case the applicant had sufficient knowledge of those events to be able to assert any rights which he may have had after receiving the information supplied by the Swiss police during the interrogations and, at the latest, when he read the Swiss judgments.

49. The applicant claims that, broadly speaking, the events on which he relies did not become known to him until 1980, after his new lawyer, Dr Diefenbacher, had had the opportunity to study the documents relating to the criminal proceedings. He did not believe the information supplied by the Swiss police and he was not able to read the Swiss judgments, which were drafted in German. In any event, he could not possibly have known of the events relating to Dr Alder's visit to the Commission on 8 November 1974.

50. According to Article 43 of the Protocol on the Statute of the Court of Justice of the EEC 'proceedings against the Community in matters arising from non-contractual liability shall be barred after a period of five years from the occurrence of the event giving rise thereto'. That provision must be interpreted as meaning that the expiry of the limitation period cannot constitute a valid defence to a claim by a person who has suffered damage where that person only belatedly became aware of the event giving rise to it and thus could not have had a reasonable time in which to submit his application to the Court or to the relevant institution before the expiry of the limitation period.

51. In this case it must be borne in mind that the Court has based its conclusion in regard to the Community's liability on the fact that the Commission had not attempted to inform and to consult the applicant following Dr Alder's visit of 8 November 1974. It is clear from the information before the Court that the applicant could not have become aware of that fact until the preparatory inquiry in these proceedings, since Dr Alder's visit was mentioned for the first time in the Commission's defence. Therefore he could

not have sought to establish the Community's liability on that basis before the normal date of expiry of the limitation period.

52. It follows that the Commission's objection must be dismissed.

Damages

53. It must therefore be concluded that in principle the Community is bound to make good the damage resulting from the discovery of the applicant's identity by means of the documents handed over to Roche by the Commission. It must however be recognized that the extent of the Commission's liability is diminished by reason of the applicant's own negligence. The applicant failed to inform the Commission that it was possible to infer his identity as the informant from the documents themselves, although he was in the best position to appreciate and to avert that risk. Nor did he ask the Commission to keep him informed of the progress of the investigation of Roche, and in particular of any use that might be made of the documents for that purpose. Lastly, he went back to Switzerland without attempting to make any enquiries in that respect, although he must have been aware of the risks to which his conduct towards his former employer had exposed him with regard to Swiss legislation.

54. Consequently, the applicant himself contributed significantly to the damage which he suffered. In assessing the conduct of the Commission on the one hand and that of the applicant on the other, the Court considers it equitable to apportion responsibility for that damage equally between the two parties.

55. It follows from all the foregoing considerations that the Commission must be ordered to compensate the applicant to the extent of one half of the damage suffered by him as a result of the fact that he was identified as the source of information regarding Roche's anti-competitive practices. For the rest, however, the application must be dismissed. The amount of the damages is to be determined by agreement between the parties or, failing such agreement, by the Court.

On those grounds, the Courts, as an interlocutory decision, hereby:

1. orders the Commission to compensate the applicant to the extent of one half of the damage suffered by him as a result of the fact that he was identified as the source of information which led the Commission to impose a fine on his former employer, the Swiss company Hoffmann–La Roche, for certain anti-competitive practices;
2. for the rest, dismisses the application;
3. orders the parties to inform the Court within nine months from the delivery of this judgment of the amount of damages arrived at by agreement;

4. orders that, in the absence of agreement, the parties shall transmit to the Court within the same period a statement of their views with supporting figures;

5. reserves the costs.

COMMENTS

1. Unlike almost all earlier disputes under EEC 215, this case is nearer the realm of 'ordinary' tort claims. The plaintiff is a human being, not a company, and has suffered physical injury. Moreover, his complaint is not about some misguided legislation or other action in the sphere of economics, but alleges Commission bungling as regards his personal safety.

2. The ECJ expresses no opinion on whether—as a matter of doing the decent thing—the Commission ought to have pleaded limitation. It is uncertain whether, if they had not done so, the Court would nonetheless have felt bound to take judicial notice of a provision of its own Statute.

3. That provision says that the five-year period runs from the event giving rise to liability. The crucial stage of this event is held by the Court (para. 44) to be the failure to warn the plaintiff, after discovering, in November 1974, that the Swiss would prosecute him; to this must be added the imprisonment and so on. The latter is the damage caused—or contributed to, or not averted—by the former, And all was over more than five years before the writ. The Court, however, reads into its Statute a provision saying that time begins to run when the plaintiff knows of the event (the failure to warn) giving rise to liability.

4. Presumably, therefore, the Court means that what triggers liability is failure to warn when you have a duty to do so: and time begins when the plaintiff knows both failure and duty. Yet this is not what the ECJ says:

> the Court had based its conclusion in regard to liability on the fact that the Commission had not attempted to inform and consult the applicant following Dr Alder's visit ... [T]he applicant could not have become aware of *that fact* until the preparatory inquiry ... since Dr Alder's visit was mentioned for the first time in the Commission's defence.

Now, Mr Adams must have known when he was thrown into jail that no one had warned him; and merely telling him of Dr Alder's visit would not suffice to put him on guard. What the Court seems to mean is that the Commission should have told him that Dr Alder threatened prosecution; and that when he went back to Switzerland, he did not know that the Commission ought to have known that it should warn him.

5. Thus, both knowledge that their informant would be prosecuted and failure to warn him are the constituents of the Commission's liability; and

Mr Adams did not know both of these until 1984. Yet, as held by the Court, his carelessness contributed—in 1975—to his own imprisonment; so either he was careless in respect of a risk of prosecution of which he did not know, or careless in not checking with the Commission.

6. The Court's reasoning appears to be, as American lawyers put it, 'result-oriented'. In essence, however, the decision seems to lead to the following. A writ is issued more than five years after the damage. If the defence enters only a plea of limitation, it should succeed. If, however, it pleads the merits, it risks, at the disclosure stage, revealing something pointing to liability; and so five years begins to run in respect of a writ which, when issued, was out of time. While one may have every sympathy for Mr Adams, the question remains as to whether the decision will encourage plaintiffs to issue stale writs, and defendants to plead only limitation, and not the merits.

INDEX

acte clair 36
Advocate-General 2, 4, 5, 9, 27, 32, 56, 73, 88, 116, 123, 124, 150, 189, 200, 205, 209, 217, 223
AETR, *see* ERTA
aids, State 48, 78
annulment, *see* judicial review
Assembly, *see* European Parliament
authority, official 100, 104

Belgium 10, 15, 16, 17, 20, 99, 100, 115, 122
Benelux 9
Bill of Rights 61, 67, 68
budget 171–82

capital 116
Commission 17, 19, 20, 31, 37, 47, 48, 54, 55, 61, 73, 76, 77, 81, 82, 87, 99, 108, 115, 116, 118, 122, 130, 137, 149, 164, 168, 190, 197, 198, 209, 225, 229, 236–50
common agricultural policy 62, 64, 91, 184–5, 186, 188, 194
Community acts, *see* judicial review, non-contractual liability
Community law
  nature of 19, 23, 29, 47, 55, 56
  supremacy of 19, 23, 42, 44, 46, 47, 50, 58, 60, 63, 69, 126
competition 81–6, 127, 225, 233, 237
confidentiality 240–5
constitutions
  American 69, 182
  Member State 10, 18, 21, 28, 54, 55, 57, 61, 63
Council 51, 102, 103, 149, 161, 176, 177, 190, 197, 198, 207, 208, 209, 216, 218
Court, *see* European Court
cross-border element 27, 69, 109, 122, 135
customs duties 9, 12, 13, 15–16, 23

damages 29, 184, 202–6, 236–50
decisions, *see* judicial review
declaration, action for 29
Denmark 11, 73, 115, 118, 235
direct applicability 51, 54, 56, 57, 87, 89, 101, 106, 112
direct effect 26, 31, 38, 40, 42, 49, 56, 82, 88, 89, 90, 91, 97, 101, 109, 115, 122, 124, 138
Directives 87, 88, 89, 90, 93, 94, 101, 103, 105, 112, 123, 137–45
discrimination 49, 67, 88, 93, 96, 102, 109, 112, 113, 118, 122, 127, 131, 141, 162, 193, 199

Ecology Party 171–6
Economic and Social Committee 23
education 115, 117, 120, 121
elections 171–6, 207, 211
equal pay 67, 12, 124
equal treatment 128, 137, 198, 199, 213
ERTA 149–60
establishment, freedom of 48, 91, 97, 99, 104–6, 110, 232
European Convention on Human Rights 67, 247–8
European Court 1–5, 181
European Parliament 23, 67, 69, 171, 177, 207–9, 214, 215, 216, 220
external relations 152–4

failure to act, *see* suit for inaction
force majeure 61, 66
France 135, 225, 226, 229
fundamental rights 24, 61, 63, 65, 67, 103, 135, 226, 229

Germany, Federal Republic of 9, 11, 13, 17, 20, 31, 61, 73, 81, 99, 100, 109, 135, 177
goods, free movement of 72, 76
Greens, *see* Ecology Party

human rights, *see* fundamental rights

illegality, plea of 184
internal market 27, 29, 69, 71–2, 114
international law 10, 20, 21, 22, 42, 51, 56, 96, 153
interpretation, *see* preliminary ruling
invalidity, *see* preliminary ruling
Ireland 78–80, 99, 100, 109, 127, 133, 235
isoglucose 186–7
  levies 196–200, 218
  production refunds 188–95
  quotas 207, 210, 218
Italy 41, 54, 81, 135

judicial review 29, 172, 183–5, 190–1, 199, 208, 212, 221
jurisdiction
  of ECJ 30, 33, 44, 45
  of national courts 33, 36, 44, 59

lawyer/client communications 225–35
legal certainty 35, 94, 134, 180, 194, 218
limitation period 183–4, 236, 248–9

locus standi
   of individuals and firms 44, 171, 189, 196, 206
   of institutions 149, 157, 183
   of European Parliament 162, 164, 208, 213
Luxembourg 15, 99, 100, 181

monopolies, State 49

national law 10, 13, 14, 18, 29, 31, 42, 56, 58, 75, 84
nationality, *see* discrimination
Netherlands 9, 10, 13, 15, 17, 20, 61, 99, 162, 168
non-compulsory expenditure 177–81
non-contractual liability 184, 201–6, 236–51
non-tariff barriers 72

pensions 140, 141
persons, free movement of 119
precedent 5, 30, 31, 34, 39
preliminary ruling 4, 17, 23, 32, 33, 43, 45, 58, 59, 184
professional privilege, *see* lawyer/client communications
property 67, 82, 86
proportionality 62, 68, 77, 197, 213
public law 66, 204
public policy 34, 73, 75, 77, 90, 91, 93, 95, 126
public service 87, 88

reference, *see* preliminary ruling
regulations 10, 90, 93, 94, 176, 178, 184–5, 188, 191, 196, 207, 212
remedies 29–30, 122, 184
residence 110, 113
retirement 137–145
retroactivity 216–20

scientology 87, 92
services, freedom of 108, 110, 114, 116, 168, 232
Single European Act 2, 215
social policy 127, 132, 135
standstill provisions 12, 27, 43, 49, 99, 122, 123
suit for inaction 161–70, 184
Switzerland 236, 239

tort, *see* non-contractual liability
tourism 116
transport 161–9
   air 167, 169
   road 149–60
   sea 167

United Kingdom 87, 88, 93, 99, 100, 109, 115, 118, 122, 133, 137, 177, 225, 226, 228, 235
USA 136, 182

vocational training 115, 118, 120

workers, free movement of 88, 93, 95